When the Music Mattered

OTHER BOOKS BY BRUCE POLLOCK

NONFICTION

In Their Own Words: Pop Songwriting,
1955–1974

The Face of Rock & Roll
(with John Wagman)

When Rock Was Young

Popular Music: An Annotated Index
of American Popular Songs,
Volume 7, 1970–1974;
Volume 8, 1975–1979

FICTION

Playing for Change

Me, Minsky & Max

It's Only Rock and Roll

When the Music Mattered

ROCK IN THE 1960s

★ ★ ★

Bruce Pollock

Holt, Rinehart and Winston / New York

Published in February 1984 by Holt, Rinehart
and Winston,
383 Madison Avenue, New York, New York 10017.
Published simultaneously in Canada by Holt, Rinehart
and Winston of Canada, Limited.

Library of Congress Cataloging in Publication Data
Pollock, Bruce.
When the music mattered.
Includes index.
1. Rock music—United States—History and criticism.
I. Title.
ML3534.P63   1983   784.5'4'00973   83-10853
ISBN Hardbound: 0-03-060426-5
ISBN Paperback: 0-03-060421-4

First Edition

Design by Lucy Albanese
Printed in the United States of America
1 3 5 7 9 10 8 6 4 2

Excerpt from "Ah, Look at All the Hippy
People" reprinted by permission of
Tuli Kupferberg.
Portions of the chapter on
Paul Simon appeared in *Playboy* and
The Saturday Review.

ISBN 0-03-060426-5 HARDCOVER
ISBN 0-03-060421-4 PAPERBACK

TO BARBARA,

My Homecourt Advantage

Contents

When the Music Mattered

Introduction: Expecting to Fly

My first rock 'n' roll song, an anguished, existential lament called "(I'd Like to) Buy Back Today," was published in 1969, only three years after I'd written it with my partner, Richie, and two years after our band had broken up, having learned only the one song. The band was called the Secret Ingredient: Andrea on lead vocals; her boyfriend, Howie, on Autoharp; my roommate, Richie, on blues guitar; and me on harmonica and pail. The Secret Ingredient, as in our great unrecorded albums *What Is the Secret Ingredient?*, *The New, Improved Secret Ingredient*, and *The Giant Economy-Size Secret Ingredient*. We lasted all of a month.

After dropping out of college in 1963 to write the Great American Rock 'n' Roll Novel, and then abandoning that novel in favor of a rock 'n' roll screenplay, in 1966 I abandoned the screenplay to become Byron to Richie's Keats (Simon & Garfunkel being taken), the premier songwriting team of the New Rock Renaissance. In our two-room Greenwich Village flat, we began crafting the generation's future evergreens. "Buy Back Today" was never recorded, but our next effort, an antidraft folk/rocker called "Clarrissy (In a Time of National

Peril)" was reported being held by no less than Blood, Sweat & Tears within weeks of its publication in 1969 by Southern Music. Visions of days spent poolside at Laurel Canyon, fending off fawning groupies, a life of velvet decadence and famous friends briefly blasted our otherwise exemplary cool. We were signed to a record label, courted by a manager-publisher; our apartment became Song Central for legions of as-yet-undiscovered singers.

But that was as high as it got. In fact, "Clarrissy" was performed only once in public, at a place in Brooklyn called the Dynamite Discotheque by a group named the Ralph, who blew the chorus. Blood, Sweat & Tears passed on the song. We were released from our recording contract; abandoned by the manager-publisher, who had failed to get the necessary money together; and utterly disgusted by the as-yet-undiscovered singers, who failed again and again to get anything together.

Not long thereafter, Byron & Keats broke up. Keats bought a fedora and went to work as an accountant. I got married and obtained a bachelor's degree. Like many people who grew up in the sixties, our infatuation with music had left us disappointed. Coming out of the passive fandom of fifties rock 'n' roll, in the sixties we craved action, the total intensity of passion and involvement only musicians' lives seemingly afforded. They beat up on their instruments sixteen hours a day, blew their minds in night-long jams and incessant, fantastic orgies. As a generation, we were looking for grand adventures; as a solitary prose writer, I wanted *in* on those orgies.

From the outset, the sixties promised so much more than they delivered. More than anything else, this was a decade that encouraged breaking the rules (but did not, as it turned out, entirely get away with it). Who would have dreamed, before the sixties, that a Catholic man could be elected president? And then that he'd be shot and killed before his term in office expired? Or that his assassin would be murdered days later on television? Who could have predicted, back in the fifties, that blacks would take their age-old grievances to the street in peaceable sit-ins? And then that a white southern president would sponsor the most impressive civil rights legislation in history? Still, by mid-decade those same streets would ignite into riot. It would have been incredible to conceive, until the sixties began, that white college students would adopt black tactics in their own street demonstrations over government and campus policies; that all their accumulated protests would result in America admitting it had lost a war. But countless social programs to help the poor created ballooning expectations. Massive marches provided the illusion of solidarity. Sustained affluence suggested indefinite prosperity. Abundant leisure time encouraged the use of recreational drugs, which fueled rosy pipe dreams.

For every assault on traditional wisdom that occurred in the sixties, there was a significant retaliation. For the civil rights dreamers, there were the Black Panthers. For the peace-movement plotters, there was Richard Nixon. For the do-your-own-thing libertarians, there was Charles Manson, doing his thing with a machete to the tunes of the Beatles. Acid bliss turned to junkie reality. The war intensified. Cops and hard-hats—keepers of tradition—counterattacked the counterculture. The economy withered. The music died. Johnson's "Great Society" fizzled. Solidarity was shattered at Kent State. The road to the Big Rock Candy Mountain led to nowhere. Oh, it was a wild time of confrontations, with every issue clearly defined: hawk against dove, hip against straight, life against death. You were either part of the solution or part of the problem. Every action was a statement, every stillness a statement of complicity. What an altogether schizophrenic decade to be young, gifted, and working on your first million!

Those who reached adolescence in the early sixties already knew what it meant to be part of a media generation. As the infamous "baby boom," we'd been hooked on our power and charisma ever since "The Twist" created the international hoopla known as the cult of youth in 1962. We were a vast segment of the marketplace and well aware of our ability to utterly shake up the world, if not to own it. Our principal vehicle was the radio; our language was rock 'n' roll.

By identifying with the underdog, the outcast, and the antihero, members of the young white American middle class elevated the hoody posturing of Elvis Presley, the town roust-about railings of Jerry Lee Lewis, the backwoods innocence of Don and Phil Everly, and the trembling arrogance of be-spectacled Buddy Holly into reverberating myth. Purists and tastemakers discovered the roots of rock 'n' roll in rhythm and blues—in Little Richard, Chuck Berry, and Bo Diddley—and black musicians who were even more outcast, underdog, and antiheroic than our pioneering Elvis and Jerry Lee. Some went even further, discovering the *roots* of rhythm and blues in the Mississippi Delta, where Son House and Skip James and Mississippi John Hurt had languished for several eternities. In the mid-sixties, the electrified leap from rock 'n' roll to rock would be accomplished from the shoulders of previously un-heralded déclassé champions named Muddy Waters, B. B. King and Howlin' Wolf.

The box step gave way to the twist. During the period from 1960 to 1963 outrageous horn and organ solos began to liberate us from the constraints of the fifties. Phil Spector's extravagant productions ("Be My Baby," "Spanish Harlem") utilized the high technology of the space age. Down in Green-wich Village, the urban folk scare, led by Bob Dylan, brought poetry-cum-new-journalism into the mix. And so, by 1964 rock 'n' roll was poised for its most major media event.

When the Beatles arrived, we were all still in our living rooms, glued to the TV screen, in the somber aftermath of the Kennedy assassination. Here is the deal the four rockers of-fered us on "The Ed Sullivan Show": in a mad, mad world, faced with imminent destruction, *let's get crazy.*

For the rest of the decade, our generation would proceed to break more rules. Musically, this meant adding electric in-struments to traditional music. It meant huge free outdoor celebrations instead of the traditional rock 'n' roll shows. It meant creating a new FM format on the radio, where records more than three minutes long could be heard. Only in the six-ties could you have a song about possible nuclear annihilation ("Eve of Destruction") at the top of the charts. Only in the sixties could the Queen of England award Order of the British Empire medals to the Beatles, could a scruffy folksinger like

Bob Dylan be named poet laureate of the under-thirty generation.

Before the decade was through, men would land on the
moon and the Mets would win the World Series. But more
significantly, the whole pace of American middle-class life
would be disrupted, as kids jumped off the clock and calendar
of day-to-day existence to live in caves, in communes, out of
knapsacks, out of wedlock. Decades of tradition would be
scrapped in favor of "making it up as you go along." In the
throes of such freedom you could quit school, grow your hair,
wear a T-shirt, forget about money, a career, marriage; you
could avoid the draft, avoid work, smoke dope, and ball your
brains out—and all amid abundant philosophical justification,
political upheaval, and loud music. Wherever the sound of an
electric guitar riding a searing blues progression keened over
the landscape like a lonesome freight train, you could be sure
of finding friends, fellow outcasts, underdogs, and antiheroes
sprawled below the stage, awash in freaky colors and sailing
away on waves of awe and sensuality.

I've selected a wide range from the musicians who were our
mouthpieces then, in order to set down what they saw from
the pedestals we placed them on. Their memories may tell us
exactly what it was that happened to all of us in that hazy decade of bliss and discontentment, and where and why it all dis-
appeared. So, too, most definitely, do their songs reveal the
era in which they did their finest work. In fact, the songs of the
sixties are so basic to an appreciation of the decade that I have
created a special "playlist" feature at the end of each section's
introduction, a highly personal, eclectic selection of what was
being written and heard—and sometimes even played on the
radio—during that chapter's segment of the era. For many,
songs in the sixties were regarded as nothing less than poetry—though we could still appreciate a sledgehammer backbeat when we heard it. Between the body and the mind fell . . .
folk rock. Taken in sum, these playlists will result, I hope, in a
kind of ideal song library for any adventurous radio program-
mer who wishes to discover what the real sixties were all

about. These lists illuminate both the diversity of the period's music and provide meaningful nostalgia for those of us who can't get there via Bubble Puppy and the Sunshine Company.

(The playlists are arranged in two ways: chronologically, by approximate release dates, for singles, and alphabetically, by artist and by title, for those songs of significance which never made it to the top of the pops.)

In deciding which artists to include in the book, my first preference was given to those musicians whose lives brushed up against my own in one way or another.

John Kuse, of the doo-wop group, the Excellents, lives both in song ("Coney Island Baby") and in reality in a Brooklyn neighborhood that lies but a bus line from my childhood doorstep. Jiggs Meister, of the Angels, was fortuitously discovered only a block from where I now live, in the suburbs of Connecticut.

Some, like Dave Van Ronk and Tuli Kupferberg, it may be argued, are not rock at all; others, like Peter Tork or Essra Mohawk, may be considered rock but not relevant—Tork much too plastic, Essra too obscure. These arguments, to me, are beside the point. This is not a critical history; it's a social document. Van Ronk put Dylan up at his apartment when Dylan first blew into Greenwich Village in 1961. Chairing the weekly hoot night at the Gaslight Café through the mid-sixties, Van Ronk became, for a generation of aspiring bohemians (myself included), the essence of artistic integrity. And so did Tracy Nelson, one of the finest blues singers of our time, who is now using that voice in the service of Busch beer, because her recording career can't support her. Living out the fantasies of many middle-class young women of the sixties, Tracy went from college dropout to superstar in a methadrine rush, wending her way from Chicago blues to the acid rock of San Francisco before settling down (some say retiring) on a farm near Nashville. Essra Mohawk debuted propitiously as Uncle Meat in Frank Zappa's merry band, the Mothers of Invention. She went on to become Laura Nyro's protégée and the woman who told Joni Mitchell it was okay to sing. Though every one of Essra's attempts at similar pop legendry met with cosmic detours, she remains, as the eighties commence, enthusiastic that the dreams of the sixties may be within the reach of an older, more positive generation of survivors. So, too, does Peter Tork, who actually lived for a time at the pinnacle of rock 'n' roll success, only to fritter it all away in the mistaken belief (rampant at the time) that the movie would never end.

As a generation, we could use these positive voices now, while Dylan recasts his old songs into Easy Listening, and so much of the sixties seems frozen in our memories. The FM band is a solid wall of heavy metal. The AM band is a babel of sex therapists. The rest of the world is a shopping mall of consciousness franchises and paperback romances. In the voices of our musicians were our yearnings; in their journeys, our rainbow's end. Denied the opportunity of hearing from them, we've been unable to face ourselves through rock 'n' roll, as we did in the sixties. But we need those voices raised in anger and in song again, now more than ever, as the melodies fade and the memories warp, to tell us who we are and remind us who we've been.

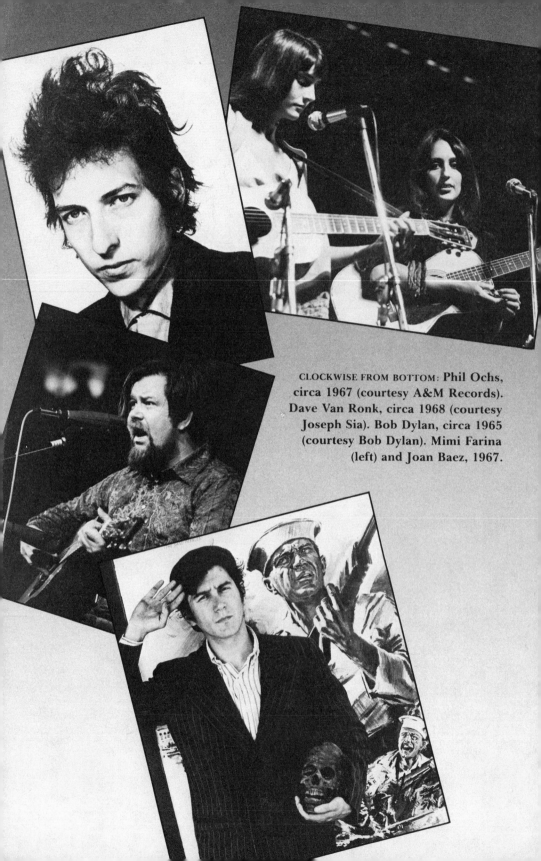

CLOCKWISE FROM BOTTOM: **Phil Ochs, circa 1967 (courtesy A&M Records). Dave Van Ronk, circa 1968 (courtesy Joseph Sia). Bob Dylan, circa 1965 (courtesy Bob Dylan). Mimi Farina (left) and Joan Baez, 1967.**

★ 1 ★

The Urban Folk Scare

From 1960 to 1963, coinciding almost exactly with the reign of President John F. Kennedy, folk music enjoyed an unprecedented run of popularity on the record charts. Nearly one hundred songs achieved at least a small measure of attention in those years, from Woody Guthrie's "This Land Is Your Land" to Pete Seeger's "Where Have All the Flowers Gone" and "We Shall Overcome." Previously regarded by the masses as the parlor music of Communists, folk's prevalence at that time was another signal that progressive thought was beginning to break through the complacent texture of American life at mid-century. Seeger, who had been a victim of Senator Joe McCarthy's witch-hunts and blacklisted from TV appearances, was one of those who placed a single on the charts, late in 1963, a witty attack on conformity written by Malvina Reynolds called "Little Boxes."

Inspired by Seeger's living legacy of commitment, this new generation of folk artists had the added benefit of the rock 'n' roll of Elvis Presley. Here was a white boy with the moves of a black man. With Elvis freely dipping into southern blues to create rock 'n' roll, it was no cosmic leap for Minnesota's Bob Dylan to rewrite folk music. After a deferential bow to forebears like Seeger, Guthrie, and Leadbelly, Dylan soon took off in a modern temper, with epic folk poems like "Blowin' in the Wind," "Masters of War" and "Hard Rain's a-Gonna Fall." From Greenwich Village, from Berkeley, from Cambridge, urban folk songs proliferated, dealing with Cuba, Vietnam, Birmingham, and the draft board, written by a literate cadre of college-educated troubadours, among them Phil Ochs, Richard Fariña, Buffy Sainte-Marie, and Eric Andersen. In this group, the idea that you could make a fortune playing folk music was generally ridiculed and scorned (along with unauthentic popularizers like Peter, Paul & Mary and the Kingston Trio), but the idea that you might change the world was not. An increasingly alienated, college-age audience found moral comfort in the words and lives of these exponents of the urban folk revival.

Following the assassination of JFK late in 1963, the sound of slick, good-time rock 'n' roll, personified by the Beatles, washed over the American airwaves. But while folk music was disappearing from the charts, the folk scene continued to be vital, with hundreds of college students (primarily white) joining the Peace Corps, working for civil rights in the South, and turning their poems into music. When Dylan heard the Animals' rock 'n' roll version of the folk chestnut "House of the Rising Sun," in 1964, he saw folk's future in a chord change. Adding rock 'n' roll instrumentation to folk music was considered heresy to some; to others it was just another rule that had to be smashed, in a decade becoming known for its stark revisionism. However, the subsequent addition of rock 'n' roll rewards to a traditional folk career proved, as many thought it would, the undoing of the scene and of most talents associated with it.

But the spirit engendered at the outset by the urban folk revival—the charismatic ambitions of Dylan and Baez, Ochs, Fariña, and a cast of thousands—would persist throughout the thrilling restlessness, the social and emotional upheavals of the era and its songs, as singers and listeners reacted with personal involvement to the political events of the decade. For the first time in memory, intellectuals had control of the music—and they were learning how to dance to it.

Playlist

Eric Andersen

"Blind Fiddler"
"Come to My Bedside"
"My Land Is a Good Land"
"Thirsty Boots"
"Tin Can Alley"
"Violets of Dawn"

Joan Baez

"Death of Queen Jane"
"Donna Donna"
"Farewell Angelina"
"Love Is Just a Four-Letter Word"
"We Shall Overcome"

Judy Collins

"The Bonnie Ship the Diamond"
"Carry It On"
"Coal Tattoo"
"Golden Apples of the Sun"
"So Early, Early in the Spring"

Bob Dylan

"Blowin' in the Wind"
"Boots of Spanish Leather"
"Don't Think Twice, It's All Right"
"Hard Rain's a-Gonna Fall"
"Masters of War"
"One Too Many Mornings"
"Oxford Town"
"The Times They Are a-Changin' "

"Tomorrow Is a Long Time"
"When the Ship Comes In"

Ramblin' Jack Elliott

"Guabi Guabi"
"San Francisco Bay Blues"

Richard Fariña

"Birmingham Sunday"
"Children of Darkness"
"House Un-American Blues Activity
  Dream"
"Mainline Prosperity Blues"
"Michael, Andrew and James"
"Pack Up Your Sorrows"
"Sell-Out Agitation Waltz"

Richie Havens

"Drown in My Own Tears"
"Follow"
"High Flyin' Bird"
"The Klan"
"San Francisco Bay Blues"

The Jim Kweskin Jug Band

"Blues in the Bottle"
"Downtown Blues"
"I'm a Woman" (sung by Maria
  Muldaur)
"Never Swat a Fly"
"Richland Woman"

Joni Mitchell

"I Had a King"
"Marcy"

Fred Neil

"Blues on the Ceiling"
"The Dolphins"
"The Other Side of This Life"
"Tear Down the Walls"
"Wild Child in a World of
    Trouble"

Phil Ochs

"Changes"
"The Crucifixion"
"Draft Dodger Rag"
"Here's to the State of Mississippi"
"I Ain't Marchin' Anymore"
"Love Me, I'm a Liberal"
"The Power and the Glory"
"Santo Domingo"
"There but for Fortune"
"White Boots Marching in a Yellow
    Land"

Tom Paxton

"Daily News"
"I Can't Help but Wonder Where
    I'm Bound"
"The Last Thing on My Mind"
"Ramblin' Boy"

Peter, Paul & Mary

"Ballad of Spring Hill"
"Blowin' in the Wind"
"Cruel War"
"If I Had a Hammer"
"Lemon Tree"
"Old Coat"
"Puff (the Magic Dragon)"

Tom Rush

"Love's Made a Fool of You"
"Panama Limited"
"Tin Angel"
"Urge for Going"

Buffy Sainte-Marie

"Cod'ine"
"It's My Way"
"My Country 'Tis of Thy People
  You're Dying"
"Now That the Buffalo's Gone"
"Universal Soldier"

Pete Seeger

"Little Boxes"
"Turn, Turn, Turn"
"Waist Deep in the Big Muddy"
"Where Have All the Flowers Gone"

Paul Simon

"Bleecker Street"
"He Was My Brother"

Patrick Sky

"Many a Mile"
"Nectar of God"

Dave Van Ronk

"Cocaine"
"Green Rocky Road"
"Sometimes I Feel like a Motherless
  Child"
"Wanderin' "
"Zen Koans Gonna Rise Again"

DAVE VAN RONK

The country was uneasy in 1960. Though the dull brown fog of conformity that had hung over the Eisenhower years showed every indication of continuing, even thickening, with the expected onset of Richard Nixon in November, the new decade brought with it ominous signs that following the leader might no longer be enough. The bomb, as always, was a major worry, but now bomb shelters were being marketed like backyard barbecues. The notion of a postbomb in-crowd of survivors was either a masterstroke of advertising con or the grim immediate future. Khrushchev was giving us the cold shoulder. When he wasn't saber-rattling over Cuba, he was embarrassing our government by shooting our spy planes out of the sky. The government denied any wrongdoing in the U2 incident, but several months later another plane was downed inside Russian airspace. The missile gap had led to a credibility gap. Inconceivable—but Ike had lied.

Closer to home, in Greensboro, North Carolina, some black college students were taking the question of racial equality into their own hands, with a landmark sit-in at a drug-store. Before the year was through, similar sit-ins would occur in one hundred other cities. They were peaceable for the most part, but a century of hypocrisy had been lifted off the back burner, and in the more liberal households people wondered how long such admirable nonviolent self-containment could last.

Even closer to home, on the same TV screen that had brought us Elvis Presley on "The Ed Sullivan Show," Senator John Kennedy began his historic charge—first, to win the Democratic nomination, and then, to beat Ike's protégé, Richard Nixon. Kennedy's attack culminated in the fall with the Great Debates. A generation that would grow to regard the appearance of Dick Nixon's face on the tube as an occasion for their choicest ripostes and cheeriest bon mots got their first close-up glimpse of his sweating upper lip during those debates. It was no contest. Kennedy was suave, a forty-year-old who kept in shape; Nixon was haggard, with a five-o'clock shadow that came out at noon.

If the excitement of a political pennant race was heady, it was also frustrating. The smart money was always with the status quo—Father Knows Best and the Yankees in Seven. As cynical teens we'd had our hopes raised before, in 1956, when Elvis gave us rock 'n' roll. Out of the fog suddenly came a lightning bolt of energy. We put taps on our shoes, grease in our hair, and waited for the millennium. By 1960 all that passion and danger had long since been drained from the music, leaving a listless crew of ducktails and bobbysoxers to stutter and stumble on "American Bandstand." Elvis was in the army, while Jerry Lee Lewis was banned from the radio for committing the indiscretion of marrying his fourteen-year-old cousin. Little Richard had found religion. And Alan Freed, rock's most vocal adult adherent, was being hung out to dry at the Senate Payola hearings. So Kennedy's gamy run had familiar echoes. Why bother to hoist those hopes, only to see them come crashing?

As sheltered children of rock 'n' roll, we of the middle class had little history to bolster us against the forces of repression, who were determined to stifle any music they deemed too dangerous for mass consumption. But down in Greenwich Village, the proponents of folk music—a left-leaning assemblage of mystic ramblers, freethinkers, and liberated women in the image of Isadora Duncan—were made of sterner stuff. From Woody Guthrie to Pete Seeger, folk music had a long legacy of front-lines solidarity, had union hymns and southern field hollers in its repertoire for moral comfort. In 1960 these tunes were trotted out by a ragged troop of Brooklyn banjo pickers and fiddlers from the deltas of Queens, when they joined hands in protest against the imminent destruction of their legendary Sunday stomping ground, the fountain in Washington Square Park.

The headline in the *Daily News* read: 10,000 BEATNIKS RIOT IN WASHINGTON SQUARE. There may have been one hundred beatniks, a couple of closet anarchists, a sleeping hobo, and perhaps even Allen Ginsberg. The rest were tourists, in from the boroughs and the suburbs to ogle the unwashed. Led by Izzy Young, proprietor of the Folklore Center, the march was staged to prevent a roadway from cutting the beloved square in two. The riot squad was sent for, and, true to the spirit of the approaching age, it was the squad who proceeded to riot. But the folkies stood fast, singing, one presumes, "We Shall Overcome." And the roadway never went in. Future Sundays in the square would owe these stalwarts a debt, as Greenwich Village would become a folk-song mecca, along with Cambridge and Berkeley. There, a musical vision of nothing less than revolution launched a change in the tone and texture of pop music for its musicians just as surely as Kennedy's upset victory over Nixon had signaled a sort of manifest destiny for the young. We were all part of a new generation, rescued from obscurity by our wit and our sophistication and schooled in the magic of rock 'n' roll.

The folk scare was upon us, with a rebellion unlike that of rock 'n' roll, one that had its roots firmly planted in *causes*, from political and racial freedom to the freedom just to ramble—and the bohemian codes that went along with it. And when this music started to get strong, to get real and to reach for converts outside its immediate hip environs, with the ammunition of Dylan's poetry, Phil Ochs's passion, and the soaring soprano of Joan Baez, no draft board could suppress it, no Senate subcommittee could address it, and no outdated concepts of morality could keep it off the air. As the decade lurched through its several bloody climaxes, it would be the folksingers, turning into rock singers, whose spirit, presence, and songs would constitute the literature of this aching chapter in the nation's history. With the intellectual idealism of folk music attached to the anger and abandon of rock 'n' roll, there was nothing a generation burned by Kennedy's assassination couldn't envision. Even without him we would save the world, unite the races. White kids would play the blues. Black kids would play quarterback.

The Gaslight Café opened in 1959 as the Gaslight Poetry Café, a flight below MacDougal Street, featuring Roy Berkeley as the house folkie, sandwiched between a lot of howling poets. Around the corner, the Café Bizarre was hiring. Lee Hoffman, under the auspices of the Folksinger's Guild, was sponsoring monthly concerts off-Broadway. Within a year these showcases would ripen into a viable scene, an actual living for a number of plucky pickers, chief among them Dave Van Ronk. Van Ronk had been hanging out since 1954, when he arrived at the informal sessions at 190 Spring Street, on the outskirts of the Village, a sixteen-year-old high-school dropout from Queens, whose main ax was the tenor banjo and whose main gig was as a part-time messenger.

At 190 Spring Street, players like Roger Abrams and Paul Clayton, John Cohn, Freddy Gurlaich, Luke Faust, and John Herald weaned Van Ronk from traditional Dixieland over to folk blues. But by the time the clubs on MacDougal Street were ready to tap these sainted rustics for their appointed hour in the spotlight, many had already abdicated their chairs in favor of something more secure. Van Ronk himself had been shipping out as a merchant seaman since 1957. Nineteen sixty found him playing six nights a week at the Gaslight, ten sets a night, for $125 a week plus a share of the basket. In 1960 that was a decent living. By 1964 the money would be much more plentiful. The whole country was listing toward the left, and the Gaslight was the focal point of the Greenwich Village music scene, populated to bursting by what seemed to be half the nation's young intellectual folk poets, each one a new Bob Dylan. As the host of innumerable Tuesday night hoots at the Gaslight, Van Ronk was the linchpin of the underground movement, an uncle figure to a generation of neophyte bohemians and radicals.

Hunkered down over his guitar, a large, bearded man with a recalcitrant forelock, smile turning to a grimace, Van Ronk stitched together precise guitar accompaniments to tunes like "Winnin' Boy," "Green Rocky Road," "Cocaine Blues," "One Meatball" and "Song of the Wandering Aengus"—a personal and eclectic repertoire. Stepping up the pace, as he'd usually do long about the third set, at three or four in the morning, he whacked away at his instrument as if bashing flies, swiped at the hair in his eyes, while his voice wheezed and keened like a nervous steam engine: not a pretty figure, not a pretty voice—the rough edges of authenticity. A self-taught hard-knocks cum laude, Van Ronk, for one night a week at least, offered those in the audience, as well as those hordes of incoming folksingers who took refuge in his apartment, shelter from the stultifying restrictions of the straight life, the academic grind, the ever-looming cold war. And even when his followers cleared out of the Village, as the fervor of the sixties turned to embarrassed giggles, hitting the highway for the suburbs and real life, it seemed incomprehensible that the big man wouldn't always remain, holding down that chair at the Gaslight, just in case some of us needed a night off.

And so he has. The Gaslight became a Ukrainian cookie factory in 1975. The Night Owl, the Au Go Go, the Bitter End, Figaro's, and the Garrick are gone—like Ochs, Tim Hardin, Tim Buckley, and so many other scattered, silent voices. Still, Van Ronk has hung tough in his rent-controlled Sheridan Square apartment, surveying the rubble and the Italian restaurants, watching with equanimity the humdrum noodlers in the park and the panhandling junkies—all of them on roller skates. The question is, has he been sustained by the curative power of the blues, confident of a return someday of a new, spirited generation of pickers? Or has he merely been stuck, stuck in his tracks when the street collapsed, and stuck in the past, unable to move or cry out?

"I remember going somewhere on the train with Paxton around 1970," says Van Ronk, "and we were talking about the business end of the business, and he said, 'I saw this great cartoon in *The New Yorker* last week: one brontosaurus was talking to another, saying, "I don't know about you, but frankly this cold snap has me a little worried." ' " He lets loose his famous cackle and sips a bit of iced tea. "I've always been a doom cryer," he says. "For years I'd been predicting grass growing on MacDougal Street, so I think it gave me some satisfaction. I probably felt like a Seventh-Day Adventist on the day the world really ended."

Divorced through most of the seventies, Van Ronk now lives in a typical bachelor pad, Greenwich Village style, thick with memorabilia, old tapes unspooled and dripping from their boxes, classic LPs and paperbacks, both with their spines broken; dust that I'm sure is from the sixties. Occasionally his dog, Glencannon, wanders through the long shadows of the living room. Occasionally the phone rings: one of his guitar students, an agent, the landlord. The apartment itself, a smallish three-roomer, is one of the few tangible rewards of Van Ronk's reputation. The landlord's daughter had been a folk-music fan. Otherwise, some notable pieces of African art notwithstanding, it's clear his relationship with the high life was merely a flirtation.

"I'm living very hand-to-mouth now," he admits. "I lived hand-to-mouth then, but I had a lot more money. Actually, I probably had about the same amount of money, but it doesn't do what it used to. And it was a kind of situation where if I didn't have the money, I could make a record or get another gig and then do what I wanted. There was an awful lot of money kicking around in 1965. My God, it was the Big Rock Candy Mountain. There was incredible prosperity for all of us. I must have spent three years living in New York without ever being on a subway. To me that sums it up, because I'd been a messenger as a kid, and I can't stand the subways.

"We had five or six real fat years. Some people bought houses in the country, some people built recording studios, some people acquired expensive drug habits. And all of it was taken for granted. Every time you went out and had a couple of drinks with somebody you heard that someone had just landed some kind of bonanza, so and so just signed a contract with Columbia for mucho buckos, and all of a sudden a townhouse is being renovated on Commerce Street."

By 1969 the cold snap had set in. "A lot of things started to happen," Van Ronk recalls. "The rock 'n' roll revival cut into business. When political protest moved over to rock 'n' roll, I think we lost a lot of our constituency. You had that business around Saint Marks Place—the Fillmore East, the Electric Circus. There were all kinds of little joints that came and went on that block. I think the most important thing was the raising of the rents. Suddenly all those little dustbins on Bleecker and MacDougal started to look like gold mines to the landlords, and they would jack up the rent literally every month. But in a club, there's just so much you can charge for a cup of coffee, especially when the wave you're depending on is petering out anyway."

Back in 1964, the going rate for coffee was $1.05 at the Bitter End, where all the commercial folk acts played—slick entities like Simon & Garfunkel, Peter, Paul & Mary, and the Chad Mitchell Trio. The genuine funky article was being dispensed more cheaply around the corner at the Gaslight. Here were people who shared a kindred sensibility, aware and alive observers of their world. The standard folk bag at this time consisted of songs like "If I Had a Hammer," "This Land Is Your Land," "Green Pastures of Plenty," and "Where Have All the Flowers Gone"—familiar summer-camp favorites, in their own way as lulling as the Beatles version of late-fifties rock 'n' roll that was heating up our radios. But folksingers like Phil Ochs and Eric Andersen, Patrick Sky, Tom Paxton, David Blue, Buffy Sainte-Marie, Alix Dobkin, Richie Havens, and Dave Van Ronk were fixing their gaze on our changing lives, the real America, here and abroad. It was not a vision that could compete at first with "She Loves You" and "I Want to Hold Your Hand" or the surf-and-Studebaker commotions of California or the Motown assembly line gearing up in Detroit. But Paul Simon had just seen a college buddy, Andy Goodman, murdered in Mississippi. The Chad Mitchell Trio sang about the John Birch Society. And Peter, Paul & Mary had brought the works of Bob Dylan—"Blowin' in the Wind" and "Don't Think Twice, It's All Right"—before the masses. There had been a march on Washington, black and white together. The times they were a-changing.

"The whole thing snowballed when the Dylan storm broke," says Van Ronk, speaking of 1963. "And while New York was kind of late on the scene, as compared with Boston or Los Angeles, the typical New York attitude was If anything is worth doing, it's worth overdoing. There weren't three or five rooms to work in, there were fifteen or twenty."

When Dylan first arrived in town in 1961, Van Ronk and his wife, Terri, put him up at their apartment on Fifteenth Street near Seventh Avenue. Terri managed Dylan for a while, got him his first paid gig, at Folk City, opening for Brother John Sellers.

"He was nothing like what he subsequently became," Van Ronk recalls. "He seemed very extroverted on the stage, and he did all kinds of little Charlie Chaplin turns. His sense of timing was incredibly good, and he was hilariously funny. He was nervous; he was obviously quaking in his boots, but he used it. He had a kind of herky-jerky patter: a one-liner, long pause, another one-liner, a mutter, a mumble, a slam at the guitar. It was very effective." So effective, in fact, that before long everyone in the Village developed such a rap—the hipster-ragamuffin, quasi-poetic view of the world, which Bob himself undoubtedly lifted from Ramblin' Jack Elliot.

"Every guest set the man did, by the time he'd do the second song, the word was out on the street that Dylan was on stage, and his coterie would start pouring in. I don't think he was as sure of himself once he got out of the Village."

By far Dylan's most famous guest sets were performed with the folk world's long-haired madonna, Joan Baez. Already an inspirational figure in the civil rights movement, a favorite of the intelligentsia stationed in Cambridge and

Berkeley, Joan's career was launched through her sister, Mimi Fariña, at the Newport Folk Festival in 1959. Van Ronk was there. "Actually, I'd heard of Mimi before I heard of Joan. Everybody in Berkeley was saying, in effect, Mimi has a sister. Bob Gibson was riding high in those days, and he'd heard Joan and brought her up during his set and gave her a piece of his show. And she brought the house down. It was pandemonium."

A skilled raconteur, Van Ronk can't resist a punch line. But first another sip of iced tea. "Ten years later, during a thunderstorm, I ran into Bob under the awning of the Figaro. He was really in bad shape. I said, how's it going? He said, 'Terrible. Maybe next year Joanie will give me a piece of *her* show.'"

Baez was the first of a new generation of folksingers who would wrest control of this venerable music and use it for their own social-political (and nefarious) ends. In 1965, Bob Dylan may have wiped folk music out entirely when he appeared at Newport for several songs with the Paul Butterfield Blues Band, in all their amplified splendor. The folk fathers were outraged that such artillery should be allowed to invade this hallowed pastoral bastion, where Seeger sang of peace and freedom and where Mississippi John Hurt courted the "Candy Man." But youth was on the march by the middle of the decade, and the momentum of that force washed over the pristine New England festival.

"It became an event," bemoans Van Ronk. "People didn't care about the music. They were turning up because it was someplace to drink, to get laid—which is perfectly all right, but when you've got fifty thousand people in that frame of mind, I don't want to be there."

Like Baez, Dylan's use and alleged abuse of folk music earned him much disfavor among purists —the authority figures in power at the time—who suggested he play by the rules and within established guidelines. "Everyone thought that unless you were Woody Guthrie you couldn't write," says Van Ronk, "and Dylan disproved that rather quickly." Leaping from tradition, Dylan was verbiage run wild, venom run amok.

He attached autobiographical odes to ancient folk airs. He denounced the government in "Masters of War" and all of creation in the surreal and image-drenched "Hard Rain's a-Gonna Fall." He had the audacity to compare his own teenage odyssey, in "Song to Woody," to the wanderings of the People's Hobo himself, Guthrie, who was then on his deathbed. And many people contended—and do to this day—that he bought his first anthem, "Blowin' in the Wind," from a strung-out New Jersey kid for fifty bucks. But, among the young, who were questioning with unparalleled ferocity that supposed purity of their authority figures, whose rules, guidelines, and dreamy egalitarianism were being made mockery of down South and elsewhere, Dylan became a role model, a mouthpiece, a poet laureate. Suddenly poetry became commercial.

"I think there was more talent around the Village after Dylan," says Van Ronk, "but there was more hokey shit around, too. Money always attracts talented people; money also attracts greed."

Both the talented and the hokey had their turn on Tuesday nights at the Gaslight, surrounded by three sets by Van Ronk. The exploding folk lyrics of America were offered up by a steady round of middle-class sensitives, for the perusal of a discerning audience of their peers. "Any music is music of its time," Van Ronk says. "But the music of the sixties was *about* its time, too. It dealt almost on a one-to-one basis with the experience that people were going through."

Eric Andersen, once described by *The New York Times* as "America's answer to the Beatles," was a clean-scrubbed Hobart College dropout when his first album was released in 1965. With a heritage that was a long way from the soot-smeared Liverpool underclass of the Fab Four, he had to provoke his own downward mobility. His early songs were a catalog of freight trains boarded at dawn, magical black tramp harmonica players encountered drunk in alleys, overpowering sexual urges and discovery, the sensual thrill of Acapulco Gold. And it was all right on the money for a generation imbibing the sweetness of their independence. Later, Andersen would acknowledge the debt folk music owed to the civil rights movement, with "Thirsty Boots," a song now considered a folk standard.

Phil Ochs's concerns were always more political than personal. In college he was the editor of the radical paper. "I had an editorial saying, at the peak of the anti-Castro hysteria, that Fidel Castro is perhaps the greatest man the Western Hemisphere has produced in this century," he once told me. "This caused a giant storm, and I was taken off political stories. At the same time I went to a journalism fraternity meeting and I saw the same people who had sacked me swearing an oath to truth. I had one of my first impulses to murder, which I still haven't lost." His first song was called, appropriately, "Talking Cuban Crisis." He followed it up with odes to Billy Sol Estes, the American Medical Association, and, in 1962, warnings about America's involvement in Vietnam. Anything *The New York Times* deemed fit to print, Phil Ochs put lyrics to, often exposing in the process the *Times*'s mainstream tendencies.

While Ochs was issuing his steaming left-field editorials— "Love Me, I'm a Liberal," "Here's to the State of Mississippi," "I Ain't a'Marchin' Anymore"—Bob Dylan was approaching a psycho-socio-emotional peak, with statements like "It's Alright Ma (I'm Only Bleeding)," "Mr. Tambourine Man," and "Maggie's Farm." Tom Paxton was operating on a gentler, more philosophic level, with "Ramblin' Boy" and "I Can't Help but Wonder Where I'm Bound." Buffy Sainte-Marie, of Cree Indian descent and University of Massachusetts education, was writing "Universal Soldier," "Now That the Buffalo's Gone" and in "Cod'ine," moaning low "I feel like I'm dying and I wish I was dead." David Blue was a good deal less dire in his playful but precise portrait of the contemporary dropout—"I Like to Sleep Late in the Morning." Richie Havens's signature song was written by Jerry Merrick, an eight-minute tone poem called "Follow," that was its author's entire output. The Fugs were more known for their scatological laments, like "Saran Wrap" and "Slum Goddess," but when Havens sang Tuli Kupferberg's "Morning, Morning," he uncovered the antic Fug for the poet he was. Richard Fariña's

"Mainline Prosperity Blues" detailed with heartfelt cynicism a generation's decline, as did Patrick Sky's "Nectar of God." And Joni Mitchell's "Urge for Going," but a sliver of her prodigious creativity, defined the fever gripping this footloose and anxious crowd of American artists, as they thumbed from coffeehouse to coffeehouse, from Cambridge to Berkeley, from Minneapolis to Austin, approaching their prime in an uncertain and dangerous age.

Beyond the natural yearning for expression and recognition, Dave Van Ronk sees the omnipresent shadow. "Something happened in this country when they dropped that bomb in Japan," he says, "and something still further happened when the Russians got the bomb to drop in testing. It's like someone who is under a sentence of death—suspended. You'd get these incredible psychotic mood swings in the country—elation, depression, manic activity." On the night of the Kennedy-Khrushchev showdown over the Cuban missile crisis in 1962, Van Ronk was working at the Gaslight. "That sort of brought it all to the surface," he says with a rumble in his throat. "We had a really drunken, depressed evening of music, everybody saying, 'This is it. Adios.' Later we went down to Chinatown and did up an incredible feast. Then there was this wild party at my apartment on Waverly Place. We went through all the mood swings right there. Nobody who went through that experience came out of it the same as they were when they went in."

As much as anyone else, these mood swings affected the writers and musicians who bent over guitars and huddled in underground cellars and caves playing the new folk music. "I can't look at the sixties with much lucidity," Eric Andersen told me in an informal chat at the El Quixote Bar, next door to the Chelsea Hotel, the famed bohemian hangout that has been overrun by rock groups since the sixties. "It was a crazy era, and the streets were kind of clouded over. You could see the forces of repression at work, but the ones who were fighting that repression couldn't agree with each other. So it was a negative time, with everybody vying for attention and getting caught up in their own ego trips." Yet with great pride he compared the era to Paris in the twenties.

Phil Ochs was uncategorically effusive. "That period in the Village was incredibly exciting, supereuphoric," he said. "There was total creativity on the part of a great number of individuals that laid the bedrock for the next ten years."

Even Van Ronk was not immune to the momentum. "We were very conscious that something important was going on," he says. "Essentially, everybody was performing for everybody else. The community was the audience that counted. To get the approval of Joni Mitchell was infinitely better than a three-page write-up in the *Times*. And, of course, Joni herself was working for the same approval. I remember one time Philsy came back from a recording session. I asked him how it went. 'How did it go?' he said. 'We have just changed the entire course of Western music. That's how it went.' "

Perspective has given Van Ronk quite a different evaluation of the era's work, however. "In terms of staying power, what was happening on Broadway in the thirties was more important," he says. "The sixties as a paradigm allowed for a good deal of sloppiness of detail as well as form. A great many of the singer-songwriters of the time were writing under their capabilities, not pushing themselves. A lot of the material you just couldn't get next to unless you were the person who had written it. I'm reminded of something Lenin said in 1920. The state publishing house had brought out a book of poetry, love poems from the poet to his wife, and Lenin said, 'Don't they know there's a paper shortage? He should have printed two copies. One for him, one for his wife.' With the exception of Dylan's work and Paxton's and a few others, very little came out of that era."

Still, Van Ronk would not quibble with Andersen's description of the Village in the sixties as a latter-day Paris in the twenties. "Paris in the twenties does come to mind," he allows. "There was an awful lot of smoke there, too, and not terribly much fire. Everybody was a fucking genius on the Left Bank in 1922."

In 1965 all the geniuses were holed up in a single apartment house on Waverly Place, which became the sixties version of 190 Spring Street. Barry Kornfeld, who now teaches at the Guitar Study Center, was the first one to move in. Dave and Terri followed, and when the Van Ronks moved to larger quarters, they installed Patrick Sky in their old apartment. Alix Dobkin, married to Sam Hood, who ran the Gaslight, lived on the fourth floor. Classical guitarist Jon Lynn was somewhere in the building. At Waverly Place Dylan met one of his earliest mentors, Paul Clayton, who died in the late sixties. Paul Simon dropped by to visit Kornfeld. "Terri still keeps a basement room there for storage," Van Ronk reveals. "I think she still has Dylan's corduroy cap."

The Van Ronk apartment was the nexus of one Village crowd. There were others. "It was essentially a question of who hung around whose house. Patrick and Tom were part of one particular crowd, Eric and Phil were part of another. There was a crowd around Fred Neil—Tim Hardin, John Sebastian, Karen Dalton. Tuli Kupferberg was very close to the Waverly Place people."

Though few of those people remain even in the city, Van Ronk remembers those days with unalloyed pleasure. "We all lived in each other's pockets. I think Terri and I were the only legally married couple in that crowd. We had all kinds of rules so that we could screw. There were times nobody was allowed to barge in, which goes to show how much barging in went on. All in all they were as fine a bunch of fucked-up boyos as you ever saw in your life."

Van Ronk's crowd was composed of drinkers who also smoked dope. There was a kind of segregation in force then, he recalls, that put drinkers on one side, smokers on the other—drinkers down in the gutter, smokers up on the ethereal plane. It was not an ethos he had much use for. "Why did people have to build these enormous, rickety, theoretical, bargain-basement, mystical structures to justify getting stoned?" he cries. "I mean, you're getting stoned man, okay, fine, get stoned. I think that was a very middle-class rationalization. All those kids who were into drugs as a self-awareness trip always struck us as being silly, just plain silly. And the mystical stuff that went along with it was boring. People would sit around all day and say, 'Boy, am I stoned. Wow, I'm so stoned.'

"I met Mississippi John Hurt one time, and we were sitting around doing dope, and John wouldn't touch it. 'Where I come from,' he said, 'we used to call that poor man's whiskey.' I thought that was really sharp."

His experiences with the stiffer hallucinogens, so popular as the sixties expanded, were also inglorious. "I took peyote one time, and—Jesus Christ—I was never so sick in my life. I was ill for days. The thing about liquor is, it wears off. I noticed the peyote just kept on and on."

And yet the generation's psychic escalation from dope to acid and then to heroin was no more than an eerie parallel of the country's growing commitment to violence. In scores of urban ghettos, black citizens were uprising. On dozens of manicured campuses, students were testing their nascent power. And Vietnam occupied each day a larger and larger share of the news as well as the consciousness of millions of draft-age young men. Van Ronk did his part for the War Resisters' League, attended meetings and conventions and demonstrations, plotted and schemed with the best of them. "That's when all the postwar babies hit college," he says. "All of a sudden you had this enormous number of eighteen-, nineteen-, and twenty-year-olds, proportionately more than the country had ever seen. If it had been a period of military peace, it would have been quite different. But, confronted with the war at the same time that the ghettos were going up, the civil rights movement getting strong (you also had this massive migration of blacks from the South), all these things sort of came together."

As if to quell the soul's unrest, some buried their heads under loud music and handed flowers to the cops. Strung out in doorways in Greenwich Village, or Akron, Ohio, it was possible for the lonesome folk-music freak to feel a kinship with struggling blacks and foxhole buddies who never came back, if not to assuage a deeper sense of guilt. When Johnson stepped down in 1968, when a generation of protesters shook him loose, this guilt mingled with the joy and awe and terror of what had been accomplished. What do you do to follow such an impressive act? When asked the same question, Bob Dylan, who had been blinding us album after album, topped by the explosive passion of *Blonde on Blonde,* proceeded to nearly kill himself on his motorcycle. Heading toward the Democratic convention in Chicago, in the summer of 1968, the generation seemed motivated by the same self-destructive impulse. Once again, Richard Nixon was a central character.

"The election of Nixon in 1968 was the turning point," says Van Ronk. "Everyone who was involved in folk music certainly felt it. The whole left-wing wave had passed. Thermidor had arrived."

Perhaps no one felt it as strongly as Phil Ochs. In one of his last interviews, in 1974, he told me that songwriting had become increasingly difficult for him since the late sixties. "It could be alcohol," he speculated. "It could be the deterioration of the politics I was involved in. It could be a general deterioration of the country. Basically, me and the country were deteriorating simultaneously, and that's why it stopped coming. Since then discipline has been constantly on my mind, training—'get it together,' 'clean up your act.' I'm now thirty-three and I may or may not succeed. I haven't been able to do it yet. But the impulse is as strong as ever. To my dying day I'll always think about the next possible song."

Says Van Ronk, "Phil's songs had a very short shelf life, and he had to keep grinding out new ones as long as he was going to stay in that topical medium. It was a corner he painted himself into quite deliberately. Eventually it just got to be too much."

At the end of one particular blue streak, where he disgraced himself in several houses with his drunken shenanigans, alienating people he'd counted on as friends, Phil took his life in 1976.

"When Phil killed himself everyone knew that an important statement had just been made," Van Ronk says. "Nobody agreed on what that statement was."

It is the winter of 1982, and Van Ronk is scheduled to play a gig in Bridgeport, Connecticut. The theater is run-down, the area is pretty seedy, and the gig has already been postponed once due to sluggish advance sales. Though something of an acoustic folk revival has been taking place of late, brought on

at least in part by the decade's sorry economy, Van Ronk reflects little of it. When I arrive at the train station to give him a
lift to the club, I find him in the waiting room, a wistful figure,
a bit stooped, rubbing his hands over his guitar case. At the
club, in response to his request for three fingers of Old
Grand-Dad about five minutes before showtime, he is told
there's no liquor on the premises. He has to settle for a Pepsi
instead, as he seeks out the more stable end of the standard
folk–dressing-room flophouse couch on which to continue
our conversation.

"One gets very bad years, one gets phenomenally good
years," he says of his current situation, a decade and a half removed from the heyday. "You can't look at any twelve-month
period and say 'This is a trend,' because the trend is up and
down and then up and then down. I work more now than I did
two, three years ago, but I'm not sure if that's because there's
a greater demand or if I've just been pushing harder to get
more work because I need more money to keep afloat." He's
shared billings during this period with other remnants of the
urban folk scare, like John Fahey, Paul Geremiah, and Bonnie
Raitt, who, of the three, has most made out like a rocker in the
chilly season since Thermidor. "Frequently I'll make more
money opening for a really strong draw than doing my own
show," he says. Tonight's show is his alone, however, and neither of us has to mention the lack of a line winding around the
block clamoring for tickets.

"It's a living," he sighs, "which is probably more than I
ever expected to get out of it. It's not a fortune, which at one
time I did expect to get out of it. But that was a belief I only
came to slowly and reluctantly. My attitude in the early sixties
was, This is the way to make a decent living; it's not the road
to the Big Rock Candy Mountain. I'm a professional performer; that's what I do for a living. The people who came into it
after 1963—from between 1963 and 1968—their first expo-
sure to the business was of visions of sugarplums dancing in
their heads. For them the realization was a terrible shock."

This is not to say that Van Ronk didn't entertain the occasional sugarplum vision now and then. "My peers and I were
always on the brink of huge success—things that could have

really materialized," he recalls, unable to keep from sounding rueful. Perhaps the biggest plum he let drop was offered to him late in 1961 by Albert Grossman, the music magnate from Chicago who would shepherd the career of Bob Dylan into the stratosphere, or as Van Ronk chortled, "When you see money in terms of Dylan, you're talking about corporate wealth." For a brief time Grossman managed Van Ronk.

"He was feeling out New York City, and I was feeling him out," Van Ronk says. "I was going up to his place on Central Park West a couple of times a week, and he was starting to do a little booking for me. Finally after about a month of foreplay, he asked me if I'd like to join a group. 'We need somebody who can sing a harmony line and who's competent on guitar, and we think you're it.' 'What group?' I wanted to know. 'Who's in it?' Grossman told me, 'Mary Travers and Peter Yarrow.'

"I said, 'I think you're wrong.' And that was that." So Grossman tapped a Village comic whose specialty was imitating a flushing toilet: Noel Stookey, the Toilet Man. He suggested a slight name change, for euphony: the result was called Peter, Paul & Mary.

But even this encounter with Grossman was a good deal more satisfying than Van Ronk's initial meeting with the (even then) legendary great gray eminence at the Gate of Horn, Grossman's domain in Chicago, in 1958. Odetta had heard Van Ronk perform at the Café Bizarre and promised him she'd deliver to Grossman a tape, if Dave would provide her with one, which he did. But after dangling for some months with no word back from Grossman, Van Ronk took it upon himself to hitch out to Chicago to present himself before the legend. "I told him I was the guy whose tape Odetta gave him. He told me he never got a tape." It was an inauspicious beginning, and things deteriorated from there. "Naturally, I had my guitar, so he let me audition. I did a whole bunch of songs while Grossman sat there absolutely stone faced. I was very spooked, but I think I acquitted myself reasonably well. When I finished I climbed down off the stage and went over to where he was sitting and asked him what he thought. 'You

know who lives not far from here?' Grossman said. 'No.' 'Big
Bill Broonzy. You know who else lives in town?' 'No.' 'Muddy
Waters. Josh White always plays here when he's passing
through. So, tell me, why should I hire you?' I was drained;
I was exhausted," Van Ronk explains. " 'Grossman!' I
screamed at him, 'You're Crow-Jimming me, you cock-
sucker.' "

It's unfair to suggest in any way that Van Ronk is just another white boy infatuated by black music and basing his career on a weak approximation of it. His style is distinctly his
own; no one treats a song with more respect or fondles it with
such tenderness. His love affair with the century's literature of
music dates back to his childhood in Queens. When his parents were divorced, Van Ronk was raised by his mother—a legal secretary—her parents, and her brother. His Irish heritage
easily swamped the Dutch of his name. His grandfather played
piano. "My grandmother sang from morning to night," he recalls. "How many people do you know who can sing 'The
Gypsy's Warning' from beginning to end?" In fact, it was Van
Ronk's fine-tuned sense of musical perfection that helped ruin
his last best chance for the big bucks when in the mid-sixties
he put together the Hudson Dusters—a rock band, of all
things.

"Sometimes it'll take me years to get together a chart that
I myself am satisfied with, but I can at least do a sketch and
get it into some kind of performing shape inside of a day or
two. No way you can do that with a band. You couldn't do
anything without having to rehearse for two million hours. After three or four weeks out on the road, playing the same god-
damn things over and over again, it was really excruciating."

Ironically, Van Ronk regarded himself as the weakest
link. "Everybody there was a pretty good musician, in one way
or another, but not in the same way. It was hard to define a
common ground. The drummer was into jazz, the bass player
had played with Jimi Hendrix, the pianist was from the hippie
Haight-Ashbury persuasion. Idiomatically, the music wasn't
close enough to what I'd been doing to completely cover all
the ideas. The better the idea, the harder it was for me to mas-

ter. And when a piece of material was within my idiom, the more competent I was to handle it, the less competent the rest of the band would be. To always feel I was dragging the outfit was demoralizing."

Aside from that, it was a financial disaster. "I couldn't get any more money for the band than I could get for myself. So I was supporting the band out of my own pocket. We made an album and the record company walked away from it. We lasted six months, and all told it cost me every cent I had in the bank. I haven't had a bank account since."

Van Ronk's albums have hardly ever meant money in the bank, though they sport their share of splendid moments, snapshots from America's store of obscure treasures, black, white, gold or blue. His first two albums, *Dave Van Ronk Sings Earthy Ballads and Blues* and *Black Mountain Blues,* he would prefer to forget. "There was a tremendous drive to get recorded," he says. "If you had an album out, even if nobody heard it, you were in a position to get more work. It established you as a professional. Though, God knows, my first albums should have established me as a professional house painter. But I lobbied so hard for them." Two of his albums, *Inside* and *In the Tradition,* have been repackaged as *Dave Van Ronk.* The latter of the two originals included spirited performances with the Red Onion Jazz Band. Still in print is my own favorite Van Ronk album, *Just Dave Van Ronk,* with flawless renditions of "God Bless the Child," "Baby, Let Me Lay It on You," John Hurt's "Candy Man," and the poignant depression-era "Wanderin'." With precision, with humor, with power, he approaches each song on equal terms, as a friend.

Since 1976 he has been recording for the tiny Vermont-based independent label Philo. "They give me complete artistic freedom," says Van Ronk, with a bit of a grin. "With regard to my own recordings, I find myself as a kind of senior partner there, because most of the people have not been in the business as long as I have. If they could really sell a whole hell of a lot of records, I think that would effectively reduce the power of my seniority."

In any case, he's given voice to another couple of dozen

gems, including Joni Mitchell's "Urge for Going" and "That Song About the Midway," his playful signature, "Would You Like to Swing on a Star," and the Bert Williams vaudeville-era tune "Somebody Else Not Me." An unexpected delight to be found on the album named for this last song is Dylan's "Song to Woody," arguably the lyric that created MacDougal Street, captured by Van Ronk twenty years later (the song is as old as Dylan was when he wrote it) in a fresh, strong, and resounding fashion. No doubt Van Ronk has come by all his hard traveling honestly.

And yet I'm brought up short by a remark he makes just prior to showtime, discussing the night's projected program. The lead-off tune, as usual, he says, will be "Green Rocky Road," a song he learned from Len Chandler, who got it from a tone-deaf poet named Bob Kaufman, who remembered it from when he was young in New Orleans. "It's a very nice, steady guitar thing that doesn't change," says Van Ronk. "It's one that's very hard to botch. You don't want to botch that first tune."

This consideration stabs at me. In the sixties, when I last saw him perform, he projected an image so totally competent as to make the thought of botching anything seem out of the question, and at the same time he was so boisterously irreverent and above it all that a missed chord, line, song, or an entire night, wouldn't have bothered him in the least.

Without a dram of booze to tether him, Van Ronk lopes onstage in Bridgeport. Is he playing out the string in the minor leagues, then, or polishing the show for Broadway? It's hard to tell. The crowd isn't any better than moderate, including, in its midst, supposedly some long-lost relatives, but the room is small and they greet him warmly. I must admit I find myself nervously rooting for him to do well here. And when he nearly botches the intro to "Green Rocky Road," I feel like slipping under the table or at least running down to the package store for some equalizer. But a Paxton song about John Hurt bails him out. And a love song to New Jersey, with Van Ronk as the deranged conductor shouting out "Secaucus, Ho-Ho-Kus, Lodi . . . ," establishes his old identity as the rascally original I remembered, tilting his guitar against the windmills of fortune.

Backstage, with the aid of some purloined vino and abetted by an old friend, Van Ronk is at last able to unwind. It had been an abbreviated set, cut short by a broken fingernail, a bit untidy by Van Ronk standards. But the man still has his chops. And better days would surely find him ready. But, bolstered now by the wine, the high of performance, the relief of performance completed, he begins to lean into tales the way he used to, and before long it could be Gaslight '64 again, the heyday, when he could take over Carnegie Hall or command any room with the sound of his pauses before the punch lines.

Returning for another glimpse at the Big Rock Candy Mountain, Van Ronk tells about a lonesome folkie named Peter Tork, who climbed that fatal hill in 1966, when he was inducted into the fabricated rock group, the Monkees, and shipped off to Los Angeles for fame and fortune, if not glory.

Van Ronk ran into Tork at his favorite table at the Troubadour, L.A.'s glitziest sixties dive, and Tork brought him back to his house. "I have no idea how many rooms were in that place," Van Ronk goes on, "but there must have been twenty, swimming pool, the whole thing. And it was wall to wall with crashed-out hippies. In every room you had to step over zonked-out people, screwing couples, whatever. He took me up to a screening room. I don't know how much money he spent on movie equipment, but I was marveling to myself at the enormous amount of bread that was obviously just going right down the tubes and at the enormous number of leeches and hangers-on that he had acquired and was more or less supporting with very good will. Nothing stingy about our boy Peter, by God. He was enjoying it.

"A year or two later I was out there again, and I went over to the Troubadour, and Peter was there, probably at the same table where I'd seen him the last time. I said, 'Hi Peter, you still living at that place up in the hills?' And he said, 'Yeah, I still live there. I had to sell it for taxes, but the new people let me sleep in a room in the basement.' " Van Ronk explodes into laughter. "But he still had the equanimity, which was marvelous."

A little bit later, as I drive him back to the railroad station, he recalls the story. "That's what happened after the sixties," he says; "the economic facts of life changed. People who grew up in the sixties, who made what they thought were their final adjustments to the real world, must have found terrific consternation in the fact that the nineteen sixties weren't the real world. All that loose money ain't gonna be around forever. And the check is *not* in the mail."

On the record label:

BLAST
RECORDS

BL-205
(X-001)
Original Music
(BMI) 2:10

Arr. & Cond. by
VINNY CATALANO

CONEY ISLAND BABY
(V. Catalano - P. Alonzo)
THE EXCELLENTS

COUNTERCLOCKWISE FROM TOP RIGHT: "Coney Island Baby," cut in 1962, the 45 that briefly brought success and fame to the Excellents (courtesy BMI Records). The Angels (Jiggs Meister on right), 1963 (courtesy Maurice Seymour). Dion and the Belmonts, 1962. The Beatles with Murray the K, on set location of *Help!* in 1965 (left to right, George Harrison, John Lennon, Murray the K, Paul McCartney, Ringo Starr).

★ 2 ★

High School U.S.A.

From the moment Elvis Presley lowered his lids and shook his hips on "The Ed Sullivan Show" in 1956, teenage America knew it had a sound to call its own at last. Rough and passionate and unrestrained, rock 'n' roll was the antithesis of polite pop music. It took its identity from simple country folk and urban black men who harmonized their wistful dreams endlessly under the moon of love. For children of the privileged class, this worship of the earthy virtues of "race" and "cowboy" and "hillbilly" music was but a hint of the uprisings to follow. Yet by 1960 the mavens of American commerce had temporarily all but civilized the beast, teaching it how to jump to their commands. Taking no chances against the vagaries of trends and talent, record labels created their own manufacturing idols and fads the same way other production lines rolled out Hula-Hoops. The turf was owned by Avalon, Fabian, Rydell, Anka, Checker, Vee, Cannon, and Funicello—not a pimple among them; for Elvis and the Everly Brothers had been drafted, Johnny Ace and Buddy Holly killed, and Little Richard retired to the ministry.

Still, there was enough left in traditional rock 'n' roll from 1960 to 1963 to safely benumb all those expectant graduates who were still living at home and to isolate them from the more dire realities of the changing times, whose constant threats were the province of folk music. Under the hypnotic chatter of our nation's deejays, doo-wop music prevailed— white soul for guys who collected on the street corner to ogle the neighborhood starlets named Ruby Baby, Barbara Ann, and Darling Lorraine. As the decade progressed, the girls would get into the act as well, with names that were as sweet and naïve—Kathy Young & the Innocents, the Angels, the Chiffons, Cathy Jean & the Roommates—as their intentions were obvious. In California, where they seem to have no neighborhoods, no street corners, kids made do with wheels and surfboards, with the Beach Boys and Jan & Dean. Yet, East or West, no one had a reputation; few had even been to the Big City. The twist would change that; with its daring instrumentation and sexy cadences, it offered the baby-boom generation its first taste of a night life. And the numbers in which they descended upon the city lights, in 1962, were great enough to attract world notice. And kids noticed, too. It wouldn't be the last time that they'd realize between dances, "Hey, there are a lot of us."

The Kennedy assassination came to High School U.S.A. like a kidney punch, stopping all the dancing. The lights went out, and it was a somber world in the morning. A generation lost its virginity, emerging from the soiled sheets a bit disillusioned, but tougher and more confident. Gone were the romantic dreams proffered by the street-corner guys and girls. In their place came the sophisticated whimsy of the Beatles, pitted against the elegant evil of the Rolling Stones (for a good versus evil battle as intense, you'd have to go back to Elvis versus Pat Boone), as pop music after 1963 began to fuse with the tremors of the age. All that was necessary to add would be Dylan's atonal apocalypse; that was coming in 1965. By then the neophytes of the neighborhood would either have to take a pad in the Village with their old lady or move back home with Mom.

Playlist

1960

January:	"Where or When" *Dion & the Belmonts*
	"I Only Want You" *The Passions*
	"Darling Lorraine" *The Knockouts*
February:	"Step by Step" *The Crests*
March:	"Cherry Pie" *Skip & Flip*
	"Gloria" *The Passions*
April:	"When You Wish upon a Star" *Dion & the Belmonts*
	"The White Cliffs of Dover" *The Mystics*
May:	"Image of a Girl" *The Safaris*
June:	"Over the Rainbow" *The Demensions*
	"Trouble in Paradise" *The Crests*
	"Pennies from Heaven" *The Skyliners*
July:	"In the Still of the Night" *Dion & the Belmonts*
August:	"Diamonds and Pearls" *The Paradons*
September:	"Tonight's the Night" *The Shirelles*
October:	"A Thousand Stars" *Kathy Young & the Innocents*
	"Lonely Teenager" *Dion*
	"Isn't It Amazing" *The Crests*
	"Will You Love Me Tomorrow" *The Shirelles*
	"Angel Baby" *Rosie & the Originals*

1961

January:	"Dedicated to the One I Love" *The Shirelles*
	"There's a Moon Out Tonight" *The Capris*
	"Once upon a Time" *Rochell & the Candles*
February:	"Baby Blue" *The Echoes*
	"Please Love Me Forever" *Cathy Jean & the Roommates*
	"Tonight I Fell in Love" *The Tokens*
March:	"Where I Fell in Love" *The Capris*
April:	"Mama Said" *The Shirelles*
	"Life Is but a Dream" *The Earls*
	"Barbara Ann" *The Regents*

"Those Oldies but Goodies" *Little Caesar &
the Romans*

"In My Heart" *The Timetones*

May: "Tell Me Why" *The Belmonts*
July: "Mr. Happiness" *Johnny Maestro*
August: "Don't Get Around Much Anymore" *The
Belmonts*

"Juke Box Saturday Night" *Nino & the Ebb
Tides*

September: "I Love How You Love Me" *The Paris
Sisters*

" 'Til" *The Angels*

"Look in My Eyes" *The Chantels*

"Please Mr. Postman" *The Marvelettes*

October: "Runaround Sue" *Dion*
November: "Once in Awhile" *The Chimes*

"There's No Other (Like My Baby)" *The
Crystals*

"The Wanderer" *Dion*

December: "Baby It's You" *The Shirelles*

1962

January: "Cry Baby Cry" *The Angels*
February: "She Cried" *Jay & the Americans*
March: "Soldier Boy" *The Shirelles*

"Uptown" *The Crystals*

"Shout, Shout" *Ernie Maresca*

April: "Playboy" *The Marvelettes*
June: "Little Diane" *Dion*
July: "Come On, Little Angel" *The Belmonts*

"You Belong to Me" *The Duprees*

September: "He's a Rebel" *The Crystals*
October: "Don't Hang Up" *The Orlons*

"My Own True Love" *The Duprees*

November: "Love Came to Me" *Dion*

"Chains" *The Cookies*

"Coney Island Baby" *The Excellents*

"Tell Him" *The Exciters*

"Remember Then" *The Earls*

December: "He's Sure the Boy I Love" *The Crystals*

1963

January:	"Ruby Baby" *Dion*
February:	"He's So Fine" *The Chiffons*
	"Don't Say Nothin' Bad About My Baby" *The Cookies*
	"Sandy" *Dion*
	"My Foolish Heart" *The Demensions*
March:	"Foolish Little Girl" *The Shirelles*
April:	"Da Doo Ron Ron" *The Crystals*
	"This Little Girl" *Dion*
June:	"My Boyfriend's Back" *The Angels*
	"One Fine Day" *The Chiffons*
	"Till Then" *The Classics*
July:	"Heat Wave" *Martha & the Vandellas*
August:	"Be My Baby" *The Ronettes*
	"Sally Go Round the Roses" *The Jaynettes*
	"Then He Kissed Me" *The Crystals*
September:	"Donna the Prima Donna" *Dion*
	"A Love So Fine" *The Chiffons*
October:	"Have You Heard" *The Duprees*
	"I Wonder What She's Doing Tonight" *Barry & the Tamerlanes*
	"I Adore Him" *The Angels*
	"Walking in the Rain" *The Ronettes*
	"Unchained Melody" *Vito & the Salutations*
November:	"Drip Drop" *Dion DiMucci*
	"Quicksand" *Martha & the Vandellas*
	"Popsicles, Icicles" *The Murmaids*
	"Girls Grow Up Faster Than Boys" *The Cookies*
	"I Have a Boyfriend" *The Chiffons*
December:	"Baby I Love You" *The Ronettes*
	"Thank You and Goodnight" *The Angels*

John Kuse *(The Excellents)*

Jiggs Meister *(The Angels)*

Despite the cold-war breezes blowing in from Russia during the early sixties, the continuing Cuban crisis, the missile gap, the megaton gap, the freedom rides down South, the Berlin crisis, Sputnik, the red menace, and the constant suppressed anxiety over the bomb, those of us in High School U.S.A. somehow found enormous confidence in young President Kennedy's ability to handle all this with consummate aplomb, with enough time left over in the evening to escort his wife, Jackie, down to the Peppermint Lounge, where all sorts of senators and socialites and truck drivers were doing the twist. Thanks to JFK's New Frontier, the spotlight of international notoriety had been focused on the youth. Our music and our dances, our taste in clothes and what we liked to eat for breakfast suddenly was the stuff of cover stories. Disquieting as it may have been for us to have to share the music with our parents, that was a small price to pay for the inflated sense of self-importance the cult of youth had given us.

Under a blanket of loud rock 'n' roll, we would remain snug and secure through 1963. In New York City our guardian angel was named Murray the K, who tucked us in each night from seven to eleven over WINS. A cherished high-school flame, Murray rode out the last days of rock 'n' roll in an open convertible, commanding all the attention and respect of any big-time greaser worth his tap shoes. And if from 1960 to 1963 we were coming under an increasingly bland collection of sounds—the product of the vinyl mills in Hollywood and Philadelphia, forgettable and contrived attempts to separate the youth from their growing budgets—the K's nightly swinging soirees held up. While doo-wop breathed its last on the street corners of our cities, Murray kept playing the Duprees and the Crests. Underneath his radio Elevated Line, girl groups like the Ronettes and the Shirelles ferociously snapped their chewing gum and cha-chaed in place. Countless submarine-race-watchers nodded in tune to the K's mangled language, shaggy-dog introductions, and sick jokes, hanging on every nuance of his programming genius. The buzzers and bells, the imitation pig-Latin—called Me-uss-urray—the Swahili chants, and the kettle drums ("Ah-bay!," etc.) were one thing. But the highlight each night was his Boss Record of the Night contest, in which a generation of incipient rock critics got to vote for their favorite among the day's five best new releases, while a generation of singers and groups, the same age, pinned their futures on the results.

I talked to John Kuse one day in 1982 at his home in Brooklyn. Once the lead singer of a doo-wop group named the Excellents, Kuse's claim to immortality was called "Coney Island Baby." Naturally, the group dropped the record off with Murray the K soon after its release. Then they promptly forgot about it. "I was sitting in a movie theater, watching the picture," Kuse recounts, "and a bunch of kids run in. 'John, it won the Boss Record contest!' Unbelievable! Everybody's screaming; everybody jumps up and we all go out to a restaurant. It was unbelievable, all the screaming and yelling. So now it's going up for Boss Record of the Week. Needless to say, the whole of Pelham Parkway—a thousand kids—are waiting for the countdown. Here we are on the number-one avenue in the Bronx, the top Jewish neighborhood going, and there must have been hundreds of people out their windows, on the streets. Anyway, the countdown: number five, number four, number three. Finally we heard number two—and we knew we were number one! Unbelievable. And then the chimes come on. 'Boss Record of the Week—"Coney Island Baby!" ' Oh, it was fabulous. There was yelling and screaming and jumping all over. It was like New Year's Eve."

Murray the K's stage shows were just as terrific, rivaling in energy and excitement those rock 'n' roll extravaganzas of Alan Freed, the man the K succeeded on WINS. Virtually no rocker of the era is without a Murray the K tale.

"We'd signed up for one of his Labor Day shows at the Brooklyn Fox," recalls Jiggs Meister of the Angels, during our interview at her house in suburban Connecticut. "It was for the most puny amount of money imaginable. I won't even tell you what he was paying us, because I'm too embarrassed. By the time the show came around, our record was number one. It was a big, big show, and it was fun, but not only wasn't he paying us enough; to top it off, he wouldn't even mention the name of our song when he introduced us. I mean, the only satisfaction we could get was going up to him and saying, the least you could do is give us more of a buildup—our record is number one. So it wound up being, 'And now the group with the number-one record in the country, "My Boyfriend's Back"—the Angels.' I have a live recording of it, so I can hear him say that."

Unfortunately, the K's gnarled tongue never quite survived the coming of the Beatles. Musically, the revolution marched by him as surely and as swiftly as it marched by the groups whose records he programmed from 1960 to 1963. Though he would call himself the fifth Beatle—much as he called himself the K, from the mundane Kaufman—like most of our Top 40 heroes of youth, like the girl groups and the street-corner guys and their writers who worked at the Brill

Building, he failed to make the transition from rock 'n' roll to rock.

But before the bullets in Dallas and before the twist, before the multitrack recording studio ushered in the space age, the a cappella spontaneity of sidewalk, stoop, and schoolyard reigned in the cities. It was a sweet time, and this was a working-class sound, with something ragged about it, unsteady, as if it had had a few too many beers after work and might lurch out of key at any minute. The feeling was right at the surface: "I love you so/never let you go" sung to a thousand different tunes in a hundred different neighborhoods, from the Pittsburgh of the Skyliners to the Los Angeles of the Coasters to the Bronx of Dion & the Belmonts. The concerns of the music were smaller then, not global at all, but as important as the school dance, the Saturday night date, and the cheerleaders you ogled from the boardwalk at Coney Island named Kathy-O and Cindy, Oh Cindy and Donna and Jo-ann.

"We went to sing at a rock 'n' roll show at Palisades Park, and, needless to say, we got booed off the stage," John Kuse remembers. "We were singing about Coney Island at Palisades Park." When he made "Coney Island Baby" in 1962, Kuse and his friends lived in the Bronx near Dion & the Belmonts. The Demensions ("Over the Rainbow") went to their high school—Columbus. The Regents ("Barbara Ann") lived in the neighborhood. Kuse had been to Coney Island only once or twice. But he lives in Brooklyn now, on the edge of Prospect Park, not in the best of neighborhoods, he admits, but it's coming back.

"We sang in Atlantic City on the Steel Pier, and it was piped into Philadelphia. Supposedly, that was a buildup for us to go on 'Bandstand.' They told us we were going to go to Philly to sing on 'Bandstand,' but it didn't materialize. We would have been set if we'd gone on 'Bandstand.' "

Unlike Alan Freed, Dick Clark tap-danced his way through the Payola hearings of 1959–60, suffering little more than a severely scuffed left shoe. By 1962 his dance show, "American Bandstand," had become so powerful that indeed just one appearance on it was often enough to shoot an ordinary record into the Top 10. It was Clark, in fact, who auditioned dozens of singers until he found one who could do a letter-perfect imitation of Hank Ballard on an obscure Ballard B side called "The Twist."

Like a Top 40 single, Kuse's career vanished into the airwaves before he got a chance to memorize the lyrics. But, after twenty years, there's still that nervous taunt of melody, itching at the back of his skull. "How they managed to get us onto that Atlantic City show beats the hell out of me," he says. "I don't know of any other groups that sang on that show. But it was the Steel Pier, and it was on TV in Jersey and parts of Pennsylvania. 'Let's get these Coney Island kids in there, you know, maybe we'll stick them on "Bandstand."' It disillusioned the hell out of me, the way we had to travel there and pay our own way. We even had to bring our own uniforms. We were all in matching blue blazers. When we got there the promoter threw off my jacket and gave me a gold one. I said, 'But we've got our own.' He told me, 'Here, wear the gold.' Nobody from the record company showed up. We didn't see anybody there. We sang on TV and that was it. And that was supposed to set us up for Philly? To me it was a fiasco. A couple of weeks went by and nobody called us. What was happening? 'Are we going to Philadelphia? Why are we going to Philadelphia? This is crazy. I don't believe we're on "Bandstand" at all.'

"I guess we weren't that gung-ho about singing as it was. We liked to sing, but that experience at Atlantic City threw us and knocked us for a loop, after trying for a year and a half, two years, walking around with our demos. I didn't think I was that good. We thought we were just normal, run-of-the-mill singers and maybe we shouldn't pursue it any further. So we said the hell with it. We got into a pretty big argument with the record company after that, and they wound up saying, 'We don't want the five other guys, we just want the lead singer, John. We can get anybody to mouth the words behind him, but we want him in Philadelphia. We're suing for five hundred thousand dollars if he don't show.'

" 'Me? Now they're saying to hell with my friends? I'm telling ya, what kind of a place is this?' But when we got into the contract, we were underage; they couldn't have done a thing to us.

" 'I don't want to go down this hole, Ma. I'm scared.' I know it sounds screwy," says Kuse, grinning sheepishly, "but I really didn't trust these guys. I had a girl friend at the time; I wanted to stay with her. And I really don't know if we would have gone on 'Bandstand' or what, but they didn't prepare us for anything, and we thought it was just a flimsy operation, and we were afraid. We were kids; we didn't know what we were doing."

"Coney Island Baby" never made the Top 40, and the Excellents soon disbanded. "We remained friends. I think we sang until about sixty-three or sixty-four. But the guys went off with their girls and whatnot. In sixty-four or sixty-five we drifted apart."

But for Jiggs Meister and the Angels, the comedown from rock 'n' roll was even more precipitous. All the way from number one. "We were just so confused as to what to put out next," Jiggs told me. An ex-twirler in high school, now divorced and the mother of a teenage girl, Jiggs is still an Angel, operating on weekends out of Connecticut. "Unfortunately, the choice that was made was really horrible. I hated it. It was just a big bomb." Although "I Adore Him" reached number twenty-five, "Thank You and Goodnight" was released only a month later and failed to make the Top 40. "Wow Wow Wee," released the same month the Beatles invaded America—February 1964—was the Angels' last appearance on the charts.

After 1964 the mood of the music changed. The revolution created by the Beatles was one that called for autonomy of music and of the musicians, and girl groups were thought to be mindless marionettes, controlled by their producers. This is not to say that girl groups, individually and as a genre, didn't provide a barely postpubescent generation with its most enduring teen dreams—one part lust, one part melody. The first girls on the block to wear eyeshadow and actively cultivate bad reputations, these girl groups live in memories of thwarted adolescents as eternal vixen-virgins in slinky skirts, beehive hairdos, as at home on the back of a motorcycle as in the backseat of a T-bird. And if they were controlled by their producers, as far as label-copy credit goes, who can say for sure who really did the controlling.

Certainly history has recorded how an exotic stagewalker named Ronnie Bennett, who sang with her sister and her cousin in a group called Ronnie & the Relatives, so charmed the boy-legend record producer of the Bronx, Phil Spector, that first he changed their name to the Ronettes, then he produced their future number-one single, "Be My Baby," and finally he went all the way with the teen-dream fantasy, changing Ronnie's name to Spector and keeping her a virtual prisoner for about a half-dozen years of marriage.

"We weren't tough at all," says Jiggs. "We were sort of sweet looking, in chiffon dresses and big skirts with high heels." Born and raised in the New Jersey suburbs, what else could they be? "Our whole image was not in keeping with what was happening," Jiggs remarks, "so I guess that's why we went in a different direction. By 1966 we were doing a kind of supper-club act, choreographed by Donna McKechnie, of *A Chorus Line*, who was married to our manager at the time. It was away from rock 'n' roll—more sophisticated."

In 1964, however, while Lesley Gore was still holding out for at least a charge plate at Fortunoff's, a folksinger named Gale Garnett was presaging the New Age with "We'll Sing in the Sunshine," a pre–flower-power homage to free love. The hippie chick in a sack dress—purity personified—would supplant the girls of the avenue in a flash: the bourgeois suburban princess gave way to the earth mother.

By 1966 the sorority of "good girls" had been raided by the advance guard of the sexual revolution. In the music business, aside from black groups like the Supremes and the Marvelettes, few of the prerevolution ladies had much success. Nancy Sinatra was wearing boots and swearing she'd walk all over anyone who got in her way. Cher had long straight hair down past her backside and lived with an older man. The new earth mother was epitomized by Mama Cass Elliot of the Mamas & the Papas, all two hundred-plus pounds of her, and on the other side was Michelle Phillips, the svelte blond California sylph, all sinewy and fashion-model remote.

In the summer of 1966, who should turn up on WOR-FM, New York's (if not the nation's) first underground rock station, but Murray the K, the gnarled tongue looking for another groove in the post-Beatles heyday of the album cut. The quality control adhered to by the Beatles had inspired every working rock band. Instead of being content to issue albums with one or two good songs, as had been customary in the past, the Beatles came up with six, nine, or even twelve gems each time out. Therefore, to keep pace, the entire level of professional music-making had to be lifted, and because of that, the common denominator of pop taste hovered at near-epic standards. Opuses of rock-song autobiography burst forth, borrowing a bit of Dylan's verbosity, a tad of the Beatles' buoyant melodic flair. Unable to contain the overflow, or stanch the impassioned assault of fervid youth and music unleashed, AM radio conceded this territory to its weak sister, FM, which had been up to that juncture a static-ridden babel of foreign-language programs and the occasional Longine's Symphonette.

One morning, out of that static came in rapid succession, without introduction and without commercial separation, "Nowadays Clancy Can't Even Sing," "Time Has Come Today" and "7 and 7 Is." It was possibly the first time three non–Top 40 rock songs had been played on the radio, certainly the first time they'd ever been played *in a row*—and without deejays! Definitely a new world was upon us. It was a total break with the past, designed for a generation intent upon breaking at least one rule a day. Now we were dropping out of school, sampling the evil weed, living with the opposite sex and off the fat of the land. And our power was so great that it had even been recognized by the radio.

And then, after only a few weeks of glory, there was that unmistakable nasal twang wrapped around some seminal flower philosophy, announcing all the names of the groups we'd been digging in their sublime anonymity—Buffalo Springfield, the Chambers Brothers, Love. The bloom was off the underground. Murray the K had invaded love land. We'd been co-opted.

We didn't need Murray now: we were a radical bunch, no longer the naïve high-school kids he'd once seduced. Living in packs and sleeping on mattresses on the floor, we sure as hell didn't want any adults leering at or trying to horn in on our new bedroom arrangements. We'd seen what a travesty they'd made of the world (to say nothing of the twist). No way would they ever understand how the dawning of the FM dial would serve to unify a generation by the strength of its music, bonding us to unseen brothers and sisters in the night, at last to politicize us under a banner proclaiming a rock revolution.

The girl groups and the doo-wop guys stood resolutely on the sidelines as the rock parade passed by. "I was into the groovy stuff," says Kuse. "I got high and whatnot, until I met my wife." He was also working on Wall Street—part of the problem.

"My father was having heart surgery in the Georgetown University Hospital in Washington, D.C., at the time of one of the marches," says Jiggs. "I was down there visiting him with my mother, and the doctor came in and we had to wait downstairs, and all these bloody and battered kids were pouring into the hospital lobby. It was really amazing. In fact, there were two guys hugging each other, sort of comforting each other, and my mother turned to me and asked, 'Are those both guys?' I said yes. That was all that was said about it. It was very moving."

Like who-knows-what percentage of the real America, Jiggs was well insulated from the extremes of the sixties. Though, in some sense, for a suburban girl, the dream of a career in rock 'n' roll may have been rebellion enough. "Well, in the early sixties there was pot and stuff like that around," she says, embarrassed. "But even if the band smoked—we would use house bands, or whatever band they had—I mean, maybe all this stuff was going on and it just passed right by me; but, as far as I know, we weren't exposed to anything like that."

As the music raged to impossible heights, the blood flowed in the streets. Dancing and fighting became interchangeable. Rock 'n' roll receded into a pristine memory. In 1969, at the great sad final bash for the warriors of the rock revolution, the Woodstock Festival, unnoticed in the tumult and the acid bliss was the big reception given a group of Columbia University students, named Sha Na Na, when they offered their loving parodies of greaser passion, a series of gold-lamé epiphanies, recapturing our innocent youth in the days of Top 40.

Jiggs Meister, her sister Barbara, and Peggy Santiglia, the same Angels of "My Boyfriend's Back," returned to the road on the "oldies circuit" in 1969. Off and on, they've been working ever since. A few years ago, nearing the big four-oh herself, Barbara decided to hang up her spikes. Jiggs told me, "She said, 'I just can't make it my whole life anymore, and if I don't really make it my whole life, then I can't do it halfway.' In a way I was thinking this probably would be a good thing for me, because I'd spent my whole career working with her, but as it turned out, nobody was able to replace her. We weren't comfortable with anyone else. So eventually Peggy and I said, 'Well, let's work as a duo.' Peggy's an excellent singer," says Jiggs. "She can sing almost anything." In 1971 Peggy put out two records with a group called Dusk; both made the bottom of the charts.

"She *was* Dusk," notes Jiggs. "I think her records did pretty well, considering that there was no group. We've done a lot of recording, but it's hard for us right now. We don't know whether to do our records as a completely different group and just take our chances or stay with the name the Angels. As the Angels some people might pick up a record and listen just because they know our old songs. But, on the other hand, they might say, 'Oh, we don't want oldies. We want fifteen-year-old girls.' "

Now almost forty herself, Jiggs claims to be rocking harder than ever. In their stage show she sings Bruce Spring-

steen's "Fire," the Sam & Dave classic from 1968, "I Thank
You," the Ad-Libs' 1965 chestnut, "The Boy from New York
City." Together with Peggy, Jiggs does Edgar Winter's "Keep
Playing That Rock 'n' Roll" and Bob Seger's "Old Time Rock
'n' Roll," not bad for a couple of pampered suburban girls,
the product of easy times. Even so, Jiggs is preparing for the
inevitable moment when she'll no longer to able to rock 'n'
roll all night.

"I exercise a lot," she tells me. "I use the Nautilus ma-
chines, take a jazz class and aerobics. I'm also into doing fa-
cials. I'm getting my equipment together, and I have a friend
who has a place I can use for a while. Eventually I want to have
a little skin-care business of my own, so I have something for
myself that's steady." But not quite yet, thank you. "They always have WCBS-FM, the oldies station, on at the Spa, and
I'm sitting there doing my stretches and 'My Boyfriend's Back'
will come on. I walked in there the other day and they said,
'Oh, we saw you on the Sha Na Na show on Saturday night.' It
just cracks me up, really, that here we are, after all this time,
and there are still people who immediately know you when
you walk out there. They know all your records. It's nuts; it's
really crazy."

The dream of harmony refuses to die. And nowhere is it
more alive than among the members of the United in Group
Harmony Association, a bunch of aging adolescents in leather
tuxedos, who periodically return to their high-school days at a
meeting hall in New Jersey. One of their newest members is
John Kuse.

"I thought everything died out," he says. "Now I can get
together once a month with all these characters. You walk
around, and everybody has that one thing in common—they
all sing. Tommy Crup of the Hudsons—never heard of them
in my life. Then I heard some of their records. They were
great. Now I know it didn't die. Where else are you going to
get forty guys doing harmony on 'Just Two Kinds of People in
the World' in a bathroom? Unreal. Here I am going to the
bathroom and there's forty guys at least—the whole bathroom
is full of these guys. Thirteen falsettos, nineteen leads. I got

some compliments when I sang there: 'You still got it, John.'
That made me feel good."

Kuse is leaning dangerously over the pit now. I can see
the signs returning of that old desire for fame, the hunger
dripping with adrenaline. "At work they don't stop," he says.
"It's Mr. Cool, Mr. Coney Island Kid. Assistant vice-president
of operations—they call me Coney Island Kid." Yet he is
quick to inform me that "Coney Island Baby" is number 119
on the WCBS-FM list of Golden Oldies, down from number
53 last year. At Clifton Music, the top oldies store in Jersey,
it's in there at number 37. "My feeling now when I hear my
voice on the radio . . . it kills me," he says. "Only in the past
three or four years have I really heard 'Coney Island Baby' on
the radio. They started saying my name on the radio, too.
That really got me—'John Kuse.' That killed me."

The shouts of a Saturday-morning snowball fight invade
the hollows of Kuse's brownstone as we stand at the record
player, knee-deep in sentiment, pedaling back toward High
School U.S.A. A tune by the Elegants, the group from which
the Excellents fashioned their name, soars from the box as
Kuse attempts to sing along. Wisely, I remain silent, sunk in
my own reveries. Walking me to the door, Kuse recalls the Excellents' final performance, circa 1975:

"It was the first time we'd gotten together in eight or nine
years," he says. "My sister-in-law called me up, and she says,
'I heard you're singing in Queens.' I said 'We are?' She said,
'Yeah, the Excellents are appearing in Queens, at Grover
Cleveland High School.' She'd heard it on the radio or whatever. Holy mackerel. I've got to see who these guys are. We'd
heard about a group the record company had supposedly
signed to impersonate us after 'Coney Island Baby'; now we'd
finally get to see them. So we went out there, five of us. Chuck
was in Florida and couldn't make it. Before we went we practiced. We still had it. We always had it.

"So we go over to Grover Cleveland on a Friday night.
But the Excellents don't show. Vito & the Salutations were
there, the Channels, Earl Lewis. We weren't looking to show
anybody up, but we said to the guy, 'We're the Excellents;

we're the real Excellents. Can we get up there?' And the guy announced it that way. 'We were supposed to have the Excellents tonight, but instead we wound up with the Excellents.' And he gave us a little help. 'They're not prepared. They just got back together for the first time.' We did three numbers, 'Vows of Love,' 'Coney Island Baby' and 'The Closer You Are'—a cappella, no music, no movements. And they got a pretty good hand. My sister-in-law got it on movie film. The sound is there. I'm up there; I see myself. I showed it to the neighbors in the backyard on the wall."

Kuse is in the pit of forbidden dreams now, the foaming lather devouring him in a fog of forsaken desire. At my car, he leans in through the window. "We went to a Christmas party at the Little Sisters of the Poor on Eighty-fourth Street and Seventeenth Avenue, and my wife mentioned that I sing. So here's this little crippled nun in a wheelchair coming over to me with a guitar. 'Could you please sing for me?' I agreed to sing, but evidently they forgot to announce me, and I wasn't going to push it, but at the end when everyone is piling out, here's the nun coming over and begging me, please sing. So I sang to her, with about twenty people around us, no music or anything, just a little nun in a wheelchair. She was just about to go through an operation to try and make her walk again."

For some reason I think of Nick Kenny, the inspirational columnist for the old *Daily Mirror*. I'd love to put Kuse together with him, but I'm sure Kenny died a long time ago.

"I still have the voice; I know I do," says Kuse.

Rock 'n' roll will stand. It was meant to be that way. "I knew I'd really made it," Jiggs Meister recalls, "when I would switch the button on my car radio to the four big New York stations and we'd be on all of them, one after another."

But WINS is all news now; WMCA is all talk; WMGM turned to WHN long ago, all country music; and the last holdout, WABC, just threw in the towel, joining the all-talk crowd. In the winter of 1982, while sipping coffee in a local restaurant where businessmen gather to grumble about the economy and the radio plays "beautiful music"—the soft, muffled cotton sound of repression—I hear that Murray the K is dead of cancer at the age of sixty. And while the news does not hit me with the same thumping shock as the murder of John Lennon, the loss is real enough, like finding out my old high school had just burned down.

Maybe rock 'n' roll is dead, too—certainly it's been reported missing. But though it's tough these days, we'll just have to keep the faith, Murray.

I don't care what people say.

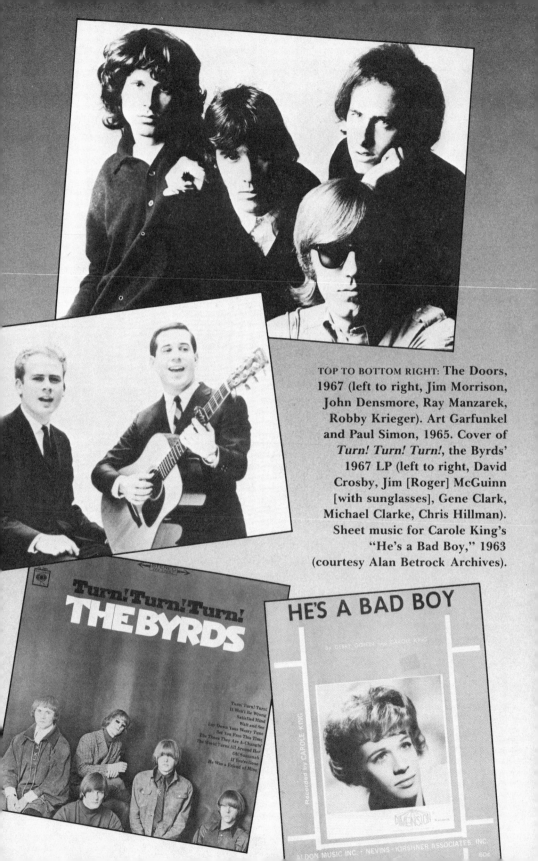

TOP TO BOTTOM RIGHT: The Doors, 1967 (left to right, Jim Morrison, John Densmore, Ray Manzarek, Robby Krieger). Art Garfunkel and Paul Simon, 1965. Cover of *Turn! Turn! Turn!*, the Byrds' 1967 LP (left to right, David Crosby, Jim [Roger] McGuinn [with sunglasses], Gene Clark, Michael Clarke, Chris Hillman). Sheet music for Carole King's "He's a Bad Boy," 1963 (courtesy Alan Betrock Archives).

The Suburban Midcentury White Young America Blues

Paul Simon, after failing to make it in rock 'n' roll as Jerry Landis, as Tom & Jerry (with Art Garfunkel as Tom), or as Tico, in Tico & the Triumphs, journeyed to England in a sort of self-imposed exile. It was 1964, and naturally enough, while over there he came under the spell of the Beatles. Roger McGuinn, then known as Jim, suffered a different kind of exile in the early sixties, playing backup guitar and banjo for the Chad Mitchell Trio in South America and for Bobby Darin in Las Vegas. In 1964 he left Greenwich Village, where everyone was under the spell of Bob Dylan, and went to Los Angeles, where the Beach Boys had yet to confront the civil rights movement.

Adding a sonic boom of back beat to melodies by Dylan and Pete Seeger, McGuinn's rock band, the Byrds, blazed a Top 40 path down which Paul Simon's "Sounds of Silence" rolled like a red carpet late in 1965, hastening Simon's triumphant return from England. Quickly enlisting Garfunkel for vocal aid and comfort, Simon would attach folk lyrics to Top 40 melodies and proceed to create folk-rock East. McGuinn, on the other coast, adorned his folk melodies with Top 40 lyrics, plus that incomparable sonic boom, to father folk-rock West. Its ancestors, Dylan and the Beatles, meanwhile, were having an encounter, from which the Beatles emerged opened to the myriad possibilities of folk music. Dylan, at the same time, it must be said, was greatly moved by the fact that the Beatles, during one week of 1964, occupied all five slots of the Top 5. Of such concerns, artistic and commercial (folk and rock) was folk rock undoubtedly composed.

By 1966 the cerebral concerns of folk music were being celebrated by millions of rock 'n' roll fans. Never before, or since, has the common denominator of a popular art form been raised to such elitist levels. It was as if every youth in the country were white, middle class, politically progressive, pro–civil rights, antiwar, and attending the college of his or her choice. This was obviously not the case, as bands of marauding blacks in Watts could attest, if any of their number had cared to put it into folk rock. Meanwhile, in America, whatever subversive twist the century had yet devised to pit child against parent, student against university, citizen against government, was finding expression in the Top 40. Mind-altering drugs had come out of the pool hall and into the study hall; students had come out of the study hall and into the streets. Thus, radio officials had no qualms against purveying for the masses the often desperate or at least uneasy sentiments embodied in songs like "Eve of Destruction," "Help!" "(I Can't Get No) Satisfaction," "It Ain't Me Babe," "Eight Miles High," "For What It's Worth," "Universal Soldier," "Where Have All the Flowers Gone," "Along Comes Mary," "The Dangling Conversation," and "Subterranean Homesick Blues."

This epidemic of rule breaking had its euphoric side as well, best defined by the Lovin' Spoonful in "Do You Believe in Magic." The Beach Boys, always up for fun, got into the spirit of the times, with "Good Vibrations." Even the Monkees, a bunch of TV actors (to actors, of course, the Monkees were a bunch of singers), had a spiritual bent, in "I'm a Believer." But there was a backlash brewing. The top song of the year was "Ballad of the Green Berets," strongly supporting American involvement in Vietnam. And by 1967, the Top 40 would be backing away from songs deemed too threatening for tender ears. But as the Top 40 attempted to restore order out of chaos, the music of protest erupted into rock fury, as life itself became too threatening for the tenderhearted. Fighting for their freedom, people dropped out, trying to avoid the war machine. The hippie fringe got politicized, the black influence became profound and the streets seethed with incense and injustice.

Playlist

1964

January:	"Little Boxes" *Pete Seeger*
	"The Marvelous Toy" *The Chad Mitchell Trio*
	"Jailer, Bring Me Water" *Trini Lopez*
	"Little Boxes" *The Womenfolk*
February:	"Tell It on the Mountain" *Peter, Paul & Mary*
March:	"Don't Let the Rain Come Down" *The Serendipity Singers*
	"Four Strong Winds" *Ian & Sylvia*
April:	"Beans in My Ears" *The Serendipity Singers*
	"Today" *The New Christy Minstrels*
May:	"Oh, Rock My Soul" *Peter, Paul & Mary*
June:	"Silly Ol' Summertime" *The New Christy Minstrels*
	"Frankie & Johnny" *The Greenwood County Singers*
July:	"Michael" *Trini Lopez*
August:	"We'll Sing in the Sunshine" *Gale Garnett*
	"My Back Pages" *Bob Dylan*
September:	"House of the Rising Sun" *The Animals*
November:	"As Tears Go By" *Marianne Faithfull*
December:	"For Lovin' Me" *Peter, Paul & Mary*
	"Someday Soon" *Ian & Sylvia*

1965

February: "Come and Stay with Me" *Marianne Faithfull*
March: "Baby the Rain Must Fall" *Glenn Yarbrough*
  "When the Ship Comes In" *Peter, Paul & Mary*
  "Play with Fire" *The Rolling Stones*
  "Subterranean Homesick Blues" *Bob Dylan*
  "Maggie's Farm" *Bob Dylan*
  "Gates of Eden" *Bob Dylan*
  "Mr. Tambourine Man" *Bob Dylan*
  "She Belongs to Me" *Bob Dylan*
  "It's Alright Ma (I'm Only Bleeding)" *Bob Dylan*
April: "Mr. Tambourine Man" *The Byrds*
  "Catch the Wind" *Donovan*
May: "(I Can't Get No) Satisfaction " *The Rolling Stones*
  "This Little Bird" *Marianne Faithfull*
June: "I Got You Babe" *Sonny & Cher*
  "It's Gonna Be Fine" *Glenn Yarbrough*
  "Silver Threads and Golden Needles" *Jody Miller*
  "All I Really Want to Do" *The Byrds*
July: "Help" *The Beatles*
  "Eve of Destruction" *Barry McGuire*
  "You Were on My Mind" *We Five*
  "It Ain't Me Babe" *The Turtles*
  "Colours" *Donovan*
  "We Gotta Get out of This Place" *The Animals*
August: "Like a Rolling Stone" *Bob Dylan*
  "Positively 4th Street" *Bob Dylan*
  "Ballad of a Thin Man" *Bob Dylan*
  "Desolation Row" *Bob Dylan*
  "Highway 61 Revisited" *Bob Dylan*
  "Just Like Tom Thumb's Blues" *Bob Dylan*
  "There but for Fortune" *Joan Baez*
  "Universal Soldier" *Glen Campbell*

"Baby Don't Go" *Sonny & Cher*
"Do You Believe in Magic" *The Lovin'*
Spoonful
"Early Morning Rain" *Ian & Sylvia*
September: "Sinner Man" *Trini Lopez*
"Child of Our Times" *Barry McGuire*
"The Sins of the Family" *P. F. Sloan*
October: "The Revolution Kind" *Sonny*
"Turn, Turn, Turn" *The Byrds*
"Don't Think Twice" *The Wonder Who*
"Let's Get Together" *We Five*
November: "Sounds of Silence" *Simon & Garfunkel*
"You Didn't Have to Be So Nice" *The*
Lovin' Spoonful
"It Was a Very Good Year" *Frank Sinatra*
December: "A Well Respected Man" *The Kinks*
"It Won't Be Wrong" *The Byrds*
"Set You Free This Time" *The Byrds*
"Can You Please Crawl Out Your
Window" *Bob Dylan*

1966

January: "California Dreamin' " *The Mamas & the*
Papas
"Elusive Butterfly" *Bob Lind*
"Homeward Bound" *Simon & Garfunkel*
"My Generation" *The Who*
February: "Walking My Cat Named Dog" *Norma*
Tanega
"Daydream" *The Lovin' Spoonful*
"Hey What About Me" *Ian & Sylvia*
March: "Eight Miles High" *The Byrds*
"Sloop John B." *The Beach Boys*
"Truly Julie's Blues" *Bob Lind*
"Cruel War" *Peter, Paul & Mary*
"Rainy Day Women No. 12 & 35" *Bob*
Dylan
April: "One Too Many Mornings" *The Beau*
Brummels
"I Am a Rock" *Simon & Garfunkel*

"Did You Ever Have to Make Up Your
Mind" *The Lovin' Spoonful*

May: "Along Comes Mary" *The Association*
"Paperback Writer" *The Beatles*
"I Want You" *Bob Dylan*
"Hey Joe" *The Leaves*
"5D (Fifth Dimension)" *The Byrds*

June: "Summer in the City" *The Lovin' Spoonful*
"Blowin' in the Wind" *Stevie Wonder*
"Visions of Johanna" *Bob Dylan*
"Just like a Woman" *Bob Dylan*
"Memphis Blues Again" *Bob Dylan*
"Leopard Skin Pillbox Hat" *Bob Dylan*

July: "Eleanor Rigby" *The Beatles*
"The Dangling Conversation" *Simon &
Garfunkel*
"A Younger Girl" *The Lovin' Spoonful*
"Sunshine Superman" *Donovan*
"The Other Side of This Life" *Peter, Paul
& Mary*

August: "See See Rider" *The Animals*
"Mr. Spaceman" *The Byrds*
"Changes" *Crispian St. Peters*
"Mind Excursion" *The Trade Winds*

September: "If I Were a Carpenter" *Bobby Darin*
"Rain on the Roof" *The Lovin' Spoonful*

October: "Mellow Yellow" *Donovan*
"A Hazy Shade of Winter" *Simon &
Garfunkel*

November: "Nashville Cats" *The Lovin' Spoonful*
"Hard Lovin' Loser" *Judy Collins*

December: "So You Want to Be a Rock 'n' Roll
Star" *The Byrds*
"Hello, Hello" *Sopwith Camel*
"Pushin' Too Hard" *The Seeds*
"Coconut Grove" *The Lovin' Spoonful*

PAUL SIMON *(Simon & Garfunkel)*

ROGER McGUINN *(The Byrds)*

Located at 1619 Broadway, in the heart of Tin Pan Alley, the Brill Building is sacred turf in the romantic history of rock 'n' roll. Booming from its hallways, slipping and sliding out from underneath the rows of glass doors that housed from 1958 to 1965 perhaps half the music publishers in New York (if not America), came a noble literature of teen dreams, from "Yakety Yak" to "A Teenager in Love" to "Will You Love Me Tomorrow." Written by specialists like Jerry Leiber & Mike Stoller, Doc Pomus & Mort Shuman, and Gerry Goffin & Carole King, the product of the Brill Building had international reverberations.

"The biggest kick I ever had was when I met John Lennon," Doc Pomus once told me, "and he said that one of the first songs the Beatles ever did was a song I wrote called 'Lonely Avenue.' Originally, all they wanted to do was to reach a point, like Morty and myself, or like Carole King and

Gerry, where they could make enough money to survive writing songs."

Ironically, it was the extent of the success achieved by that prolific team of Lennon & McCartney that would all but doom the other stalwarts pacing in their cubicles and pounding pianos in the Brill Building. "After the Beatles started to grow and get real good," Gerry Goffin once told me, "it suddenly appeared that going in and writing songs for whoever you were writing songs for was not the way anymore."

The new people charging through the corridors of rock 'n' roll tradition weren't wordsmiths, paid by the song. They weren't rock 'n' roll slave laborers assigned to write an answer song for "He'll Have to Go," a follow-up in the mold of "Up on the Roof" for the Drifters, or a sure-fire surf single for the Shirelles or Jimmy Clanton. They were songwriters after their own hearts, inhabiting that phantom dreamspace where wishes became melodies, complete with a beat and a hook that wouldn't quit.

Among those early rebels who brought rock 'n' roll down from the office building to the street was Paul Simon, who, in fact, knew well the layout of the Brill. Going under names like Jerry Landis, Paul Kane, and Tico & the Triumphs, he'd been perfecting Brill techniques since the late fifties, sculpting 45s into works of art. While still in high school, in 1958, he had a minor hit under the alias of Tom & Jerry, "Hey Schoolgirl," sung with a kid he'd known since sixth grade, Artie Garfunkel. But that one proved to be a fluke, and the two New York buddies from the borough of Queens suspended operations for the "more appropriate" alternative of college. Although Paul's father had once been a musician, going so far as to play the bass in the Garry Moore Show orchestra, even he had returned to school to become a college professor. Rock 'n' roll was a slightly unsavory profession, after all, for the scions of middle-class prosperity.

Yet Paul Simon was not quite cured of the obsession, the dream that would haunt so many similarly besneakered dawdlers, who huddled in their rooms at night, listening to Alan Freed and Symphony Sid and Jocko Henderson on their radios. It was a dream of re-creating Top 40 magic, setting off that magnificent explosion they'd felt so many times, on a record of their own. As a freshman at Queens College in 1959, he would venture with another freshman, Carol Klein, from Brooklyn, back down to Brill.

"Carol would play piano and drums and sing. I would sing and play guitar and bass," he told me. "The game was to make a demo at demo prices and then try to sell it to a record company. Maybe you'd wind up investing three hundred dollars for musicians and studio time, but if you did something really good, you could get as much as a thousand for it. I never wanted to be in groups; I was only after that seven-hundred-dollar profit. I always tried to get my money up front, because you were never sure of getting your royalties if they put the record out. You were dealing with a lot of thieves in those days."

Eventually Carol met someone in her chemistry class named Gerry, who had been writing lyrics since the age of eight, and they started to collaborate. When she quit school, it was to take a job as a songwriter in the Brill Building. She adopted the professional name of King, added an "e" to her first name, and proceeded to create the stuff of teenage legend. Paul Simon went back with his original collaborator, but it wasn't until he left law school in 1964 that he released an album under his own name. *Wednesday Morning, 3 A.M.* was produced by Tom Wilson, Dylan's producer, on Dylan's label, Columbia. Though Simon & Garfunkel was a catchy moniker in the Brill Building tradition, the resulting album reeked of folk music. These were boys who'd appeared as crew-cut teens on "Bandstand," yet they were singing "Last Night I Had the Strangest Dreams," "You Can Tell the World," "The Times They Are a-Changin' " and a song Paul had written about a classmate at Queens College, Andy Goodman, one of the three Freedom Riders found dead the past summer in Mississippi, "He Was My Brother." They had short hair, they lived at home, but there was something subversive about their choice of music. Radio stations didn't know what to make of it, in 1964, while the Beatles were blissfully singing love songs.

The album sank from sight, and Paul Simon packed his bags and left for England, seeking to become the American Donovan.

While Simon was in England in 1965 and Garfunkel was studying at the Columbia School of Architecture, strange hands were moving in the music business. The clock was striking the hour of folk rock. The year was simply one of unparalleled surprises on the radio dial. From the symphonic blue-eyed soul of the Righteous Brothers' "You've Lost That Lovin' Feelin'," produced by Phil Spector, to the MacDougal Street jollity of the Lovin' Spoonful's "Do You Believe in Magic," it was actually happening—the merger of rock energy with folk reflection, the body twitching, the mind wigging out. All it took was one verse of Dylan's majestic "Mr. Tambourine Man" for the Byrds to reach number one that summer. Even Dylan had honed his vitriolic lyrics to within pop parameters; actually, the parameters had been redefined around *him*, with "Like a Rolling Stone" and "Positively 4th Street." Rumor had it he'd been hanging out in England with the Beatles. This fateful meeting had its effect on the Beatles, too. By the end of the year they'd come out with *Rubber Soul*, easily their best work to that date, with complex classics like "Norwegian Wood," "I'm Looking Through You" and "In My Life." No doubt about it, the lads had lost their virginity. The Rolling Stones, meanwhile, had never had it to begin with. In 1965 they seethed with "Satisfaction" and "Get Off of My Cloud." The Kinks and the Animals were becoming acculturated. The Zombies checked in with "Tell Her No." The Yardbirds, one of England's seminal blues-rock bands, gave us "For Your Love," with Eric Clapton on guitar. In San Francisco the Beau Brummels were hot with "Laugh Laugh," and in Los Angeles Sonny & Cher were all the rage with "Baby Don't Go" and "I Got You Babe." All of it was based on the impassioned, somewhat-nasal Dylan whine, which coursed through the charts like poison ivy that year.

Neither was the Top 40 as removed as it had previously been from the grim verities of the real world. While in 1963 Dylan's pacifist anthem "Blowin' in the Wind" had done respectably, more people were bewitched by the Singing Nun and "Dominique." In 1965, however, when Barry McGuire sang about the world exploding in "Eve of Destruction," the single raced to number one! Not only was the international scene trembling on the brink in 1965; at home the cork was about to pop in Watts, the black ghetto in Los Angeles, land of the Beach Boys, where the rioting would go on for seven days.

Not surprisingly, in 1965 most black Americans had more pressing concerns on their mind than the folk-rock hijinks of the white middle class. They wanted in on the shopping-center world surrounding them, promulgated by the movies, TV, and the radio. It had been a world dominated by the young, ever since Chubby Checker did the twist, but now Chubby was twisted out of shape, and the civil rights movement had stalled. They had little use for the abstract complaints of folk rock, but the message of the kids was coming through nonetheless. Up in Berkeley the students had been winning their fight for free speech, and on Sunset Strip proto-hippies lounged around in multicolored hair. These white kids had learned some precious lessons from the protesting blacks down South, had borrowed and adapted their own version of urban angst, becoming street-wise scholars in their image, just as they had borrowed rock 'n' roll in the mid-fifties from rhythm 'n' blues. Now it was black America's turn to do the studying.

In 1965 only a quarter of the action on the pop charts belonged to blacks, and half of that to one company—Motown Records in Detroit. In 1966 it would drop to 20 percent, as looting and rioting and gunfire would spread to thirty-eight cities, Detroit among them; By 1967 the figure had risen to a solid 33 percent. Perhaps by then they'd guessed where the true black power lay.

In this fertile atmosphere, it was only a matter of time before rock 'n' roll would look to the preppie sensibility for inspiration. The single "Sounds of Silence" was lifted from Simon & Garfunkel's buried album late in 1965, approximately one year after it had been declared dead; some electric instruments were overdubbed and, quicker than you could say Barry McGuire, the Brill Building folkies were back in business.

With a title that could have come from Sartre or Camus or Herman Hesse, "Sounds of Silence" was received with great joy by those intellectual pop fans who were always reading the paperback edition of Dostoevsky's *Notes from Underground*, or at least incessantly flaunting it on subways. Before long "Homeward Bound" took its place on the charts, followed by "The Dangling Conversation" and "I Am a Rock." The thinking man at last had singles he could relate to. The cardigan-sweater–team-jacket world of Goffin & King, meanwhile ("Take Good Care of My Baby," "Chains," "The Loco-Motion"), had become as outdated as an Archie comic book.

At first exercises in English composition, Paul Simon's early works nevertheless reflected the position of most young white middle-class Americans at the turning point of the sixties. Especially if you were of the segment of the generation whose experiences tended more toward the Volkswagen than the Harley, the Saturday-night date as opposed to shacking up, the ski-weekend trip rather than the acid trip, Simon's troublesome miniatures struck much closer to home than Dylan's frenetically eloquent dissertations. At the same time they were meatier by far than Lennon & McCartney's adolescent trifles.

Here you were, still in school and somewhat alienated and repressed ("Sounds of Silence"), trying to explain yourself to women ("The Dangling Conversation") or to yourself if they wouldn't listen ("I Am a Rock"). But even though your head weighed approximately twice as much as the rest of you, sometimes, unaccountably, you felt good ("The 59th Street Bridge Song"). So, if Lennon & McCartney were still essentially foreigners, and if Dylan had leaped one too many synapses to reside in the perpetual ozone of the stoned poet, Paul Simon lived closer to Ozone Park, Queens, New York. Actually, right across the Fifty-ninth Street Bridge from it, on the Upper East Side of Manhattan, a short jog from Gracie Mansion.

"It was a neighborhood largely unaffected by the youth

culture," he told me when I interviewed him at his monumental apartment, a city kid's dream, with picture windows that encompassed all the ball fields of Central Park. The maid had just served us lunch. "Simon & Garfunkel never drifted into the pop hierarchy like John Phillips (of the Mamas & the Papas). We didn't know how to do that. We were fairly isolated from other musicians and mostly stayed together. I wasn't involved in anything. I was just by myself. I was crazy most of the time, high, and relatively depressed throughout those years."

He never had the hair for the sixties; it was too thin and curled a little at the ends when he let it grow past his ears for the photograph on the cover of Simon & Garfunkel's soundtrack album for *The Graduate* (1968). Definitely he was on the wrong side of the mind-body split that separated college graduates from street people, dope from acid, folkies from rockers. However the sixties' lust for parsley, sage, rosemary, and THC distracted his bloodstream, Simon managed to evince a portrait of control, the straight-arrow, house-plan image that had haunted him for years.

"We took drugs, we just didn't sleep in teepees," he said. "We were quiet about it. I never wanted to be busted in Des Moines, you know? So we just played it straight, and it made life a lot easier and safer. I didn't believe the hippie thing, anyway, that laid-back, minimal-vocabulary California existence. I didn't believe all the smiles. I thought there was a lot of vindictiveness behind them."

As the sixties turned the corner, though, nonbelievers were distinctly out of fashion. "We thought at the time that it was the cultural revolution," Simon said, "or even the Revolution that everybody was talking about. We thought it was really going to come into effect and that Simon & Garfunkel were going to be artifacts of the New York-eastern-early-sixties days, which could no longer continue because we didn't understand about things like the ecology."

Though Paul had spent much of his youth down in Washington Square Park, where the girls ironed their hair and the boys played mandolin, Simon & Garfunkel had not been part of the Village folk scene, either. The supposed purists at the

Gaslight Café did not buy their polished choirboy sound. I remember one particular Tuesday night when I saw them; they bounded onstage for a set, dressed like a couple of accountants, in suits and ties.

"We were being represented by the William Morris Agency," Simon explained with real agony in his voice, "and they were looking for a way to sell us, with typical disregard for the content. They wanted us to be the Smothers Brothers. I arrived at the Gaslight that night with a terrible sense of foreboding, because I used to go there to watch the other acts—in normal attire—and now here I was knowing I shouldn't be wearing this jacket. I told our agent we were making a terrible mistake, and he said, 'It doesn't matter what the audience thinks, there are television people here.' "

A year later, when Simon returned from England a pop star, the last place he wanted to visit was Greenwich Village. "I was keenly aware that we hadn't been accepted by the Village crowd," he said. "Suddenly we were very desirable to the folkies, but I resented them."

If it seems his hard-won fame had been dissipated by a classic case of New York City neurosis, the middle-class blues, Simon was quick to amend that impression. "It was really a good run," he said. "We got knocked, but the overwhelming majority of people treated us with great affection. We had far more success than we ever anticipated. If I felt at a certain time that I wasn't getting enough credit for writing the songs, I don't feel that way now. In the middle of things you can get competitive or petty. I know there were a lot of demands on me, pressure to put out records, self-induced pressure to write when it was difficult, drug stuff clouding up my brain, tensions between myself and Artie as our careers grew. There were times when it seemed pretty miserable. But looking back on it, it wasn't miserable at all."

Certainly the hits kept coming, although songs like "At the Zoo" and "Fakin' It" were among his most insubstantial works. But *The Graduate* revived Simon's profile, opening up the duo to hip mass appeal. Coming out a month later, *Bookends* revived his and Garfunkel's career and showcased what was Simon's best song to date, "America," recounting the story of a very specific all-American malaise, as experienced by a generation of thumb-struck children of Jack Kerouac. Nevertheless, Simon the writer wasn't entirely satisfied.

"For me the significant change occurred around 1969, after I wrote 'The Boxer,'" he said. "At that point I stopped smoking grass and I never went back. I told a friend of mine, a really good musician, that I had writer's block. And he said, 'When are you going to stop playing this folkie stuff, all the time the same G to C chords? You could be a really good songwriter, but you don't know enough, you don't have enough tools. Forget about having hits—go learn your ax.'"

In the era of repression ushered in by the election of Nixon in 1968, everyone would have to learn their ax if they hoped to survive. Though 1969 was championed as the year Aquarius dawned, in actuality the darkness was spreading. Martin Luther King, Jr., had been murdered. Bobby Kennedy had been murdered. Gene McCarthy had abdicated. The peace movement had failed to end the war. There was widespread quarreling among the ranks, paranoia, FBI infiltration. The solution was becoming part of the problem. No one could agree on what the hell the solution was. The Beatles had been to India and back, with little to offer but "All You Need Is Love." Fat chance. The seeds of their acrid disentanglement from each other were even then being sown in the recording studio, where they chafed inside the prison of their fame.

In other quarters, folk rock's leading lights were going on the dim. Bob Dylan's 1966 motorcycle accident was an ominous sign to a generation that had been traveling too far too fast. After his drawn-out recuperation, subsequent albums *John Wesley Harding* in 1968 and *Nashville Skyline* in 1969 revealed a country singer, his caustic edge and poetry gone. He was married now, nearing thirty. Could we trust him anymore? By 1968 Macdougal Street lay nearly deserted, with all the traffic moving to the psychedelic experience on the Lower East Side. Phil Ochs was suffering from an irreversible writer's block. The Lovin' Spoonful had broken up amid ugly drug-informant rumors.

The high had been stupendous—we'd grown our hair

longer than we'd ever thought possible—but it proved to be a rather limiting preoccupation. "Don't forget," said Simon, "involved in that hippie ethic was a very strong anti-Protestant-ethic thing. It was all 'Get out there and feel it. Just let it happen.' But that doesn't work." Certainly not for Paul Simon. "I started to study theory. I began listening to other kinds of music—gospel, Jamaican ska, Antonio Carlos Jobim. 'Bridge over Troubled Water' was a gospel-influenced song. It was very easy for me to feel at home with gospel, because it sounded like the rock 'n' roll I grew up with in the early fifties."

"Bridge over Troubled Water," as Simon recalled it, was partially written in the recording studio, at Art Garfunkel's urging. "I wrote a third verse, which doesn't really fit in as well as the other two, and we decided to throw in the kitchen sink on it." It became their biggest hit. "Paradoxically, *Bridge over Troubled Water* was our most intense success, but it was the end of Simon & Garfunkel. As the relationship was disintegrating, the album was selling ten million copies. And by the time I decided I was going to go out on my own—you can imagine how difficult it was telling the record company there wasn't going to be any follow-up to an album that sold ten million. But for me it really saved my ass, because I don't think we could have followed it up."

The unprecedented musical rush of the sixties was never really equaled either. Joni Mitchell wrote perhaps her finest collection of songs on the trenchant *Blue* in 1971, and Simon himself, in the seventies, compiled an impressive body of work, but Dylan's much anticipated masterpiece (as alluded to in his 1971 song "When I Paint My Masterpiece") was never written. The individual Beatles had their occasional moments of inspiration, but mostly they lived off the fat of their reputation. Laura Nyro, Neil Young, Eric Andersen, Tim Buckley, John Sebastian, Buffy Sainte-Marie, and so many others seemed to have left it back there, somewhere in a smoke-filled room with the incense and the laughter and the dreamy camaraderie. Jimi Hendrix and Janis Joplin killed themselves in 1970, and Jim Morrison died in 1971. In their place came the Carpenters, the Partridge Family, and Three Dog Night, an enforced tranquillity echoed by the Beatles in their swan song, "Let It Be."

"My feeling is that it bottomed out about 1971," Simon reflected. "People were so angry by 1971 that the ones who still had their wits about them and had talent and had enough energy and drive to do something started working." It was no shock to Simon as hippie after hippie turned thirty—and found that he could no longer trust himself. "Sooner or later you become the mainstream," he observed. "You're willing to take responsibility because you want the power. I don't think we were as conformist as other generations, but I think we were just as materialistic, despite the rejection of materialism in the sixties. I think the sociological phenomena was interesting and important," he said. "But I don't think there was an essential change."

Simon gave much of the credit for his own survival to the analysis he began at the end of the Simon & Garfunkel period. "It was really good for me," he noted. "I was in analysis for a long time, and I feel like I'm okay now. I'm not totally happy or unneurotic, but basically I can take care of my problems— I'm a grown-up now. I've been through a marriage and divorce, children, successes and failures, and I think I'm now a very competent cripple. I can absolutely navigate my way across the street. Not in the most graceful manner, perhaps, but I can definitely get from one curb to the other."

Through the seventies, Paul Simon managed to stay acutely in touch with his audience, as he continued the attempt to transcend terminal adolescence through rock 'n' roll. "I can say things in a song that I would never say otherwise," he told me. "It's a way of telling the truth, but not intentionally. It just turns out that way." But whether he's reflecting on the past ("My Little Town"), feeling lost and disenfranchised ("American Tune"), commenting on a marriage gone awry ("50 Ways to Leave Your Lover") or a personality run amok ("Still Crazy After All These Years"), Simon remains attuned to the concerns of growing up in this time and this place. Meanwhile, he's managed to reach the masses through the vehicle of the 45.

"There's something in me that's singles-oriented," he

stated, unashamedly. "I've been making records for twenty years. That's my profession. You start to make a track, and all of a sudden it's got a great feel to it. A kind of magic happens that you couldn't have predicted. 'Let's pull out all the stops and make an AM record'—that sentence comes up a lot in the studio."

In a recording studio not far from the Brill Building, where he keeps his publishing office, I next caught up with Paul Simon as he rehearsed his band prior to his first tour in four years. The movie he'd been working on during this time, *One Trick Pony*, and its concurrent soundtrack album with all new songs, was about to hit the streets, and he was enduring a protracted state of panic, although the advance single from the LP "Late in the Evening," as rousing a song as he'd ever done, was whipping up the pop charts. Its ascent prompted him to remark that he had a shot now to reach number one in three different decades.

"There's this guy in the garage where I park my car," Simon was telling me. The eternal adolescent, he was wearing a T-shirt and dungarees. For concerts he donned a sport jacket. "A black guy in his fifties. Somebody there must have tipped him off about me. So one day he comes up to me and says, 'Who are you? Are you famous?' So I said, 'Well, yeah, you know, to a degree I'm famous.' He asked, 'What do you do?' So I'm trying to grope for the broadest common denominator that anyone would know. I said, 'Did you ever hear of Simon & Garfunkel?' 'No.' Then I said, 'Did you ever see *The Graduate*?' 'No.' 'Do you know that song Aretha Franklin sang, "Bridge over Troubled Water"?' 'Yeah!' I said, 'I wrote that.' He called his buddies over. 'Hey, he wrote Aretha's song.'"

Ten years later, the question of black and white doesn't seem so black and white anymore. The war is over, and all the flower children of 1967 have also staggered back to middle America to cut their hair and join the family business, trading in their stereos for color TV sets. Even FM radio betrayed the cause, transforming itself into a junior AM band once it too discovered it had something to lose.

It was only with the shooting death of John Lennon that a fragmented generation could find the impetus to gather around the radio once again, more than a decade after Aquarius rose and fell at Woodstock, breaching the tacit vow of silence that seemed to be in force, the protective blackout of memory and emotion taken up to spare some the embarrassment of having to recall those fabulously wasted years. In enduring the days of Lennon's music and poetry that followed, the poignancy of his message (and how dated it seemed) at times overshadowed even the tragedy of his death. Imagine no possessions. Come together over me. Nothing to get hung about. Love is all you need. Just like starting over. A lot of refugees from Woodstock Nation, ex-freaks, ex-dreamers, in public and private eulogies mourned not only Lennon and their lost youth but their lost adulthood as well. In losing their music, their poets, their voices, they'd become stunted, apathetic, lacking community, commitment, and emotional direction.

But Lennon's death revealed, if only for an instant, that those buried dreams were not quite suffocated. They were only looking for an occasion to shine forth. And such an occasion was provided, less than a year later, by Paul Simon, when he reunited with Art Garfunkel for a free concert in Central Park in front of nearly half a million people and within earshot of John Lennon's bloodstained doorstep at the Dakota apartment building. Though *One Trick Pony* had met with muted critical and commercial reaction, the concert was an astounding success. It was made into a double record album; it was taped for a cable TV special; it was released on videotape for a growing market of video-cassette-recorder owners. Calculated or not, the concert proved beyond a doubt that the audience was still there, still yearning for the purpose and idealism that gave the music of the sixties its special enduring flavor.

In a horrible irony, however, underscoring, perhaps, the flip side of that era, the image that lingers from viewing the Simon & Garfunkel videotape takes place during a touching song called "The Late Great Johnny Ace," a newly written tribute by Simon to several fallen idols: Johnny Ace, John Kennedy, John Lennon. An unexpected visitor vaults the stage and hurtles past the camera, brushing into Simon before being nabbed by security (who are, as usual, two steps behind the action). "Paul," he's reported to have said, "I have to talk to you." On the tape it's impossible to tell if this kid, too, was carrying a copy of *The Catcher in the Rye*, as had Mark David Chapman, the deranged Beatle fan who was Lennon's assassin.

"Paul, I have to talk to you." In their own sad way those pathetic words sum up the revolution that occurred in rock music in the sixties. With Simon & Garfunkel as its representatives, the middle class found its voice. These guys did not hail from Hollywood, charm school, or the conservatory. They were not deprived high-school dropouts or street urchins. Neither were they from the ghetto or the sticks. They came from the old neighborhood.

This was a neighborhood in which rock 'n' roll had rarely trod before to find its audience. And when the white middle-class collegiate sensibility overtook rock, the concerns of the audience became the concerns of the rock stars, because they were us and we were them. Never before was the line between artist and audience so consciously vague and often breached. If you didn't actually play an instrument then, you probably knew someone who did, and wrote songs with them or sat in on the harp. If not, you became an expert on the anglo sound, or a devotee of the sitar, or got carried away by the delta blues. You may have written a review or two for one of the many publications created just to put your fevered words into print. At the very least you adopted the tie-dyed T-shirt of the extended adolescent, for a time, and rolled in the aisles at screenings of *Reefer Madness*. The point is, if you were a rock fan in the sixties, a real rock fan, you also lived the music.

Paul Simon's accessibility may have been an illusion, but it was a seductive one, and surely no accident. It meant that to be Paul Simon you could be small and shy and bright and write poems, you didn't have to reinvent yourself a hobo past or lease a mattress in Nirvana. You could be yourself and still one day get to play basketball with Connie Hawkins, make a movie with Woody Allen, wear sneakers with a tux, or a chicken suit on "Saturday Night Live." You could become a legend on your old block. It's all there in the photo in the souvenir book that comes with the double album of their Central Park concert, the one with Paul and Artie in front of Paul's childhood home in Queens.

"I took my son back there recently," Paul told me. Harper is nine. "I drove him around the neighborhood. I took him to Artie's old house. I took him to my public school. We went down to the candy store where I used to hang out and place bets on the trotters. I bought him an eggcream. The guy in the candy store recognized me. He knew what had become of me, but he related to me the way he'd always related to me. He called me Paulie."

One of the songs Roger McGuinn—a solo artist now, divested of his feathery friends the Byrds—sings in concert these days concerns a man, maybe not so young anymore, who sounds suspiciously like someone you might call a sixties survivor, one who weathered the trips and tragedies of that decade and emerged from them "without a scar."

"I wrote that song with Jacques Levy, for a play," McGuinn told me, "but I can identify with it. The guy in the play did all these things, went through all these different scenes, and he got out of it clean; you know, it didn't affect him. I feel like I got out of it pretty clean."

Somehow they are thought of as survivors, these ragged renegades who've been drifting home for the last ten years to pick up threads of lives abandoned or obliterated in the sixties. They were street people and sidewalk revolutionaries, beatniks and Beatlemaniacs, freedom riders and free lovers, hippies, peaceniks, draft dodgers and finger pickers: veterans of the war, the riot, or the party that dominated the heads and the headlines of a generation's collective coming-of-age. Scratch the modern three-piece-suit composure of your local businessman and you might find a previously hash-addled resident of the Haight or the Village, who marched at Selma and cried at Woodstock, who can quote you to the hour and minute the beginning and the ending of his personal sixties odyssey. Ask about the skinny details, though, the rooms and profiles from those days and years in between, and you may draw a blank. Reached by phone in England, Paul McCartney chuckled. "The sixties went by in a bit of a blur for me, you know?" he said.

I met Roger McGuinn at a Holiday Inn in New Haven, Connecticut, in the spring of 1982, the morning after his successful show at Toad's Place, the eminent rock club in town, where he and his twelve-string had aroused the crowd with spirited re-creations of hippie splendor. "So You Want to Be a Rock 'n' Roll Star," "Eight Miles High," "Chimes of Freedom," "Ballad of an Easy Rider," "Mr. Tambourine Man," "Mr. Spaceman," "I Wasn't Born to Follow" and "My Back Pages" weren't so much exercises in nostalgia as they were testaments to the staying power of those visions, however brief, of a better world through chemistry, communion, and rock 'n' roll. At forty years old, McGuinn seemed in fine shape, looking like a cross between Bruce Jenner and Van Morrison. Unlike many of his fellow musicians up there in the eye of the sixties storm, he'd retained his perspective, or at least regained it.

"We were superstars overnight," he said, with more than a touch of irony. "Actually, we were only up there for a short while. After sixty-six we took kind of a dive, saleswise. We had a moderate resurgence around seventy with *Untitled*. After that there was really nothing to speak of, as far as chart action."

Of course, the sixties, as a cultural concept, was not an entire decade long, either. Though the image of Bob Dylan that was struck for eternity on the front cover of his *Freewheelin'* album in the spring of 1963, arm in arm with Suze Rotolo, walking down that wintry West Fourth Street, collar up against the wind, was alone probably enough to send a funky regiment scurrying toward Washington Square Park in search of the same suede coat, it wasn't until the Beatles played "The Ed Sullivan Show" in February of 1964 that the seeds of the sixties were planted among the masses. The civil rights movement expanded, the free speech movement erupted; eventually both were superseded by the peace movement. On the decade's clock radio, the Beatles left a cosmic wake-up call for 1967, at which time their psychedelic message imploded upon the consciousnesses of the remaining holdouts like a magic-mushroom cloud. By then the lines were well defined between black and white, hawk and dove, straight and hip, just as the lines were becoming blurred between rock and folk, folk and blues, Dylan and the Beatles.

"Yeah," said McGuinn, "Dylan was real and the Beatles were plastic. Then the Beatles got more authentic and Dylan got more Top 40." Like the sixties, the Byrds' impact was far greater than their longevity would suggest. They hit, hit hard, burst brilliantly, then flamed out. Two of their 1965 singles, "Mr. Tambourine Man" and "Turn, Turn, Turn," went to number one. They sang the words of a dust-caked radical poet (Dylan) and a suspected Commie folksinger (Pete Seeger) on every car radio from New York City to the Golden Gate. Their exquisite Beatles harmonies on "It Won't Be Wrong," "Here Without You," "You Won't Have to Cry" and "Set You Free This Time" were sung with a Dylan snarl. It was folk rock with a vengeance.

McGuinn's sixties started in 1959. From a well-to-do Chicago family, the rigorous Latin School, the progressive Old Town School of Folk Music on weekends, he had his first job lined up even before he graduated. Alex Hasilev of the Limelighters had spotted him playing banjo at the Gate of Horn. A few months later, in June, Hasilev's graduation present to McGuinn was a plane ticket to Los Angeles, where McGuinn joined the Limelighters as a backup instrumentalist. He performed the same role soon thereafter with the Chad Mitchell Trio. Essentially clean-cut, in the image of the Kingston Trio, Chad's crew distinguished themselves with the occasional bit of protest material, such as "John Birch Society," which actually hit the charts in 1962. But McGuinn was not content to be a hired hand. "I'd be back there where they couldn't see me, doing little pantomime stuff to the lyrics," he said.

A stint with Bobby Darin followed. "He did a folk thing in his Vegas act," McGuinn said. "He'd take off his jacket, roll up his sleeves and do some Harry Belafonte. Then I'd come out and sing with him and play twelve-string and banjo, and we'd do three or four songs. Then I'd leave and he'd go on with his 'Mack the Knife' and stuff. The most important thing he taught me was to get out in front of an audience as much as you can."

McGuinn also did some significant moonlighting down in Greenwich Village, a little closer to the front lines of the coming revolution. "I was doing folk rock when there was no such thing as folk rock," he noted. Bob Dylan, meanwhile, was just another scuffler, sharing from the same baskets as John Phillips, John Sebastian, Peter Tork, and McGuinn. "He was playing Woody Guthrie songs, and all I knew was that the little girls liked him a lot. But I thought of him as just another guy. I was really shocked when he took off."

Of course, McGuinn had something to do with that take-off, from the monosphere of folk music to the stereosphere of rock 'n' roll, when he and his band, the Byrds, cut Dylan's "Mr. Tambourine Man" as their first single in 1964. "We all took turns singing it," McGuinn modestly allowed, "and I won the audition." But the credit for discovering their launching vehicle he gives to their manager, Jim Dickson. "He had the vision to hear 'Mr. Tambourine Man,'" McGuinn said. "It didn't sound like a hit to me."

Not long after the Kennedy assassination, McGuinn moved to Los Angeles, into a hotel room for fifteen dollars a week, across the street from Capitol Records, home of the Beatles. "When I saw the Beatles, I knew I wanted to get a band together," he said. "It looked like a very attractive proposition. In fact, I remember walking down the street just before I left New York, and there were these club owners who said, 'What we need is four of him.' That's when I knew I had something that would work."

In a large measure, the story of the sixties was just that: isolated folk musicians casting their lots together in electric bands—John Phillips (the Mamas & the Papas), John Sebastian (the Lovin' Spoonful), Peter Tork (the Monkees), Roger McGuinn (the Byrds). Even Dylan found the Band to be his house accompanists. In the same way, the members of the audience found their strength in numbers, in protest marches, radical organizations, and communes. When the sixties ended the band members split for solo careers; the musical richness of collaboration was gone; the political solidarity shattered.

So, after a solo gig at the Troubadour in L.A. in 1964, McGuinn was approached by another folkie, Gene Clark, and the incipient Byrds had their wings. Later on, David Crosby joined them, and the Byrds had their beak. Mike Clarke and Chris Hillman were added on drums and bass, respectively. They called themselves the Beefeaters. Jim Dickson had access to a recording studio at night at no cost, and the five holed up through most of 1964 with a four-track tape machine, occasionally venturing out to appear at a bowling alley. The demo they finally produced was good enough to get them a contract at Columbia records, good enough to be released when the Byrds were on a downward spiral in 1969 as *Preflyte*.

Nineteen sixty-four was still in the era of the small bucks for rock groups. But the Byrds would change those figures dramatically with their success. At first, though, no one at the label knew what to make of them. "They had no idea what they were doing," McGuinn said, "they just wanted to get some kind of young thing going on. Terry Melcher was the only young producer Columbia had on staff, so they just sort of stuck us with him."

In 1964 and 1965 groups still had to prove themselves with singles before the parent company could be persuaded to shell out the large sums necessary to produce an entire album. If the single bombed, there wouldn't be an album. (Later on, this process would be reversed, with the album becoming the main focus and the single, most often, no more than its three-minute commercial. By the late sixties albums could sell even without benefit of a hit single—a revolution, you might say, in the music business.) The Byrds' problem in early 1965 was that Columbia wouldn't release their single. They let it sit in the can for five months.

"At that point Dino Valenti approached me, wanting to start up a band," McGuinn revealed, "and I almost went with him." But by June, McGuinn's nearly lapsed faith was rewarded. "Terry Melcher picked me up in his Cadillac and turned on the radio and said, 'Listen to that.' " It was "Mr. Tambourine Man," on its way to number one. The youth of America was ready for Dylan's words by then, his outraged, bittersweet, and feverish poetics. After Kennedy had raised their hopes so high, the cold, brutal fact of his death had yet to find adequate response. Among black youths, the message of his death was even more devastating. In 1965 in the Los Angeles ghetto of Watts, they began finally to take what had been promised them.

The Byrds became America's rock 'n' roll release from our extended mourning period. At Ciro's, a dilapidated nightclub on the Strip, they were a fixture, bent on ripping down the frothy scenery of the California myth, propagated by the Beach Boys and Jan & Dean, of sand and sun, cars and girls, and, most especially, the holy surfboard. McGuinn, with his imposing twelve-string guitar, his Ben Franklin glasses, and knowing, intellectual smirk, had surfed but once in his life "and got carried out to sea."

Following in his landlocked footsteps, the new Los Angeles groups would favor an even more extreme and dramatic vision—backed up against the edge of the continent, cornered and scared but defiant. Jim Morrison, dressed in leather, declaimed his fierce poetry to the Doors' organ-drenched backbeat, urging his legions to "break on through to the other side," "light my fire," and swim with him to the moon. Buffalo Springfield took intense notice of the troubled L.A. street scene in "For What It's Worth"—the Man with the gun, the young people carrying signs. They understood and defined the concept of "our side." Frank Zappa, with the Mothers of Invention, was much more overt and desperate, chronicling the same freak parade that was Sunset Strip in "Hungry Freaks," "Trouble Comin' Everyday," and "Who Are the Brain Police," from *Freak Out.* The extended rioting in Watts had shown up in white music. "Good Vibrations," offered by the Beach Boys, were clearly not enough. The generation demanded something extravagant.

"There was just a wild thing going on at the time," McGuinn said. "The economy was pretty plush. It was between wars—although the Vietnam war was starting up, nobody really knew it—so it was kind of peaceful. People had a lot of money to burn and nothing to do. It was a big party."

Revered by the folkies for their intelligence, their commitment to Dylan, and by the "Louie Louie" set for their melodies, a debt owed to the Beatles, the Byrds were among the guests of honor, arriving in McGuinn's Mercedes with "Byrds 1" on the license plate, or, more often, in a limo. "The limo was a protection device, because the fans would kill you if you weren't in something," explained McGuinn. "I remember running for one. They parked it about ninety yards away from the gate, and I had to run across this field to get to it, and I didn't make it. The little girls got me and started tearing me apart. They were trying to get a piece of me for a souvenir."

On the bootheels of "Mr. Tambourine Man" and "Turn, Turn, Turn," all sorts of weird and wonderful scenes opened up to the Byrds in 1965 and 1966, among them, getting to meet the Beatles. "We'd seal ourselves up in a bathroom or something, get the security guys out of there, and all take acid and sit on the floor and play guitars," McGuinn recalled. McGuinn credits himself for turning George Harrison on to Eastern mysticism. "George didn't believe in anything when I first met him. I remember his response, because I thought it was really odd. He said, 'We don't believe in God.' Like he didn't have a personal mind or ego of his own. It was a group consciousness. Well, we don't know what to think about that. They were kind of neat the way they worked, the Beatles. They used to all protect each other; it was like a little gang. If you do something to one of them, they'll get you. Anyway, I told him about Ravi Shankar and all that Indian stuff, and he got into it after that."

McGuinn had first tried LSD back in 1961, when it was decidedly underground and still legal. "There were five of us in a commune in the Mission district of San Francisco," he said. "One guy started drawing weird stuff on napkins, and then he got crazy. We had to hide all the knives. I got into music. I remember testing myself to see if I was out of control. I got into the shower and I said, 'Well, if I'm out of control, I'll turn the shower on and get myself wet.' So I stood there and decided, no, I'm not gonna do that."

Experiences like those were then intensified by the prose-lytizing of the Byrds, the Beatles, and Dr. Timothy Leary. As the decade wore on, it seemed as though there were a couple/three freaks in every neighborhood who paraded about in open defiance of Sal the barber, espousing a gloriously sensual life-style, much sex, loud music, and a righteous belief that this was the one and only way to knowledge, bliss, and eternal contentment. The acid rock of 1966 and 1967 came not only with a beat and a new hidden language but also with a whole philosophy of life. "We were going to change the world," said McGuinn, without irony this time."It was going to be love and peace and justice and freedom and all kinds of great stuff."

But like the freedom riders before them, like the peace movement after them (like Alan Freed!) what they found at the end of that rainbow was repression. "That's what killed us," agreed McGuinn. "We got blackballed after drug allegations in 'Eight Miles High.' It was climbing up the charts, and then the *Gavin Report* came out and panned it. They said it was a drug song, and all these stations stopped playing it, and I don't think they wanted to touch us after that."

Before long, McGuinn became convinced that the group was being followed by the FBI. "They'd been chasing after us because somebody left some hashish in the airplane coming back from England," he said. "So they came down on us in a recording studio and said, 'Whose is this?' Of course nobody claimed it. But I remember one time not long after that when we were out on the road. David Crosby was on the balcony of this Holiday Inn, and he had a slingshot with these little .22 caps that you put in a blank gun. He was shooting them against the brick wall, maybe thirty feet down, and they were exploding, right? Okay, well down at the end, right where these things were blowing up, there was a bunch of rednecks playing poker. And they came out and started climbing over the balcony, screaming, 'Guys died in Iwo Jima for punks like you.' They were pounding on Crosby, when suddenly the FBI appeared. You know, 'FBI, son, break it up.' They took these guys out and sent them off to their room. I don't know if it was just a coincidence, but what were they doing in the middle of Iowa? From then on I used to be looking over my shoulder, thinking that the government was after me."

Like a lot of less-visible counterparts, merely turning on in the privacy of their bedrooms, the Byrds and others waited for that knock on the door. The government, which had tolerated the protests of the early sixties, the overthrow of the traditional values of the thirties, forties, and fifties, was beginning to assert itself. The same AM band that had given the top-song spot throughout the early sixties to Simon & Garfunkel, the Byrds, the Lovin' Spoonful, Bob Dylan, the Beatles, the Rolling Stones, Donovan, and the Mamas & the Papas voted Staff Sergeant Barry Sadler's "The Ballad of the Green Berets" number-one song in 1966. It was an affirmation of the president's position on Vietnam, as opposed to the people's dissent. Later, the Monkees were created—a toy of the oppressors, a tool to further enforce this vision of calm, even as the country seethed.

In 1967 the Monkees had the top song of the year, "I'm a Believer," certainly an unintended double entendre. What the Monkees believed in is not known. The true believers of the revolution weren't waiting to find out; they proceeded en masse to Monterey for their first and possibly best political convention. Representatives from the East (Simon & Garfunkel, Laura Nyro) met representatives from the West (Janis Joplin, the Byrds, the Jefferson Airplane). Jimi Hendrix was the representative from Mars. Otis Redding represented soul. And topping it off, Ravi Shankar represented to the Western World the timeless music of India. "All the cops had orchids on their antennas," said McGuinn. "Everybody was freaked on acid. It looked like what we were shooting for was happening, for one day anyway. I saw my first synthesizer there. You could make any kind of musical sound on that thing."

The event marked the blossoming of rock's maturity—the coming of the big bucks. The film of the Monterey Pop Festival was an event in itself. With their career drooping, the Byrds could have used that stage to boost themselves. Instead, as McGuinn recalled, David Crosby used it as a platform. "He said stuff like 'The *Warren Report* is a lie,' and 'Paul McCartney said everybody should take acid.' The crowd loved him. But that's the reason we didn't get in the movie."

A few weeks later the Byrds were auditioning new members for Crosby's vacated slot. The Monterey rap was only part of why he was dismissed, but his dismissal was indicative of the problems that plagued the Byrds once they'd reached their destined treetop. Battles over power and control could invade the most idealistic group—commune or band. "I was the leader, in name at least," said McGuinn. "I did the lead vocals and lead guitar, plus got a lot of recognition. Crosby wanted to be the top man and kept pushing for that, and there was just this ego battle going on all the time. I mean there were fist fights and all kinds of stranglings. So Chris Hillman and I got rid of Crosby, because he was so outrageous, and then Hillman started wanting to be the top guy. You can't win. The only way to do it is not to have a group, I guess."

The largely unexplored problems of group living proved to be a major factor in undoing both the rock world and the counterculture. Through the remainder of his tenure with the Byrds, McGuinn would change the group's personnel frequently. Offstage he went through three marriages and is currently on his fourth. Where once he compared the sound of a generation to the roar of a transcontinental jet, now he is back to the horse and buggy of an acoustic guitar. With the perspective of a decade between the monumental highs of the late sixties and the monumental lows that followed, McGuinn admitted, "I've reevaluated some of my drug-culture mentality. We thought acid was a panacea: it would make dull people bright, take hateful people and make them loving. It didn't work that way. I don't do drugs at all anymore."

Drugs, for McGuinn, were always connected to his search for a new religious awareness. "I was looking for God, you know?" he said. "I came out of the Catholic church, and I didn't like God there. I was kind of rebellious, too, so maybe I didn't give it a chance. So I went through about seven or eight years of agnosticism and was pretty happy with that, until I read *The Power of Positive Thinking*. The Byrds were built on positive thinking, as far as I was concerned." McGuinn said that the quote attributed to him in the liner notes for the Byrds' first album, "I trust everything will work out all right," comes straight from Norman Vincent Peale.

"I was looking for God, but I didn't know where to find him," continued McGuinn. "I didn't believe this Jesus stuff. So one day I was walking around the block in Greenwich Village, smoking a joint with another guy, and we passed by someone named Richmond Shephard, who was a mime in the area, and he said, 'You know, I've got something better.' " That something better was a form of Eastern mysticism called Subud. "I thought it was something you put in your coffee," said McGuinn.

Nonetheless, he agreed to check it out. "It was kind of weird, like the Holy Rollers. They separate the men from the women and go through these dances. There's chanting, but you don't memorize the chants—it's sort of spontaneous stuff. Changing your name was optional," McGuinn recalled. But he decided to toss in his given name, Jim, for the new, improved Roger. "A guy in Indonesia sort of pulled it out of the air. It had something to do with vibrations."

From 1967 through the end of the decade, McGuinn practiced this strange form of religion, presaging, just as his music did, the fate that would overtake so many stoned believers in the onslaught of the straight world's backlash. In 1967, while the Beatles were isolated in the recording studio, safely removed from contact with the people on the street and approaching a technical peak with *Sergeant Pepper's Lonely Hearts Club Band*, McGuinn's Byrds began a drift toward country music, with two Chris Hillman songs on *Younger Than Yesterday*, "Girl with No Name" and "Time Between." The LP also featured the cynical "So You Want to Be a Rock 'n' Roll Star" and the critical "Everybody's Been Burned." Not only the Byrds were reacting to the burnt end of the rock 'n' roll candle. "Mr. Soul" by Buffalo Springfield was a commentary on the changes wrought when your "head is the event of the season." "Broken Arrow" was an excruciating parable of devastation. Neil Young's poignant "Expecting to Fly" presented a generation poised on the edge of their feathers with no place to go but down. Jim Morrison and the Doors responded in 1967 with a battle plan for "When the Music's Over." Briefly, it read "We want the world, and we want it . . . now?" No answer. "Now?" Still no answer. "*Now!!!*" But the world was to be denied the "us" implied in Morrison's "we." Frank Zappa took a dimmer view of all things countercultural, in *We're Only in It for the Money*, an honest enough statement for an ex-advertising man. But songs like "Concentration Moon," "Flower

Punk," and "Who Needs the Peace Corps" went beyond cynical parody. Even the Beach Boys tried to express their malaise, with their legendary *Smiley Smile* album, but though critically coveted in the underground, it went unreleased.

Dylan's *John Wesley Harding*, released in January 1968, made the disquieting country-influenced trend official, even though just two months before the Beatles had come out with some of their strongest pro–New Age consciousness material in *Magical Mystery Tour*—"Penny Lane," "I Am the Walrus," "Strawberry Fields Forever" and "All You Need Is Love." Once again the camps divided, those choosing to stand and fight for rock 'n' roll with the Beatles, those cutting out of the madness with Dylan. "All Along the Watchtower" told where he stood in his battles with the businessmen, who were calling the tune. His terse, epigrammatic songs came as a shock to Dylanographers who kept expecting him to expand—not only his mind, but the limits of the song form itself. Dylan chose not to do this, at least not in the way it was expected of him.

With Gene McCarthy running—actually, more or less ambling—for president and Dylan a recluse in Woodstock issuing cryptic jingles, an eerie passivity reigned, while violence echoed in the distance. For a short time optimism lingered, but the party was about to end . . . with a bang.

"I was sitting in my house in L.A. with Jacques Levy," McGuinn told me. "We were watching the California primary with the sound off and working on some songs. Then Jacques said, 'Hey, something's happening up there on the TV,' and we turned the sound on, and, oh man, my reaction was, I couldn't sit down for two hours. We'd just done a benefit for Bobby Kennedy two weeks before, and then he was dead. It really tore me up. And Jacques said, 'Oh Roger, this country's in trouble.' "

In August, on the streets of Chicago, with the whole world watching, the peace movement unraveled disastrously. In November, the torch was passed to Richard Nixon. The man whom Kennedy had defeated at the decade's outset—a defeat that gave us a taste of unheard-of liberation—had come back to ring down the curtain. If the anxious rock constituency was waiting for a statement from its leaders concerning this absurd irony, the message couldn't have been plainer. The Byrds' *Sweetheart of the Rodeo*, released that month, was a country album, complete with homey hymns like "I Am a Pilgrim" and "Christian Life." Dylan's *Nashville Skyline*, coming out in April 1969, was hokey enough to make you feel the man had gone Republican. The Beatles' 1968 double album was a last gasp of creativity from the mop-tops; from there they sank into animated cartoons before the final dissolution. McGuinn's biggest personal success came in 1969, when he wrote "The Ballad of an Easy Rider," for the movie *Easy Rider*, which quite accurately portended what longhairs would have to look forward to in the coming Nixon years.

In 1970 McGuinn became disenchanted with Subud. In its place, his wealth allowed him to deteriorate in style. "I did a lot of cocaine," he said. "My voice got real hoarse. You can hear that on the live part of *Untitled*. That's a cocaine voice." The seventies was a period of little sustained music for McGuinn. The Byrds broke up, and he issued several well-regarded solo albums, which failed to sell. "There were times when I wouldn't pick up a guitar for weeks," said McGuinn. "It would just be sitting there on the wall, out of tune. I remember once the guys from the New Lost City Ramblers came to visit me. They went over to this nice-looking guitar and they all strummed on it and went 'eeeuuu.' It was so out of tune. I was really ashamed of myself." By 1977 he hit bottom. His career was going nowhere. He was in the midst of his third divorce. He'd even tried a Byrds reunion album, but it fell flat.

"I said, 'Oh God, how can I keep from feeling like this?' And I got this sort of . . . not a loud voice or anything: 'Well, you could accept Jesus.' So I said okay, and I felt good again."

Dylan converted, as well. What was the meaning of this exodus to Jesus in the late seventies by two of folk rock's founding fathers? Was it a consequence of enduring the wild extremes of life at the top in an era when musicians were themselves considered gods? John Lennon had said that the Beatles were bigger than Christ. That would make Dylan at least the equal of the Buddha, right? McGuinn? Nothing less than "Harry" Krishna. In the seventies it might have seemed only natural to want to align yourself more closely with like Divinities. On the other hand, the motive might lie in the glide through country music that both Dylan and McGuinn experienced. Country, and its concomitant worship of the simple values, could have been just the right tonic for a couple of road-weary rockers to chug after a decade and a half of speed and acid visions that all too often had come to compose their day-to-day reality.

Finally, these were cats, after all, who had put their guts on the line and taken a generation with them. However reluctant they may have been to dwell too much on past accomplishments, it would be hard for them not to believe that their best highs were behind them. They'd outlived their moment; they were relics, affluent, obese dinosaurs. And with such a loss of love on the worldly plane (on the personal plane, Dylan, too, was having a domestic upheaval at about the time he saw the Light) where else to find its replacement but on the cosmic?

Regardless, the saved McGuinn (if not the saved Dylan) looks and sounds great. Under the spotlight he could be a whippersnapper of twenty-five, crashing out a post–rock-folk song with elemental ease. Except the songs reflect a passage not so much to God as through Hell. Still, I thought he sang "So You Want to Be a Rock 'n' Roll Star" with a new and much-deserved sense of self-worth. "When we wrote it we were a little angry," McGuinn observed. "I don't take it all that seriously now. I think it's funny. I'm sure there are greater achievements."

This, however, sounds to me like blasphemy, coming from a sixties survivor. It was a time when the words of our musicians were regarded as the gospel; in their lyrics, we were sure, was the key to the universe. But perhaps their words were all an illusion. Certainly the musicians themselves will never tell. The best evader of the lot was Dylan. I recall an interview he had with *Rolling Stone* magazine, the journal of the counterculture, where its editor, Jann Wenner, lunged from the merely pathetic to the archly comical in his attempt to pin Bob's wings to the wall. Over and over again Dylan refused to explain himself, define, interpret, comment on, or take credit for the experience of the generation that fell under the spell of his songs. Wenner begged, Bob did an old soft shoe. Wenner tried to get serious, Bob backpedaled out the door. It was ultimately tragicomic.

More than a decade later, the silence on the part of our reluctant poet laureate continues to say something troubling about our sixties experience. But what?

"People imagined all these things going on," McGuinn responded. "Oh, this guy's a great spokesman, a great statesman, a great artist. I think it was definitely an overestimation of the people involved. The fact is, it's just punks trying to play music, usually."

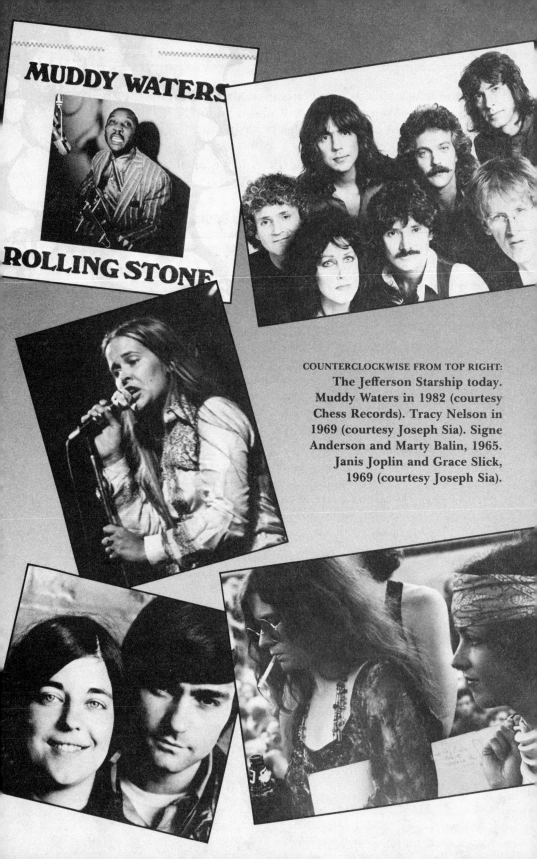

MUDDY WATERS

ROLLING STONE

COUNTERCLOCKWISE FROM TOP RIGHT:
The Jefferson Starship today.
Muddy Waters in 1982 (courtesy
Chess Records). Tracy Nelson in
1969 (courtesy Joseph Sia). Signe
Anderson and Marty Balin, 1965.
Janis Joplin and Grace Slick,
1969 (courtesy Joseph Sia).

★ 4 ★

Pipe Dreams,
Cheap Thrills

Bo Diddley once said of the King: "I don't hate Elvis Presley. I never have disliked the man. But at one point I thought he could have gotten his own act and left mine alone." In the sixties, young whites borrowed freely from the black man's act, from drugs to slang to music to that certain swagger that comes from living at the edge of danger. Long before the confrontations on the Berkeley campus in 1965, black college students were fighting for their rights in North Carolina, Mississippi, and Alabama. It was the black man who was the first to reach, with fists through a plate-glass window, for the elusive promise of an American Dream that America seemed determined to deny them. As the decade advanced, whites too would get to experience the billy club of oppression, as their chosen life-style, garb, and manners, their vision of right and wrong, made them the target of discrimination.

Since its inception, rock 'n' roll has made abundant use of black music. Purists were devoted to deejay Alan Freed because he always stood by the original rhythm 'n' blues recording of a hit song rather than play the innocuous white cover version—usually by Pat Boone or the Diamonds. Blacks were thus rewarded with prominent access to the pop charts, with Chuck Berry, Little Richard, Fats Domino, and the Platters becoming stars, though not quite the superstar that Elvis was. Music fans too pure for rock 'n' roll appreciated delta blues for its exquisite simplicity and grace under pressure. It was music from the gut, the back porch of black reality; many young middle-class white kids ached to empathize with such deeply earned despair. In elder statesmen like Lightnin' Hopkins, Mississippi John Hurt, Son House, and Skip James, they found father figures who could preach to them of things that mattered, matters of the soul rather than matters of the business world their own fathers offered them.

In the mid-sixties, when Dylan added an amplified guitar to folk music, with a blues band behind him, many other white kids were starting to pick up on the electrified blues of urban blacks. No less urgent and yearning than delta blues, Chicago blues had more rage, supplied by eloquent blues guitarists like B. B. King, Otis Rush, and Buddy Guy. The deep, sad eyes of Muddy Waters were as much a tribute to human endurance as his bottomless voice. The blues lines that charged the remainder of the decade ripped through the intellectual wordplay of folk rock and spoke to something basic in the heart. Like the step from the easy, flowing discourse provided by marijuana to the potentially horrific or blissful images of LSD, it was a commitment to emotional release, an irrevocable opening-up. Blacks were remembering a history in chains and therefore considering the possibility of violent assertion in the studio as well as in the streets. Whites had other options available. So with the blues as a common denominator, blacks took the low, down-to-earth road to Motown in Detroit and Soul music in Memphis, while whites took the high, blissed-out road, to acid rock in San Francisco.

A boundless, internal music, acid rock subverted the blues into a soundtrack for a party. Every rock band was a festival, everybody was a poet—better yet, everybody was a *poem*. A generation stopped to smell the flowers, to *become* the flowers, to hand the flowers to the cops. At its best, acid rock was an ode to unrepressed joy; at its worst, just another scene that failed to move beyond its grandiose promises. Its supposedly immune figureheads were as susceptible as anyone to the bloodless lure of the TV cameras and the big bucks. As the overture to the Summer of Love in 1967, a glorious paean to sensory overload, acid rock seduced a lot of instant converts; as the underscore for the Democratic convention in Chicago in 1968, it produced more than its share of innocent victims. The enemy beat back the disorganized troops; the energy evaporated. Musicians who journeyed from folk to rock through blues to acid, in the attempt to fashion a sound for the era's malaise, next took to the mountains, to the backwoods. Was it a diversionary retreat, prelude to a massive retaliation? Or were they irreversibly burnt out?

Playlist

Blood, Sweat & Tears

"I Can't Quit Her"
"I Love You More Than You'll
Ever Know"

The Blues Project

"Alberta"
"I Can't Keep from Crying"
"No Time Like the Right Time"
"Two Trains Running"
"You Can't Catch Me"

The Paul Butterfield Blues Band

"Born in Chicago"
"Born Under a Bad Sign"
"East-West"
"I Got My Mojo Working"
"Mellow Down Easy"

"Mystery Train"
"Walkin' Blues"

James Cotton Blues Band

"Jelly, Jelly"
"Knock on Wood"
"Turn On Your Lovelight"

Country Joe & the Fish

"Flying High"
"Grace"
"Janis"
"Not So Sweet Martha Lorraine"
"Who Am I"

Cream

"Four Until Late"
"I'm So Glad"
"Sunshine of Your Love"
"Tales of Brave Ulysses"

The Grateful Dead

"Golden Road (to Unlimited Devotion)"
"Good Morning, Little Schoolgirl"
"Morning Dew"
"New, New Minglewood Blues"

John Hammond, Jr.

"Drop Down Mama"
"Goin' Down Slow"
"I Live the Life I Love"
"No Money Down"
"Who Do You Love"

Tim Hardin

"Danville Dame"
"How Can I Hang on to a Dream"
"If I Were a Carpenter"
"The Lady Came from Baltimore"
"Misty Roses"
"Reason to Believe"

The Jimi Hendrix Experience

"Foxy Lady"
"Hey Joe"
"Manic Depression"
"Purple Haze"
"The Wind Cries Mary"

The Holy Modal Rounders

"Half a Mind"
"Random Canyon Blues"
"STP Song"
"Werewolf"

John Lee Hooker

"Decoration Day"
"It Serves You Right to Suffer"
"One Bourbon, One Scotch, One
  Beer"
"Seven Days and Seven Nights"
"Sugar Mama"

Lightnin' Hopkins

"Bottle It Up and Go"
"Penitentiary Blues"
"Shake It Baby"
"Trouble in Mind"

Mississippi John Hurt

"Candy Man"
"Coffee Blues"
"Make Me a Pallet on the Floor"

The Incredible String Band

"Blues for the Muse"
"First Girl I Loved"

The Jefferson Airplane

"Come Up the Years"
"It's No Secret"
"Let's Get Together"
"Plastic Fantastic Lover"
"Somebody to Love"
"Today"
"White Rabbit"

Janis Joplin (& Big Brother and the Holding Company)

"Down on Me"
"Women Is Losers"

B. B. King

"Every Day I Have the Blues"
"How Blue Can You Get"
"It's My Own Fault"
"Sweet Little Angel"
"Sweet Sixteen"
"Ten Long Years"

The Steve Miller Band

"Children of the Future"

Moby Grape

"Naked, if I Want To"
"Omaha"

The Mothers of Invention

"Brown Shoes Don't Make It"
"Help, I'm a Rock"
"Hungry Freaks, Daddy"
"Plastic People"
"Trouble Comin' Every Day"
"Who Are the Brain Police"
"You Didn't Try to Call Me"

Tracy Nelson (& Mother Earth)

"Down So Low"
"House of the Rising Sun"
"Living with the Animals"
"Mother Earth"
"Starting for Chicago"

Otis Rush

"It's a Mean Old World"
"So Many Roads, So Many Trains"

Muddy Waters

"Honey Bee"
"I Just Want to Make Love to You"
"I'm a Man"
"I'm Your Hoochie Coochie Man"
"Mannish Boy"
"My Home Is in the Delta"
"Rollin' and Tumblin' "
"Rollin' Stone"
"Same Thing"
"You Can't Judge a Book by Its Cover"

Junior Wells

"Good Morning Little Schoolgirl"
"It Hurts Me Too"
"Messin' with the Kid"
"Stormy Monday"
"Vietcong Blues"

Howlin' Wolf

"Evil"
"How Many More Years"
"Howlin' for My Baby"
"I Asked for Water (She Gave Me
   Gasoline)"
"Red Rooster"
"Smokestack Lightnin' "
"Spoonful"
"Wang-Dang-Doodle"

The Yardbirds

"For Your Love"
"Heart Full of Soul"
"I Wish You Would"
"Shapes of Things"
"23 Hours Too Long"

The Youngbloods

"Four in the Morning"
"Get Together"
"Grizzly Bear"
"The Other Side of This Life"

TRACY NELSON *(Mother Earth)*

MARTIN BALIN *(The Jefferson Airplane)*

There was North Beach in San Francisco, Venice in Los Angeles, the Oldtown section of Chicago, Dinkytown in Minneapolis, and Greenwich Village in New York—cornerstone bohemian enclaves where coffeehouse poets howled and the plays and films of the avant-garde drew somber appreciation. In the waning days of Ike and into the early hours of JFK, the beat philosophers encamped on doorsteps in those several neighborhods represented just about the only signs of encouraging oddity on an American landscape dominated by processed housing and processed foods and still in the grip of the red scare and the cold war.

By the mid-sixties nearly every college town in the country would be similarly madcap, with shaggy, ragged, barefoot citizens collecting in the quads around adhoc orators or harmonicas, as the nation tilted dangerously toward the zany.

More people than ever were attending college in the sixties, or had recently dropped out and were still to be found fraternizing with friends in the all-but deserted pastures along fraternity row. Politically conservative, pro-war, antidrug, the beer-bellied Greeks were gradually being replaced in campus status by the freaks, whose tastes in everything ran toward the extremes. The intelligentsia at leading-edge campuses of state universities in Berkeley, Madison, Ann Arbor, and Austin majored in Marxism, street theater, and macrobiotics; musically they favored the authenticity of the blues to manufactured rock 'n' roll. Fats Domino and Chubby Checker they dismissed; Josh White and Harry Belafonte they disdained. The only true and committed music was the delta blues. Though collectively their experience leaned more toward the deli than the delta, many of them had marched for civil rights and had picketed in sympathy with southern blacks, and many more would spend their summers ringing doorbells in Mississippi and eagerly signing up for the the Peace Corps. At Newport and other folk and blues festivals, they paid tribute to recently unearthed originals (still in their original overalls) like Mississippi John Hurt, Son House, John Lee Hooker, Lightnin' Hopkins, and Skip James. The music of Bessie Smith and Big Mama Thornton was also popular on campus.

"There were a lot of people who tried to be real earnest and intellectual about black music," Tracy Nelson told me. "It was the music of the people, and blacks personified the people, so they intellectually embraced the music for that reason. I just heard it and it moved me tremendously and I loved it." A jeweler's daughter, born and raised in Madison, Tracy had been into blues since high school, when she used to drive around at night in her father's 1955 Chevy convertible listening to WLAC coming out of Nashville—vintage Bobby Bland and gospel music. She attended the university for a couple of years, majoring in social work, but six months off as an aide at a city-run day-care center cured her of that ambition. By 1965 she'd made an album of acoustic blues for Prestige, called *Deep Are the Roots*, and was gigging around town with a rhythm-and-blues group dubbed, in classic collegiate reverse irony, the Fabulous Imitations. Days she worked near the campus at Discount Records, and nights and weekends, whenever she wasn't playing, she caught a bus for Chicago, where she haunted the South Side bars, enjoying sets by master urban blues musicians like Muddy Waters, Junior Wells and Buddy Guy, Otis Rush, Howlin' Wolf. No less blue than their delta relatives, the proponents of Chicago blues specialized in a searing electric-guitar sound that would dominate rock 'n' roll once it took hold mid-decade.

Many of Tracy's white contemporaries used to jump right up there on those South Side stages and jam with the black musicians, among them Charley Musselwhite, who'd played the harp on Tracy's album. "Charley knew Muddy and Howlin' Wolf, and he'd play with them regularly," said Tracy, who preferred to sit and watch. "They accepted him because he was very good and really a simple country boy. He wasn't some college punk trying to do the blues."

Another superior harp player was Paul Butterfield, who was also befriended by Muddy Waters. "When I first saw him at Smitty's Corner, on Thirty-fifth and Indiana, I was about fifteen," Paul told me, "and it was like magic to me. Muddy was a spiritual influence on my life. When I first started playing, I couldn't do a lot on the harp. He encouraged me tremendously. He said, you got it, now play."

Tracy was also friendly with Steve Miller. "Their attitude toward him was tolerant," said Tracy. "They kind of thought it was amusing. Also, in a real weird way, they felt it enhanced their status somehow for a white kid to come in and play with them. This was before any of the serious consciousness-raising among the blacks. I could walk around on the South Side at night by myself, walk into any club and feel perfectly safe. Those people were lovely to me. That period of my life is when I had the most fun. The music was so good it was just a total pleasure and nothing else."

To Tracy's middle-class parents, however, her habits were less pleasurable. "My parents thought it was terribly morbid that I listened to that music and hung around with those Negroes all the time," she said. "Once I brought Charles home for dinner, and they thought he was a nice boy, but, you know, rather lower class."

Like a great percentage of her privileged counterparts, Tracy's slumming deepened into a life-style once she dropped out of school. Again her parents were understandably mortified. "They didn't like the idea, of course," said Tracy, "but they had pretty much decided that I was going to do what I was going to do, so they didn't make things terribly difficult. They didn't support me; I took care of myself. So there really wasn't anything they could say or do about it anyway. I have an older brother who was a lawyer then; now he's a judge. He was the good guy in the family, who got married and had kids. He's a very liberal person, but he did things more conventionally than I did. He kept my parents off my back, I think, because he'd dropped out of school once, too, and *he* went back, so they kept thinking, 'Oh, it's just a phase.' By the time they figured out that it was not a phase I was going through, I had a record deal and was earning a pretty good living. They were still not thrilled about my choosing music as a career, but at least they were pretty sure I wasn't going to end up on their doorstep, strung out."

Other parents weren't as fortunate, as the decade drifted toward anarchy and students dumped their college programs in favor of the university of the streets, the tuition paid, in many cases, with money from home. Panhandling became a source of subsistence income; mooching became an advanced art. In college towns everywhere, the free speech movement, which had begun as an academic issue, rapidly became a literal and visceral struggle. In heated battles with school administrators, the townspeople, and the police, college kids took their cues from Berkeley and Madison and began to emulate the radical and desperate actions of their black neighbors who rioted in the inner cities in 1965 and 1966. At times these battles spilled into the street and made the evening news.

"I was officially a nonstudent agitator in those days," Tracy said. "My mother keeps a scrapbook on me, and she has a picture in there that appeared in the *State Journal*, of me in bare feet and blue jeans, playing my guitar to all these people who had just occupied the adminstration building, I think to protest the dropping of the 2S deferment. It was the first time anything like that had been done there." But not the last. "The serious riots and student unrest happened after I left," said Tracy.

By that time—late 1966, early 1967—a lot had changed in Tracy's old Chicago stomping grounds. "Within a couple of years after I moved from the Midwest, there was no way you could go down to the South Side anymore," she said. "In fact, they had to move Pepper's—where Muddy used to play—uptown, because they had a middle-class clientele that was afraid to go down there. As soon as the black people started rioting and getting overtly hostile, white people's interest in that music changed."

The blues, as such, would soon become nearly extinct. But blues-influenced electric rock 'n' roll would go on to be the sound of the sixties. The invasion of Chicago blues would be launched on the playing fields of the delta aficionados at Newport in 1965, when Bob Dylan employed the Paul Butterfield Blues Band to back him up on several new high-powered amplified numbers. The camps would split in two after that historic set—pro-technology and con-. In the final analysis, most would follow the map laid out right there, down the path to the unlimited treasures of mass appeal.

Butterfield had left Chicago for New York in 1964. "We were just playing this bar in Chicago," he said, "and within two weeks—bam—a whole bunch of people wanted to sign us." He went with Paul Rothschild and Elektra Records as the label's first electric band. With a National Merit Scholar on rhythm guitar, Elvin Bishop; a Jewish upper-middle-class virtuoso on lead, Michael Bloomfield, and a black rhythm section, the Butterfield Blues Band would lay waste to the distinctions between urban blues and delta blues, folk blues and rock blues. "We were just working all the time," said Paul. "We traveled all in one van and set up our own equipment. Finally we got a guy to help us. We had no idea how popular we were on any kind of national scale, which was probably to our benefit." After the Butterfield Blues Band staked out the territory, hundreds of young players took up guitar arms: Danny Kalb with the Blues Project in New York,

Jerry Garcia with the Warlocks in San Francisco. Jimi Hendrix and Eric Clapton would emerge from England as giants: the guitarist as existential hero, machine-gunning everything that got in his way.

Tracy Nelson headed toward the West Coast, tossing in her knapsack with the children of the future in San Francisco. First there was a stopover in Los Angeles, paid for by Randy Sparks, a folksinger who had created the New Christy Minstrels, an expanding apple-cheeked contingent that had enjoyed considerable popularity in the early-sixties commercial folk boom. After leaving that group he formed comparable ones to tour the college circuit, usually sponsoring as part of the package a folk-talent contest in which first prize was $250 and a two-week engagement at his club in Los Angeles. When the Sparks troupe hit Milton College in Milton, Wisconsin, Tracy entered and won the contest with "I Know You Rider" and two other acoustic tunes.

"I took the money, but I didn't intend to take the job," she said, "I was into electric instruments by then. But I decided rather abruptly that I wanted to leave Madison, and this seemed like a good way to do it." The trip out couldn't have been less thrilling. "This was during the airline strike, so I had to take a bus from Chicago to Los Angeles. There was this black guy who sat next to me part of the time who kept telling me he used to play with Otis Redding. I stayed pretty slack on Robitussin most of the way. I remember waking up in the middle of the night and this guy was all over me. I had to literally boot him out of his seat. It was pretty grim."

In L.A. with her Martin guitar, Tracy found that Randy Sparks also had designs on her. "Actually, his reason for running these contests, aside from using them to help get gigs, was to scout new talent to put together more of his groups. What he really had in mind for me and the other winners was for us to be in these groups and wear gingham and smile a lot. It wasn't what I wanted to do at all. After I did the two weeks at his club, he told me, 'You'll never make it as a folksinger, you're just too much of a nonconformist.'"

Tracy packed her bags again and journeyed up the coast.

"I'll tell you what I saw when I went to San Francisco," Frank Zappa once remarked to me. "Whereas in L.A. you had people freaking out, that is, making their own clothes, dressing however they wanted to dress, wearing their hair out—being as weird as they wanted to be in public and everybody going in different directions—in San Francisco I found everybody dressed up in pretty specific psychedelic garb. It was like an extension of high school, where one type of shoe is the 'in' shoe, but it was the costume of the 1890s in this case. They had a more-rustic-than-thou approach. It was cute, but it wasn't as evolved as what was going on in L.A."

I had my own rather quixotic affair with San Francisco in the sixties, venturing out there on several occasions. In the summer of 1965 I attended the summer session at San Francisco State, as Marty Balin often did. I went to an Allen Ginsberg reading in Berkeley and wrote fourteen furious short stories. My first date in San Francisco not only knew the work of Tom Rush, an obscure but eloquent Boston folkie, she'd *lived* with him. My last San Francisco liaison was with an otherwise unremarkable young lady who suggested we sniff Contac cold pills for a good time.

I'd like to tell you I ran into Marty Balin on that fragrant pink campus at the end of the trolley line, that together we hitched to Mexico, high on Contac. It would be nice to say I was in the opening-night crowd at Marty's club, the Matrix, that I saw the Jefferson Airplane when Signe Anderson was still the lead singer, the Grateful Dead when they were still the Warlocks, and Grace Slick when she sang with her husband and brother-in-law in the Great Society. I saw none of that. My only brush with the counterculture, aside from the Ginsberg histrionics, was when a young girl on a trolley asked me if I were a Beatle. I shrugged and said yes. Then I got off the trolley before she asked me which one.

In the spring of 1966 I was pulled back there again—passing through Madison on the way, to visit a friend and to purchase a record from Tracy Nelson. My S. F. State roommate was living on Frederick Street, in the Haight-Ashbury district and working at the post office, then something of a haven for the San Francisco left wing. I had progressed from MacDougal Street regular to Greenwich Village resident, from short stories to an epic novel. I had prowled the three squares of the Village—Sheridan, Washington, and Tompkins—in an ankle-length Air Force–blue woolen 1910 overcoat and a black Mormon-preacher hat that I bought for fifty cents at a rummage sale in Williamsburg. I had consorted with winos, bums, and songwriters. But despite it all, I still felt like Frankie Avalon, caught on the wrong side of Kings Highway, casing the terrain for his little lost Sicilian jailbait bride. On Haight Street (or was it Ashbury Street?) I walked among men of mountainous beards and scents and great toenails leering up at me from leather-thonged sandals and women of unbridled breasts bobbling beneath pioneer-age dresses and uncombed hair. In Golden Gate Park, where the Human Be-in had been staged and where nude nymphets, I'd heard, customarily cavorted, blasted out of their minds on wacky weed, I encountered nothing but a Japanese flower garden. Bitterly depressed and horny, I gravitated, in the grip of my Brooklyn heritage no doubt, to the deserted Golden Gate Lanes, where I proceeded to bowl a 227, my all-time record. Just down the block was the Straight Theater, where the marquee announced the Grateful Dead. I did not peek in. I wasn't in the mood to sit through another avant-garde play. At San Francisco State I visited my old writing instructor, one T. Mike Walker, who suggested I seriously consider dropping acid. What was acid? Something was definitely happening in San Francisco; I didn't know what the hell it was. My ex-roommate told me I was repressed, a typical New York affliction. In San Francisco they'd found the cure for repression—a mixture of climate and chemical, the lavender hills and a preponderance of young adults, free, curious, and living on their own.

In 1968 I was once more to the Golden Gate, arriving on the day after Bobby Kennedy was shot. The Jefferson Airplane's free concert, scheduled for that day in Golden Gate Park, was canceled. My ex-roommate now lived on Ashbury Street with eight others in a seven-room brownstone. The talk was of music and politics. I jokingly told the assembled throng that I was in San Francisco courtesy of a New York State grant for creative writing—unemployment insurance. Nobody laughed. "Under socialism," I was rebuked by a recently liberated American Indian, "there would *be* no unemployment insurance." My politics were by no means radical—I followed the then-very-popular politics of the oblivious—but back where I'd come from, it was certainly acceptable. Here, because, for instance, I had not as yet gotten a gun, I was termed "part of the problem." Saving the trip somewhat, my ex-roommate's ex-girlfriend seduced me in my ex-roommate's current bed. But I had a feeling my ex-roommate put her up to it. I was disconcerted. If this was the revolution, it was going badly. I feared our side wouldn't win. In San Francisco I was provided with instructions on how to cheat the airlines out of first-class tickets and the phone company out of long-distance calls. I didn't think that would quite cover it when the shooting started.

Marty Balin, it turned out, quit San Francisco State before I even got there. After attending three straight summer sessions, he only lasted a month once they gave him a scholarship to major in drama full time. The summer I was lazing around the campus taxing myself with courses in intermediate tennis, creative writing (tutorial), and film appreciation, Balin was working. He was hoping to save some money toward a trip to Europe. At the age of twenty he'd attempted the same thing, with a marriage and a daughter behind him. Fleeing from a factory job, he hitched with a friend to New York City in 1961, planning to board a freighter. Instead he heard Dylan and wound up bringing Dylan's first LP home to San Francisco.

"My friends thought he was weird," Marty Balin told me. "I said, 'But listen to the energy that guy's putting out.'" A few years later, after bouts with sculpture, painting, commercial folksinging, and street-corner poetry, Balin, like so many others, became his own Dylan, by living his dreamsong to the hilt. "When I started to put a band together," he said, "I realized there was no place an electric rock band could play in the city. So I had to buy a club for us to play in." He borrowed nine thousand dollars and in 1965 converted an old bar on Fillmore off Union into the Matrix. He built the stage, painted it, hassled with the city over permits, did the wiring, and even designed the posters out front. From acoustic blues to acid folk, all the early exponents of the new San Francisco gold rush now had a place to go. Balin's work was done. "I was there a big month after it opened. Then the Airplane took off."

According to Marty, Jorma Kaukonen came up with the name, after a friend's dog, Thomas Jefferson Airplane. Grace Slick had another explanation. "We named it after Blind Lemon Jefferson; Jorma was into blues," she told me. "And Paul Kantner has been wanting to go to the moon for forty years; so there's the Airplane. It's sort of a cross between Jorma and Paul." Whichever version is closer to the truth, that the Airplane made an instant impact is beyond question.

"The first night we played we went out and put up stickers telling everybody about the Jefferson Airplane," Balin recounted. "We covered the town with that name, and everybody came just to see what it was, including the record labels."

What it was was a sensory-saturated brew, the aural equivalent of an acid trip—not at first perhaps, but in its second stage, after the folkish influences were shed in *Jefferson Airplane Takes Off* and Grace Slick had replaced Signe Anderson, who went to Oregon to have a baby. *Surrealistic Pillow* came out in February 1967 with two hit singles, "Somebody to Love" and "White Rabbit." The Summer of Love in 1967 became a psychedelic inevitability.

"When we started to play there were no expectations," Balin said. "For us to show up and play, that was the only expectation. It didn't matter what we or any of the other bands did musically. It was that we all came together; people all came together because of this music."

So, into the neighborhood came the folded, the spindled, the lame, the halt, and the mutilated, to make their stand against the Industrial Revolution. Once again a sense of solidarity fostered by an indigenous music caused the walls of the city to shake and its rules to crumble.

"I liked the people around me. I liked what everybody

was trying to figure out," recalled the proprietor of the Print Mint on Haight Street, where the original psychedelic posters, the visual equivalent of acid rock, were dispensed. "It was the first time all these different kids from all across the country felt they could accomplish something since the great disappointment of the Kennedy assassination."

At the Human Be-in of 1966 it became clear that the incipient hippie community was larger than anyone suspected. Dr. Timothy Leary, its resident acidhead guru, was reported to have suggested afterward that "for every person on the street with long hair, there are ten hippie sympathizers."

So if you multiply the sixty-thousand head count of the Be-in by the Leary equation, you can see why Marty Balin might have felt the millennium had arrived, with a butterfly on its cheek and a flower in its hair. "I thought it was a great feeling, at first," he said. "In fact, I remember one time talking to a guy at *Time* magazine, when it was just hitting and Haight Street was like a tourist attraction and people were dressed in colorful costumes like you see at the Renaissance Fair. I told him, it's great you're publicizing this and telling people about all this spirit and everything that exists here. He looked at me and said, 'Fastest way to kill it.' He sure was right."

If there were a San Francisco equivalent to Mount Rushmore, there would be room only for two faces, the classically chiseled model's beauty of Grace Slick and the craggily drawn homely gusto of Janis Joplin—twin monuments to the San Francisco music scene, the one a cool, controlled siren of psychedelia, the other a combustible slave of the blues. Tracy Nelson had identity problems right from the start.

"Everybody was looking for another Janis Joplin," she said. "I had nothing but hassles with my record label over that. Whenever I gave them something they would immediately reject it because it wasn't as wild as what Janis was doing."

Janis Joplin intended to be a teacher when she enrolled in the University of Texas at Austin, but she quit school after her first year, when she was voted Most Ugly Man on Campus. By then she was a regular at the Flamingo, Austin's blues and folk nightclub, where she sang at the Monday-night hoots. Upon leaving Austin, Joplin embarked on a route familiar to the beat generation, all those Kerouac-inspired cats and chicks who bounced endlessly in Desotos across the sad night of America in the late fifties. She hitched to San Francisco in 1964 with a classmate named Chet Helms, but didn't remain long. In New York City she scrounged for food in garbage cans. Her boyfriend was a speed freak. She dropped to ninety pounds. Her career frustrations were epitomized by the night that Bob Dylan accidentally broke her guitar at a party.

By 1965 she was back in school, at Lamar Tech in Beaumont, Texas. She was off alcohol, off drugs, had gained some weight, and was seeing a psychologist. "She was bored as hell," a friend recalled. "She said, 'I haven't even been laid in six months, that's how good I've been.'" In San Francisco Chet Helms was involved with a band called Big Brother & the Holding Company. They had a good sound, but their lead singer had a speech impediment. What they needed was a ballsy new chick singer. Chet got word to Janis back in Texas to come to San Francisco to try out. The audition was held at 78 Henry Street, an abandoned firehouse, otherwise known as Mouse's poster studio, where Big Brother rehearsed and acid impresario Owsley Stanley mixed LSD. Janis got the job.

Tracy Nelson knew Janis only slightly, though she played on many bills with her. It's not surprising that the women never became friends, considering the context in which Tracy generally came into contact with Janis's name. "The first time we played the Avalon Ballroom," Tracy said, "we did a pretty good set, and I remember I came down off the stage and this little guy, the guard at the dressing-room door, said to me, 'Well, you're okay, but you're no Janis Joplin.' I could have creamed him. But that was exactly what was going to be happening to me from that point on."

If it wasn't Janis's name that was invoked, it was Grace's. "We'd be rehearsing," said Tracy, "and we'd have these guys in shiny suits come around, trying to act real big. One time we got some people from the William Morris Agency, these guys

in Hart, Schaffner & Marx suits. If they hadn't been slightly
sleazy looking they would have looked like Feds. We started
doing a tune, and all of a sudden this guy starts yelling in a
German accent up at the stage 'Do you do "White Rabbit"?' I
don't know who he was or what he was doing there, but every
time we'd stop he'd say 'But don't you do "White Rabbit"?' I
got so angry that I threw something."

"White Rabbit" was the chemically suggestive song that Grace
Slick, a northern California banker's daughter, had brought
with her from the Great Society. The song was a cunning take-
off on the *Alice in Wonderland* motif; in it Grace espoused, as a
prescription for dealing with life's exigencies, the all-consuming motto "Feed your head." And as the decade moved from
the delirious high of instant liberation through sex, drugs, and
rock 'n' roll to its dire denouement—with Johnson stoking the
war with young bodies, the inner cities igniting, and campus
vigils proliferating—in one San Francisco neighborhood, at
least, the party continued virtually unabated.

"I was never determined to be a great singer," said
Grace. "Basically I was determined to be a great fuck-off. I
was just sort of going with whatever looked like a good time."
In California, as the Beach Boys would have put it, life was
"Fun, Fun, Fun." Grace Slick concurred. "If you have sunny
days and you're going out and playing your music at night and
everybody's having a good time, that's fine," she said. "It's a
bit different in the slums of Detroit. Most California musicians
are very lucky; you don't have that same struggle for survival,
'cause California's a kind of a dreamland. If you don't have
any money you can go to sleep in the hills. That's why, basically, none of us know how to plug in a damn light socket, let
alone survive."

But the Jefferson Airplane never had to worry about survival. Even before their gold records they were the first San
Francisco band to hit pay dirt. "My feeling about playing music for money was always, you get some money and you pay
your rent," said Marty Balin. "When I first went to L.A. to ne-

gotiate a contract, I walked into an office and the guy asked me what I wanted. I said, we want fifty thousand dollars. He said, 'Okay, what else do you want?' Done! I had said it off the top of my head, jokingly, and he said okay, what next? I didn't know what else to say."

Soon enough San Francisco promoter extraordinaire, Bill Graham, would become the Airplane's mouthpiece. Said Grace, "His instinct was always You better keep at it, you better get it while it's hot. And we always thought he was nuts, going crazy trying to get the bucks, not because he was totally money oriented, just because Bill's instinct was to make sure of everything, watch everything, control everything; it could all fall apart at any second. We didn't have that attitude. We never went on the road every day of the year, really pushing hard—let's make it to the top in five minutes. We had a looser attitude. We were very conscious of not overloading. At least the rest of the band was. I wasn't. I'd overload at any given time. Say the word *overload* and I'd overload. The group was not like that. I'm probably still around now partially because they were more laid back."

Nose to nose, breathing fire and fury into the music, Marty and Grace created a sonic excitement that took over the entire town. Other bands were quick to sense the tremors. Big Brother & the Holding Company went into business. The Quick (Quicksilver Messenger Service) and the Dead (the Grateful Dead) personified the emerging spirit. Dino Valenti, the Quick's lead songwriter, penned the counterculture anthem, "Get Together," an ode to community, temporality, and love. Jerry Garcia, guitarist of the Dead, was less specific, a nonlinear type, whose very presence came to signify the drowsy, free-floating, serene, secure, acid ambiance that would pervade bohemian centers and college towns for several years in the late sixties. Bolstered by the underground press—the *San Francisco Oracle* and the proud and triumphant *Rolling Stone*—the denizens of Haight-Ashbury had every reason to believe it was all happening for them. They represented the first flowering of a new consciousness: Love is all you need. There was free food, provided by the Diggers; free love, provided by any number of pioneers, free rooms, free dope if you needed it, and free music in the park. There were endless afternoon guitar solos, within which were contained all possibilities—Indian ragas, blues progressions, rock 'n' roll flashbacks—including the idea that it would never end.

On Haight Street at the Print Mint, the euphoria was reflected in exploding sales of psychedelic posters. Originally an offshoot of Moe's Used Books, of the more serious neighboring Berkeley, the Print Mint, in just two months of operation, outstripped the volume of the first three years of the parent store. "The place was swarming with all kinds of people," the proprietor told me. "People with minks on, people with long hair, a kid with Indian clothes and a beard. It was America coming into that store, for some reason. It looked to me like the start of something good."

Tracy Nelson got a scent of those possibilities as soon as she arrived in San Francisco. "I was there with a guy I knew from Madison, and we didn't know where we were going to stay. I had relatives in San Francisco, but I had no intention of staying with them. So we were just wandering around Haight-Ashbury, and we met this guy. He said, 'I'll give you lunch if you help me move into my apartment.' He got a bunch of people off the street to help him carry his stuff. He had a beautiful apartment, and he let us stay with him for a while. Soon my friend split, but I stayed with the guy a while longer."

Tracy got herself a part-time job at the Berkeley branch of Discount Records and sampled the new product issued by the bands of San Francisco. "I thought they were all garbage," she told me. "The Grateful Dead, Quicksilver, Big Brother—I thought they played their instruments badly and that they had very little understanding of the music. You know, most of the groups considered themselves blues bands. But it was like fourth-generation stuff. Say a Michael Bloomfield comes from Chicago having been crazy for B. B. King and doing a really hyper Jewish version of that kind of blues. Well, then Jerry Garcia hears Bloomfield, so he does his version of Bloomfield's version of B. B. King. And then there were all the other guitar players who thought that Jerry Garcia was the ultimate, and they did their version of him. So people would say to me, 'Hey, why don't we go down to the Fillmore and listen to this blues band, the Grateful Dead,' and I'd go and I'd just think it was garbage. Of course, I thought the Rolling Stones stunk, too.''

Given the prevailing musical winds and Tracy's staunch if not obstinate beliefs, a career in San Francisco, let alone stardom, might well have eluded her. Tracy gave Steve Miller a lot of the credit for booting her ambitions right in the hindquarters. "When Steve came to town," she said, "he put a group together right away, and that got me kind of excited. He made a statement to me at one point that this is the happening music, this psychedelic stuff is really what's grabbing people. He really did recognize the trend as something that was going to have significance. I wrote it off.''

Miller's influence was more than merely philosophical. He also introduced Tracy to her eventual band, first Ira Kamen and Powell St. John (who later left the band), then adding Doug Sahm's rhythm section, imported from Texas. What Tracy and the band did mostly was practice.

"We'd rehearse for hours and hours cause it was so much fun playing. We were all serious and intense about what we were doing. We were making music with a capital *M*. I don't think any of us were into the blues like Butterfield, but that's all we wanted to play.''

Before their first audition, at the Straight Theater, they all got swacked on Thunderbird wine and Vicks inhalers. "We were so tanked up," said Tracy, "that we were terrible. It was the first time we'd ever performed as a unit after this endless rehearsing. But they absolutely loved us and we got the gig.'' Then Bill Graham began booking them into the Fillmore; the Avalon Ballroom opened up. Within six months, Mother Earth had a record deal with Mercury.

"I went from earning thirty dollars a week to sixty-five thousand dollars a year," said Tracy. "And, of course, we gave it all away. We were all so democratic, and everybody got their cut, and we lived high off the hog on the road. The money was

just there and was always going to be there. It made me think
that I could jerk off and do whatever the hell I wanted to and
get away with it. I didn't have to pay attention to any of the
realistic details about being in business and earning a living."

Even at the bottom end of the scale, Tracy's generational
cohorts were released in the late sixties, through the economy's unprecedented largess, from the business of making a
living. There was always another patron around to play host
to an indigent hippie. Many middle-class outlaws made do
with the occasional dope deal; some came into dangerous
windfalls. At the same time, the government had a wonderful
benefits package for the especially needy or enterprising to
take advantage of. It made for a lot of long weekends, in San
Francisco and elsewhere.

But that kind of freedom doesn't usually come free. It was
a woolly, rampant debt being run up. "That whole period of
time was so crazy," said Tracy. "The artists were given so
much credibility that you couldn't tell them anything, myself
included. I needed discipline when I was first starting out, and
I had total freedom. Now I don't think I would have accepted
any discipline if it had been given to me, but I wasn't at all
sure of what I was doing. And to be pandered to like we were
is not very valuable for anybody.

"I think part of it had to do with all the dropping out. A
lot of the people who were dropping out were highly educated, from middle- and upper-class families, and they were just
better at dealing with the corporate mind. The kids were doing a con on the corporations instead of the other way around.
So these were kids who took themselves seriously, were pretty
bright, and who just made demands that they somehow got
away with. The amounts of money that were given to people
who would have accepted so much less were just extraordi-
nary, and, in most cases, unjustified. There was total self-
indulgence for a long period, and it was nearly the ruination
of me."

Whether it was the closing down of a university and the
subsequent negotiations with the school's officials, the outrageous bargaining sessions of a bunch of ragged hippies in the
boardrooms of the Establishment, or the collective presence

of the affluent children of the middle class demanding that the government acquiesce to their grievances against the war, a momentum was building. There was a kind of magic omnipotence, a product of togetherness, the I Ching, a mushroom diet, and the natural confidence that comes from always having gotten your own way. Like a generation all going through their terrible twos at the same time—testing the powers of authority, resenting but desperately seeking some controls, on the outside and the inside—youth, en masse, created larger and larger obstacles to surmount, daring retribution. Sitting-in at the Oakland army-induction center was a nice high in 1966; the following year the trip was to levitate the Pentagon in Washington. It wouldn't take long for the momentum to turn.

"It didn't help to have a hundred thousand cars driving down Haight Street all day long," said Travis Rivers, the one-time proprietor of the Print Mint, who went on to become Tracy Nelson's manager. "They didn't even get out of their cars. It was like they thought they were in Yosemite National Park."

Along with the tourists came the media. A CBS documentary about Haight-Ashbury focused on the not-so-subtle extremes of life-style propounded by the residents of the area. "The documentary implied that all this art and music and poetry was coming out of the minds of people who were totally fucked up on drugs," said Travis. "So kids thought, 'Wow, I can just get stoned and all this wonderful stuff will come out.' It was like you sweated it. So we ended up with all these mental cripples on the street."

It was a transitionary period, from rural America to "MediAmerica," suggested Robert Hunter, lyricist-in-residence for the Grateful Dead. "As soon as the TV cameras screwed down on it, the vampire began to drink and only those with self-contained blood units survived intact," he went on. "It was ugly to watch the efficiency with which that scene was dismantled. The Abyssinians came down like wolves upon the fold. There was no bone worth picking that wasn't stripped clean and the marrow sucked."

Retribution arrived from within and without, in the form of tourists and leeches with flowers in their hair, record-company executives dangling contracts, increasing drug busts, rage, murder. The free food ran out, followed quickly by the free love. Depleted, demoralized, victims of their own mad magic, the dreamy residents were ripe for a comedown. Rock bands from San Francisco, being the most visible champions of the New Age energy, came under conspicuous heat. "Oh yeah," recalled Marty Balin, "we had to pay off a lot of judges and get out of town." If the acid experience didn't play well on the road, it had its share of problems even at home. The government, through the IRS, closed down Owsley Stanley, catching him for back taxes. (Alan Freed had been similarly fleeced by the tax man.) In 1968 a local hero drug dealer named Superspade was found murdered, stabbed six times, shot twenty-two times. Rumor had it the Manson gang was responsible. "The publicity got so bad," Balin continued, "that some of my friends wouldn't let me come into their homes. Their parents would be uptight."

In 1969 a kid, an innocent bystander, was blown off a Haight Street roof by the San Francisco riot squad, three blocks from Travis Rivers's house. "Reagan was governor, Nixon was president," said Rivers. "California was obviously their stronghold. I said, 'If this is what they have in mind for the rest of the country, I'm getting out of here.' " The neighborhood had gone to pieces by then anyway. "You had a lot of people talking to posts," he said. "They were ripping one another off, because it costs a lot of money once you get strung out on speed."

Tracy Nelson was more than happy to leave the city, too. "Here I was," she said, "right in the middle of all these people who were always proselytizing. If you didn't embrace this euphoria and this totally useless, pointless life-style, you were a schmuck, and they let you know it. They were very condescending. In the meantime, they were living like animals, begging for money on the street. The musicians who made money didn't have to beg, but they still just abused their bodies and their brains; they were jerking off and taking themselves much more seriously than they had any reason to. If they'd had any realistic attitude about how preposterous it was that they were in the position that they were in, if they'd been having fun with it, that would have been another thing. But they felt they had the world by the tail and the answer to everything. I thought they were all full of shit."

She didn't have much use for the pioneer women either. "The women were literally kept barefoot and pregnant and in the kitchen making herb tea for the guys," Tracy observed. "Either that, or they were this bizarre kind of whore image, just the total earthy sexual persona. Those were the roles for women, and I didn't fit either one."

Consequently her music-making ability suffered. "There was so much turmoil," she said, "trying to make sense out of the music business and everything else you had to make sense out of. I was contending with a lot of hassles in dealing with the musicians, trying to keep them from each other's throats, trying to keep everybody from getting drunk all the time on the gigs, dealing with promoters who treated me like garbage when I thought they should be treating me with respect—I was a great musician, after all. I tend to take charge in situations, or try to, and therefore I have always taken on these responsibilities, and I've been pretty weighed down by them. It took me a long time to recognize the things you need to worry about and the things you don't need to worry about. It's my biggest fault, always having to have a say in everything and not being able to let someone else handle something that's important in my life.

"Also, I had no recognition at the time of the kind of conflict that goes on when you work with male musicians. I didn't understand where it was coming from. They would get defensive and snotty, and I wouldn't understand why they would come down on me so hard for doing what I thought I had to do. My work suffered and my performing suffered, because by the time the show came around I'd be so tense my throat would go, or I'd just be physically exhausted."

At Woodstock in August 1969, homage was paid by the citizens of a battered Woodstock Nation to their weary warriors, their rock bands. Four hundred thousand were there, in peace and in love, according to the papers. Marty Balin was there, too. The Airplane went on at dawn. "I remember playing poker in the lounge at the Holiday Inn, waiting for the helicopter to take us there," he said. "We were totally wiped out by that time. I think the audience was asleep." Everything about the Woodstock Festival was immense, including the revived prognostications of hippie power. Four months later, at the Altamont Speedway in California, the false hope of those prognostications was shattered. Altamont was the latest and greatest free concert, a peaceful assembly brought together by rock music. The crowd, filled with loving vibes and smashed on weed, was kept in line too abrasively by the ushers: Hell's Angels, hired by the afternoon's headliners, the Rolling Stones. Fighting would be the order of the day—turmoil—which would end in a fatal knifing.

As he'd been in the beginning, at Monterey, Marty Balin again was there. "There was a fight going on when we started to perform," he recalled. "They were beating this guy up, and the audience just stepped back and watched it happen. I figured the guy needed some help, so I jumped down—and they stopped. But when I went back and we started to perform again, the same fight started up. So I joined in again and I got knocked out. That was the end of our performance."

The Rolling Stones denied responsibility; the Hell's Angels couldn't have cared less. But, to all intents and purposes, that was the end of the sixties.

Tracy Nelson wasn't at Woodstock *or* Altamont; for her the sixties ended a bit more idyllically than for most of her contemporaries, up in the woods near Nashville, Tennessee, home of country music. "The second I got here I just loved it," Tracy said. The band had come to record an album. "We all moved into this lovely old farmhouse, and the people were nice and the musicians in Nashville were very good. They enjoyed playing, but they didn't take themselves so seriously; it was their job."

When her manager, Travis Rivers, suggested they remain in Tennessee after the album was completed, Tracy was all for it. "It seemed perfectly sensible to me," she said. "There are good studios in Nashville, and it's accessible to more of the country than California. But I'm told by everyone who knows anything that it was the worst thing I ever did in terms of my career. A lot of people thought I'd just retired. It wasn't that they could say, well, I was doing country music, so I moved to Nashville. There was no progressive country in those days. You were either rock 'n' roll or you were country. So I guess I can understand why it probably wasn't a practical move, but I'm still glad I did it, because I don't think I would have lasted in San Francisco. And I wouldn't live in Los Angeles if my life depended on it."

Geographical trivialities have framed Tracy Nelson's career—Madison to San Francisco to Nashville. Stylistic inconsistencies have dogged her tracks—from acoustic blues to rhythm and blues to rock 'n' roll to quasi-progressive country-blues-rock (plus acid-rock connotations mired in soul proclivities). But more dismaying is the way these factors have frustrated what is potentially the finest voice in music. At barely five-feet-three, in a J. C. Penney dress, Tracy plants her feet like a country waitress at a biker's truck stop and, three or four times a show, lets loose a cry to raise cain, the crops, and the dead. Monumental, tidal, very nearly unharnessable, the voice was always there, even in the beginning. A mysterious gift from heaven and the genes, like the kid with a 200 IQ, born to ordinary humble farm-folk parents, the voice has been Tracy's pleasure and her curse, a living, breathing, heavy-weight responsibility to cope with every day.

"The first few years I was pretty hard on my voice," she said. "I was hoarse a lot and even when I wasn't hoarse, I sang too hard. I would frequently be agitated or annoyed or just jacked up from adrenaline, or drunk. So I would oversing. Every time I got up to sing I was just trying to get everything out all at once. If I let myself I could still just push as hard as I could and let everything out every second. But that's not good art. It's not really the best way to make music."

Including her maiden effort, *Deep Are the Roots*, Tracy's recording career stretches through largely unproductive outings with Mercury, Warner Brothers, Columbia, Atlantic, MCA, and Flying Fish, approximately thirteen albums, give or take a cutout or two, nearly nine hours of material, 150 songs, including some that will live forever in my memory, like "Down So Low," "I Need Your Love So Bad," "God's Song," and "Mother Earth," and too many others that seem hardly worth the wax; perfunctory performances of negligible tunes.

"I've always felt rushed when I've gone into the studio," Tracy explained. "It's difficult to prepare for an album when you're hustling on the road trying to keep your living together." That's part of the problem; another is song selection. Here again she's been at constant odds with her various labels. "They think my taste in music is too eclectic to be salable," Tracy said, "and I've never been able to prove them wrong. They all recognize my potential, but each time I make a record they go, 'Uh-oh, Tracy's made another of her self-indulgent albums.' I don't think they are, but they do, and it's been the same with every record company."

In fact, she's displayed an uncanny, if not perverse, ability to undermine her best chances for popular success. A classic example of this knack occurred in 1974 when she coaxed Willie Nelson, the deacon of progressive country music, to accompany her on a duet of the Conway Twitty–Loretta Lynn chestnut, "After the Fire Is Gone." Linda Ronstadt added one of her patented harmonies. "I thought it was just wonderful the way it came out," Tracy said. "The combination of people was so weird. I made a three-hundred-dollar bet with my producer that it would bomb, that people would hate it. He said it would be a Top Ten country hit." The record peaked at number thirteen. Pretty soon Tracy was getting offers for lots of country gigs.

"I had done it to myself again," she said. "I had just whimsically done a country tune, and all of a sudden everybody was thinking I was country again. I had to make a conscious effort not to follow it up." Tracy received a Grammy nomination the day after she was dropped from her record label.

Even selling out has been an ordeal for her. Consider the early-seventies episode involving a commercial she was hired to sing for Fabergé, makers of perfume for svelte and fashion-conscious women, of which Tracy is neither. "They gave us too much money, didn't make any effort to have control over it, and then when it was all done, they went crazy," she recounted. "They wanted to use my name, which I had specifically not negotiated. I was willing to take their money, but I wasn't willing to have anyone else know about it. They wanted to make little forty-fives up, with my name on them, to give away with the product, and I just said 'No way!' We had already gotten all of our money, so they had no pressure they could bring to bear, so they said, 'Well then we'll get somebody else to sing it.' And I said, terrific. I get the money and I don't even have to have the embarrassment of hearing my voice on the commercial.

"I wouldn't have done the commercial at all," Tracy took pains to explain, "except I was between record labels and really hurting for money." Not long after that, while moving to the farm outside of Nashville that she's only recently finished paying for, almost all of Tracy's record collection of rare Chicago-blues sides, the spine of her early influences, was stolen. Just carted away in boxes. "And I have always considered it some sort of karma for having done the jingle, that I did it against my principles, strictly for the money. It was something I swore I'd never do, and that was my punishment for it.

"Now what's odd about that is, I just don't have the same principles anymore. I have spent many, many years having absolute integrity about what I do. And now I've had enough. I'm perfectly willing to make some money—and I hope I do."

The decade since the fall of Woodstock has done that to many previously dollar-foolish people. Values have been rearranged, priorities reassigned. Selling out no longer has the connotations it once did. When I heard Richie Havens, my favorite MacDougal Street soul man, singing for McDonalds, I let out a cheer by far in disproportion to my taste for the product. Why not, I shouted, grab yourself a chunk of the old American pie? Even Grace Slick has been on the "Merv Griffin Show" of late. "If I were to join the Los Angeles Police Department, you could safely say I'd sold out," Grace told me. "Beyond that, I don't know what selling out is." In 1982, Tracy Nelson's fans got to hear her voice on AM radio, possibly for the first time (barring country-music-station play of "After the Fire Is Gone"). It was in the service of Busch beer.

"I had no problem with it whatsoever," Tracy said. "After a year of virtually not working, it was an offer I could not refuse. And the other people they chose to do the commercial were Muddy Waters, Ramsey Lewis, and Chuck Berry."

That's pretty fine company. But Tracy's updated ambitions are even grander. "My goal, and I swear to God I'll do it, is to have a song on the pop charts, a song on the R 'n' B charts, and a song on the country charts."

I don't have my record books in front of me right now, but the last person I recall accomplishing that particular feat was a fairly heavy fellow, upstanding role model and cultural high priest: Elvis Presley.

Grace Slick, after a few years off pretending to be a housewife (she has a daughter, China, age eleven), rejoined the Jefferson Airplane in 1981 (now known as the Jefferson Starship, with a remodeled lineup, sans Marty Balin). She seemed to feel it was possible to rock not only at forty, but well beyond. Citing the Starship, the Dead, the Rolling Stones, the Who, and the Beach Boys (three California bands out of five) as the oldest groups still around, she said, "We may be toothless and crippled and eighty years old and still getting up there to sing 'I Can't Get No Satisfaction'—mainly because we can't get out of bed."

Marty Balin left the Airplane at the top of the seventies, after participating in their masterpiece, *Volunteers*. Written at the height of the Vietnam fighting, the street fighting, and melancholy scuffling that characterized the last days of Aquarius, the title song, which he co-wrote with Paul Kantner, became a rallying cry for defiant hippies everywhere. Still at large were dreams of one day annexing Nevada, turning it into a free hippie state. The rhetoric and the fantasies would stumble into the seventies, living on in sentimental pipe dreams prompted by repeated spins of songs like "Lather,"

"Triad," "Wooden Ships," "We Can Be Together," and "Saturday Afternoon."

In 1974 Balin teamed up with Kantner again, on "Caroline," which appeared on the *Dragon Fly* album and which prompted Balin to board the Starship full-time. "It took me about a year after leaving the Airplane to come down," he told me. "I was still singing and working on songs and everything, but I just had to get out of the spotlight for a while. There was an album called *Bodacious* that came out, but I wasn't seriously doing anything. I built a house at the time. I did some work with the Indians. I was getting my head back together. The band had gone on putting out records, and I kept reading reviews where people were longing for the old days when Paul and I would write songs together. The band's albums were really kind of nowhere at the time, so I thought it would be funny to write a song with him, see if we could turn things around. So we tried it, and we did. 'Caroline' got a lot of attention, and so, after they came back from a tour, they asked me to join up, and I did."

In 1975 Balin wrote the biggest Airplane/Starship hit of all time, "Miracles." Having accomplished his purpose, he debarked again. In 1981 "Hearts" came out under Marty Balin's own name, marking his first solo smash. Touring in the wake of that success, Balin looked somewhat lost without the Starship/Airplane for ballast. He is not your typical supper-club performer. But when the crowd warms up, he warms up, and within his soaring voice he reveals the deep scars he lives with like tattoos, the unspeakable pain carved into the notches on his forehead. A lover and a fighter, a street punk with a heart of gold—in the movie of his life, Balin would have to be portrayed by the Harvey Keitel (or is Balin, in fact, portraying Keitel?) of *Mean Streets*. This is a question I never got to ask him. Backstage, after the set, he looked emaciated and seemed distracted. Not in the mood for an extended monologue.

We talked about songwriting. "People find all kinds of meanings in my songs that have no meaning for me whatsoever," he said. "It may have that meaning for them, but I didn't put it there. Then the song develops that meaning, because people give it that meaning. I used to try to write without having any specific meaning, leaving it open so that it would have so many variable meanings that it would trigger many ideas in someone's mind without specifically stating anything. Those are the best songs to write. Then you could get a myriad of meanings. Dylan does the same thing. He can string together a bunch of images that have no meaning whatsoever."

Of course, on acid, many of those songs were perfectly clear. At least reviewers said they were. "Ah," cried Balin, "a journalist has to have a meaning to everything. He has to have a pigeonhole, a label to put on things, otherwise he's frustrated. The artist doesn't ever want to be pegged or pigeonholed, so they're at odds right there to begin with. A songwriter isn't looking for meaning," Balin said. "The meaning is an emotional thing."

For a generation of runaways, escape artists, draft dodgers, professional vagabonds, the search for emotional truth was at times a devastating one. Once you opened yourself up, the wounds took a long time healing. Some never recovered from those wounds. When Dylan said you had to be honest to live outside the law, it could have been just a clever turn of phrase, or it could have alluded to a deeper integrity—a wider risk—that comes from establishing your own rules in a chaotic society and sticking to your guns at all costs. In the sixties rock 'n' roll helped us take that stand.

"If you're interested in music and exposed to it at the right time in your life," Tracy Nelson told me, "it will really just blow you away. And if you have the luxury of becoming totally involved in it, it can take over your life."

But if the debts of the sixties have been coming due for a decade, perhaps the stiffest price we've paid is the loss of most of our music. Seventy-five percent of Tracy Nelson's catalog is out of print. So many stalwarts are without current labels. Nothing is on the radio; little is in the stores. You might think someone was trying to wipe out even the memory of that odd and inconclusive decade. "Record companies are ignoring the people who came up during that freedom period," said Tracy. "There was a much longer, much more self-indulgent time for their musical tastes to become really ingrained.

There are still people from twenty-five to forty-five out there who are simply too old or too straight to get into the current trends but who really want to hear their own music, their own rock 'n' roll. I mean, there is no opportunity for people making the kind of music that I make to reach large numbers of people, even though those large numbers are there and probably very open and hungry."

Whether they were open and hungry, I couldn't say, but a fairly large crowd turned out when Tracy hit New York on a double bill with John Hammond, Jr. Tracy was in great vocal shape erupting into molten high notes (Mt. St. Tracy Nelson) at least a half dozen times. Still rusty on nuance and shading, she displayed a tendency to go for the strikeout on every pitch, and the songs quickly started sounding alike. Not for Tracy the subtle teasing of the corners: it's right down the middle every time. But when it works (as it does for me nearly all the time) and she gets up there into that groove, taking the audience with her, nothing and no one can touch her.

And her moment, among moments of occasional glory, is still her signature "Down So Low." A throbbing, gospel-flavored country ballad that keeps building and building, it was written by Tracy in 1967, shortly after she arrived in San Francisco. "I was doing a lot of speed," she said, "so I would sit down at night and write lyrics. I wrote all the lyrics for it in about forty-five minutes. But I just couldn't translate the music I heard for it onto a guitar, and it took me a year until I got to a place where I had a piano. I really had no confidence in the song at all. I only put it on *Living with the Animals* because I wanted to have some of my songs on the album. I didn't do 'Down So Low' in performance for two years. It took me a long time to realize that people had heard it and really did like it."

Another performer who does "Down So Low" is Country Joe McDonald. He hailed from Berkeley in the sixties with his band, the Fish, and was more overtly political than the neighboring San Francisco bands. Of course, he had his softer side too, as his ballads called "Janis" and "Grace" would indicate—his tributes to San Francisco's musical monuments. In fact, he once lived with Janis Joplin. As far as I know, he's never written a song about Tracy. But in his liner notes for a package of vintage Joplin performances, issued to commemorate the tenth anniversary of her death, he committed to print this rather startling, rather withering irony: " 'Farewell Song' was her last really great performance with a really great rock band, and I think her best. In the opening she sounds exactly like Tracy Nelson to me. . . ."

Survival has its occasional small rewards.

TOP RIGHT TO BOTTOM: **The Monkees, 1966 (left to right, Michael Nesmith, Mickey Dolenz, Peter Tork, Davey Jones; courtesy RCA Records). Peter Tork in 1982. The Mamas & the Papas, 1966 (left to right, Denny Doherty, Michelle Phillips, John Phillips, Cass Elliot; courtesy Michael Ochs Archives). Jimi Hendrix at Monterey, 1967.**

★ 5 ★

The Big Rock Candy Mountain

The Monterey Pop Festival of 1967, perhaps the signal event in the maturation of rock 'n' roll into rock, with the big-time dollars and respect that transition implies, was also the greatest show of youthful unity that side of Woodstock. In 1967, whether you played your music at the top of the charts or from the bottom of your soul, you were still assured a niche in the counterculture. Peter Tork, of the insidiously ebullient Monkees, was one of the hosts at Monterey; John Phillips, of the ostentatiously hippie Mamas & the Papas, was one of its organizers. Janis Joplin, Jimi Hendrix, Otis Redding, and Ravi Shankar showcased decidedly non–Top 40 music before the eager and hungry crowd. Buoyed by common music, sensuality, youth, energy, dope, mistrust of the government, faith in the Beatles, and a readiness to party, this festival sent reverberations of contagious dementia to all corners of the map.

Featuring the Beatles, the Stones, the Who, the Mamas & the Papas, the Buffalo Springfield, the Doors, the Jefferson Airplane, and the Young Rascals, AM radio in 1967 was very much a party to all this partying. Moreover, AM stars lived like reigning royalty, like gods atop the Big Rock Candy Mountain, their every whim indulged. As insulated as they may have been from the realities confronted on FM, the AM superstars were nonetheless attuned to the spiritual and sexual currents in the air. The only difference was, if you were the Beatles you didn't merely worship the Maharishi, you had lunch with him aboard your private jet. If you were Peter Tork, you didn't hang out on the corner of St. Marks Place and Second Avenue, hoping to pick up a flower-haired runaway from Terre Haute, you had round-the-clock orgies downstairs in your living room.

However, once FM began establishing itself as a countercultural force, once the counterculture began exerting itself as a socially and politically radical unity, the indulgences of rock 'n' roll crowned heads began to reek of complicity with the "enemy." Musically, they took no stand—and by taking no stand they revealed themselves to be the Establishment. In the fire storms of 1968 and 1969, with repression closing in from every angle, the government seeking to dismantle the machinery of protest, the draft heating up, AM radio contributed bubblegum music; the 1910 Fruitgum Company, the Ohio Express, the Archies, Steam—the last two groups not even groups, just studio voices augmented by the "miracles" of engineering. And if the insipidness of bubblegum didn't work, there was always the sledgehammer approach. To soothe the troubled gentry and mollify the remaining short hairs still in the system, AM provided air space to hard-rock efforts by Blue Cheer, Deep Purple, the Amboy Dukes, and Grand Funk Railroad. As the sound of protest wafted up from the street, on AM they chose to drown the mothers out.

Playlist

1966

January:　"The Ballad of the Green Berets" *S. Sgt. Barry Sadler*
"Nowhere Man" *The Beatles*
"19th Nervous Breakdown" *The Rolling Stones*

February:	"Time Won't Let Me" *The Outsiders*
	"Good Lovin' " *The Young Rascals*
	"(You're My) Soul and Inspiration" *The Righteous Brothers*
March:	"Monday, Monday" *The Mamas & the Papas*
	"A Groovy Kind of Love" *The Mindbenders*
	"Kicks" *Paul Revere & the Raiders*
April:	"Paint It Black" *The Rolling Stones*
May:	"Little Girl" *The Syndicate of Sound*
	"Hungry" *Paul Revere & the Raiders*
	"I Saw Her Again" *The Mamas & the Papas*
	"The Pied Piper" *Crispian St. Peters*
	"Red Rubber Ball" *The Cyrkle*
	"Wild Thing" *The Troggs*
	"Hanky Panky" *Tommy James & the Shondells*
June:	"Mother's Little Helper" *The Rolling Stones*
July:	"You Can't Hurry Love" *The Supremes*
	"Yellow Submarine" *The Beatles*
	"Bus Stop" *The Hollies*
	"Wouldn't It Be Nice" *The Beach Boys*
August:	"Walk Away Renee" *The Left Banke*
	"96 Tears" *? and the Mysterians*
	"Psychotic Reaction" *Count Five*
	"Last Train to Clarksville" *The Monkees*
	"Cherish" *The Association*
September:	"You Keep Me Hangin' On" *The Supremes*
	"Devil with the Blue Dress On and Good Golly Miss Molly" *Mitch Ryder & the Detroit Wheels*
October:	"Good Vibrations" *The Beach Boys*
November:	"Words of Love" *The Mamas & the Papas*
	"I'm a Believer" *The Monkees*
December:	"Ruby Tuesday" *The Rolling Stones*
	"(We Ain't Got) Nothin' Yet" *The Blues Magoos*
	"Gimme Some Lovin' " *The Spencer Davis Group*

1967

| *January:* | "Strawberry Fields Forever" *The Beatles* |
| | "For What It's Worth" *Buffalo Springfield* |

"Then You Can Tell Me Goodbye" *The Casinos*

"Dedicated to the One I Love" *The Mamas & the Papas*

"Penny Lane" *The Beatles*

"Love Is Here and Now You're Gone" *The Supremes*

February: "Happy Together" *The Turtles*

"A Little Bit Me, A Little Bit You" *The Monkees*

March: "Creeque Alley" *The Mamas & the Papas*

"The Happening" *The Supremes*

"Groovin' " *The Young Rascals*

April: "Respect" *Aretha Franklin*

"She'd Rather Be with Me" *The Turtles*

"Sunday Will Never Be the Same" *Spanky & Our Gang*

May: "C'mon Marianne" *The Four Seasons*

"Let's Live for Today" *The Grass Roots*

"Up Up and Away" *The Fifth Dimension*

"San Francisco (Be Sure to Wear Some Flowers in Your Hair)" *Scott McKenzie*

"A Whiter Shade of Pale" *Procol Harum*

"Windy" *The Association*

June: "Light My Fire" *The Doors*

"All You Need Is Love" *The Beatles*

"I Was Made to Love Her" *Stevie Wonder*

"Pleasant Valley Sunday" *The Monkees*

July: "Brown-Eyed Girl" *Van Morrison*

"San Franciscan Nights" *Eric Burdon & the Animals*

"I Dig Rock and Roll Music" *Peter, Paul & Mary*

"Reflections" *Diana Ross & the Supremes*

"Ode to Billie Joe" *Bobbie Gentry*

"The Letter" *The Box Tops*

August: "Never My Love" *The Association*

"How Can I Be Sure" *The Young Rascals*

September: "An Open Letter to My Teenage Son" *Victor Lundberg*

"I Can See for Miles" *The Who*

"Soul Man" *Sam & Dave*

"Incense & Peppermints" *The Strawberry Alarm Clock*

October: "Daydream Believer" *The Monkees*
"Hello Goodbye" *The Beatles*
"I Heard It Through the Grapevine" *Gladys Knight & the Pips*

November: "Judy in Disguise (with Glasses)" *John Fred & the Playboy Band*

December: "Green Tambourine" *The Lemon Pipers*

1968

January: "(Sittin' on) the Dock of the Bay" *Otis Redding*
"Valleri" *The Monkees*
"Simon Says" *The 1910 Fruitgum Company*

February: "Mighty Quinn" (Quinn the Eskimo) *Manfred Mann*
"Dance to the Music" *Sly & the Family Stone*
"Lady Madonna" *The Beatles*
"Cry Like a Baby" *The Boxtops*
"Honey" *Bobby Goldsboro*

March: "A Beautiful Morning" *The Rascals*

April: "Reach Out in the Darkness" *Friend & Lover*
"Angel of the Morning" *Merillee Rush*
"Yummy Yummy Yummy" *The Ohio Express*
"Mony Mony" *Tommy James & the Shondells*
"MacArthur Park" *Richard Harris*
"Mrs. Robinson" *Simon & Garfunkel*

May: "Lady Willpower" *The Union Gap*
"Stoned Soul Picinc" *The Fifth Dimension*
"Jumpin' Jack Flash" *The Rolling Stones*

June: "You Keep Me Hangin' On" *Vanilla Fudge*
"Hello, I Love You" *The Doors*
"People Got to Be Free" *The Rascals*

July: "Hush" *Deep Purple*
"1,2,3, Red Light" *The 1910 Fruitgum Company*
"I've Gotta Get a Message to You" *The Bee Gees*

August: "Say It Loud—I'm Black and I'm Proud"
James Brown
"Time Has Come Today" *The Chambers
Brothers*
"Elenore" *The Turtles*
"Midnight Confessions" *The Grass Roots*
"Fire" *The Crazy World of Arthur Brown*
"Hey Jude" *The Beatles*

September: "Love Child" *Diana Ross & the Supremes*
"Those Were the Days" *Mary Hopkin*
"Magic Carpet Ride" *Steppenwolf*
"White Room" *Cream*

October: "Both Sides Now" *Judy Collins*
"Abraham, Martin and John" *Dion*
"Wichita Lineman" *Glen Campbell*
"For Once in My Life" *Stevie Wonder*
"Cloud Nine" *The Temptations*

November: "I'm Gonna Make You Love Me" *Diana
Ross & the Supremes and the Temptations*

December: "Touch Me" *The Doors*
"Everyday People" *Sly & the Family Stone*
"Crimson and Clover" *Tommy James & the
Shondells*
"I Started a Joke" *The Bee Gees*

PETER TORK *(The Monkees)*

It was probably late 1966 or early 1967 when word first began to circulate through the Village. "You know the Monkees, that plastic-fantastic pop group, created in Hollywood, the prefab four, now ever so hot both on the pop charts and on the tube? Well, one of them is our own Peter Tork!"

Certainly nowhere near as momentous an event in pop history as Dylan Goes Electric, the transformation of Peter Tork from promising folkie to full-fledged plastic rock celebrity had the drafty cellars of Bleecker Street agog with mixed emotions. To some, he'd lucked out, plain and simple. Their jealousy was easy to understand. To others, the news was as shocking as if they had heard that Tork had become a Hare Krishna. They refused to sanction what appeared to be a radical departure from tradition. To all, it was symbolic of the extravagant changes life in the sixties could produce at any given moment, in any given body. One day you were a normal, law-abiding honor student sampling the evil weed; the next you were on the street, with no immediate prospects, liv-

139

ing in sin, in poverty, an outlaw in the eyes of society—and loving every laughing minute of it.

Of course, that may be an overly romantic viewpoint. "The thing about the Monkees operation is that it wasn't just the four guys," Peter Tork told me. "It was the producers, Burt Schneider and Bob Rafelson, Don Kirshner, who oversaw the music, Tommy Boyce and Bobby Hart, the songwriters—the whole crew. The four of us were just the front. I mean, I've heard that Mickey said later that we weren't the Monkees any more than Lorne Greene was a Cartwright, which is true. At the same time, we *were* the Monkees. It was a unique phenomenon, to be a member of a group that wasn't really a group and yet was a group. If we'd been a group, we would have fought to be a group or we would have broken up as a group. But we were a project, a TV show, a record-making machine.

"The thing that made the Monkees so successful was the incredibly adept commercial push that was behind the phenomenon, and a lot of people resented that, particularly people who wanted some of it. But I don't want to demean anybody's motives, because one of the things they wanted was a more even distribution of those goodies throughout the concerned population, and I'm in sympathy with that. But there I was, you know, racked with self-doubt: Do I really deserve to be here? And then, being a member of a synthetic group, I suffered from the criticisms—'those no-talent schmucks from the street'—while in the meantime I wasn't able to make the music I thought needed to be made. From the producers you'd run up against a lot of 'You guys are not the Lovin' Spoonful, so shut up.'

"But one of the things that's a blessing to me is that I've been able to accept things that weren't quickly describable," he said. "The phenomena are the phenomena."

The reflective Monkee, sometimes the ebullient one, a rock 'n' roll Maynard G. Krebs in a Nehru jacket, Peter Tork sat across from me in the spare room he occupied in his manager's small Manhattan apartment, a child of the sixties, approaching forty in a Beatle-bob haircut. "I don't want to have the Monkees on my back," he joked. "But I don't have to close the door on my past anymore. I don't have to try to escape from what I've done and been. Everything I am now is a product of all of what I was, and I'm not given to know the whys and wherefores of things as I go through them. Mostly I find out the whys and wherefores afterward."

Born in Washington, D.C., in 1942, Tork would live in Detroit, rural Connecticut, and Madison and Badger, Wisconsin (with an interval in Germany) before he turned ten. After flunking out of college in Minnesota twice, he gravitated to the Village in 1963 to begin picking out a minor living with his banjo and his antic persona. In 1965 he hitched to Los Angeles, where destiny in the form of folksinger Stephen Stills awaited him.

"Stephen met one of the producers socially in Hollywood, while they were holding auditions," said Tork. "They liked him a lot, liked his music, but thought his hair and teeth were wrong. Stephen and I were known in the Village as the guys who looked alike. So when the producer asked him if he knew anybody who looked like him, who was also musical, and whose hair and teeth were right, he immediately thought of me and called me up to say go try out for this thing. So I walked into the middle of the auditions and I got a part."

In November 1965 Tork, Mike Nesmith (a folkie from Los Angeles), Davy Jones (an English actor who had previously achieved fame as the Artful Dodger in *Oliver*), and Mickey Dolenz (whose credits included a stint as Circus Boy on TV), got together for the first time to make their demo for RCA. The idea of the producers was to tap into the ready-made subteen audience for an American Beatles, by duplicating on a week-to-week basis the rambunctious, good-time vibes the Beatles had created in *A Hard Day's Night* and *Help!* Similarly designed songs would be provided to sing on the show and to quickly leap into the upper reaches of America's Top 10. And if one or more of the Monkees could not play their instruments well enough, superb backup help would be provided. All in all, no sweller deal could have befallen man or ape.

Except if you were once an aspiring musician, hoping to stamp your own identity on the product bearing your name. "When the Monkees made their pilot," Tork said, "the four of us got on stage and we were supposed to be doing a dance set. Mike had his guitar, I had my bass, Mickey knew two beats on the drums. During breaks in the filming we asked the stage crew to fire up the amps, and, never having played together before on the same stage, we knocked out a song and the audience liked us. Everyone danced. When it was over they applauded. Some people from Capitol records, who had heard us, said they would have signed us even if we hadn't had a TV show.''

While this story may only serve to illustrate the depths record companies had reached in their attempts to exploit the huge numbers of young people turned on by the Beatles, it also underscores Tork's dilemma as a breathing human in a plastic machine. As a novice TV actor, he could deal with the confusion. But as a musician, there was little he could claim as proof of his existence. Recording sessions were especially depressing.

"Davy played nothing but tambourine," Tork said, "so he had his part down after the second take, and we would sometimes do fifty takes to get our basic track down. Davy's arm got tired. He got sick of banging the tambourine all day long. And Mickey lost faith in himself. He never did believe he was a decent drummer, so he didn't want to do it anymore. Mike wanted to produce his own records. He wanted to have total control. I was the only one who believed in the group per se, and so there I was all by myself, wanting a group, with nobody to be a group with.''

Understandably, his musical memories are few and tinged with ambivalence. "At the outset," he said, "the background instrumentals were almost entirely studio musicians, but the lead vocals were always one of us. On 'Pleasant Valley Sunday' I played piano, we had a studio drummer, the producer played bass, Mike played guitar. Essentially we created that record ourselves.''

Their fourth single release, after "Last Train to Clarksville," "I'm a Believer" (both number-one songs), and "A Little Bit Me, a Little Bit You" (which peaked at number two), "Pleasant Valley Sunday" continued the Monkees' seamless string of prepubescent odes to normalcy and suburban contentment—finishing its run at a comfy number three on the charts. "A notion of mine that I was real pleased with took over at one point," Tork said, "and that was having two guys sing in unison rather than one guy doubling his own voice. So you've got Mike, who was really a hard-nosed character, and Mickey, who's a real baby face, and these two voices blended and lent each other qualities. It's not two separate voices singing together, it's really a melding of the two voices. Listening to that record later on was a joy."

Tork's favorite Monkee album is their third, *Monkees' Headquarters*, released in June 1967. "At that point we behaved like a musical group," he said. "It was our record. We had the producer play bass. We had a cello player and a horn player on one cut." That cut was "Shades of Gray," which Tork feels holds up to this day. "Mike wrote the cello and horn parts; he sang them to me and I wrote them on paper and we gave them to the musicians. I wrote a little piano lick at the top and played it. That was a record we created out of our own feelings. It's like, not only are there shades of gray, God damn it, but what happened to the black and white? What happened to those clear-cut old ways that used to be?"

By 1967 those clear-cut old ways were being subjected to a veritable chaos of self-expression. The war in Vietnam was beginning to edge into mass awareness. Under a cloud of doom, a generation proceeded to freak out. A joyously contagious laziness took hold, symbolized by the spectacle of grown men wearing T-shirts! Wildly striped, splashed with crazy color, these T-shirts represented the dream of an adolescence regained—*knowing everything you knew now*. Men burned their draft cards, women burned their bras—and the weight of the world was lifted off their shoulders. Indeed, the times were too dire to think of anything else but having fun.

While Students for a Democratic Society was galvanizing incipient campus radicals and while black separatists shaped by the race riots of several long hot summers were beginning to organize the Black Panthers, the Beatles released their joyful opus *Sergeant Pepper's Lonely Hearts Club Band*. It was certainly a more pleasant option to ponder. At the same time the Yippies emerged—Abbie Hoffman and Jerry Rubin. It was revolution for the hell of it, a wide-open street theater of the absurd, suggesting that the peace movement could be fun and games too. In 1967 Yippies marched on Washington in an attempt to exorcise all evil spirits from the Pentagon. Many in the audience swore they momentarily succeeded.

On the streets, at four in the afternoon or four in the morning, grown men could be found unshaven, barefoot, giggling—with their pre-Lib women by their sides—in any number of towns, experiencing a wonderful, sudden release from traditional obligation: forty years of work and a heart attack. Self-discovery and self-indulgence were the order of the day. For a brief, exultant while, everyone conformed to nonconformity.

"Oh, I thought the New Dawn had come," said Tork. "The Dawning of the Age of Aquarius. So did everybody else. We thought everything was just going to be roses from here on out. But you have to do that. Those of us who were young and innocent and open and thrilled to be part of the age were not able—couldn't have mustered the vision—to see that it was a passing thing and that it would eventually turn around."

In 1967 the feeling of community, of safety, was prevalent and expanding. The ability to walk down a street at midday in zebra-skin jeans and a tattoo shirt, hair in a ponytail and zonked to the gills, was absolutely predicated on the certitude that no one would come up to you and break your face. "There was a feeling," Tork said, "that if you messed up, your friends would pick up the pieces for you, and that was true in a lot of contexts. There were a lot of little societies where people knew if they flipped out, their friends would take them to the beach and let them watch the ocean roll."

The ideal was often breached, however. "My brother flipped out on acid and thought he was the last humanist in a pocket of enclosing fascism," Tork told me. "He was at a party in a beach house, and he tried to get out by throwing his guitar case through the window. When I finally got to him, he was covered with sweat in a clinic in Malibu. But he came out of it all right."

In fact, as time wore on, little niggling chinks began to appear in the armor-plated fantasy. "You began to find what we call lame heads," said Tork. "At first 'head' was a compliment. Anybody who smoked grass was all right with me. I saw it as a vindication of my way of life. Then I began to perceive that it was not a matter of everybody finally waking up to themselves, but rather of simply following the style of the day."

If it was a kind of mass neurosis that overtook young men in the sixties—a collective, euphoric maladjustment—Peter Tork's position atop the rock pinnacle at the time only intensified and quickened the emergence of his latent personality disorders. Like an acid trip, the fame and the money, the status and the stimulants came in a glowing, breathless rush. But that was just a prelude to the pointy-headed monsters frothing within. "I saw myself as the victim of forces, the product not of myself, but of other people, places, and things," said Tork. "I was in therapy for about a year when I was a teenager, and I learned that whatever happens to me in life is a function of my own choices—but I lost sight of that for a long time."

Even in its early stages, the trip contained warning signs enough. The first time he attended a Beatles concert, at Dodger Stadium in 1966, in preparation for the Monkees' upcoming road shows, Tork was clearly disillusioned. "I couldn't believe the kids were not listening to them," he said. "Here was the greatest single musical operation of all time, and they wouldn't listen. It was all just screaming. The Beatles did about twenty minutes, and I don't blame them." Later, when the Monkees were on tour, Jimi Hendrix opened for them in England.

"Once Jimi came along, everybody said, 'Gee, if I turn up my amps, everybody will go berserk.' But what they were really going berserk for was Jimi Hendrix's pioneering musicianship and his art. No matter what kind of inspirational thing happens, somebody will latch on to one of the external details and call it that. It's called mistaking the finger for the moon. You point to the moon and somebody looks at the finger. It's inevitable."

Like a lottery winner rolling in the ruins of his fortune, Tork's ambivalence about the end results of his windfall cannot supersede the marvelous fact of the windfall itself. "It was a chance," said Tork. "I've always been a clown. I did comedy-variety shows and minstrel shows in high school and college. On the Village stages all you could do is throw out a few one-liners; basically you're up there to sing and pass the basket. This opened up a whole new area that I hadn't been able to explore so fully before. I was hoping to base further experience on that and eventually expand, but that didn't happen, which was disappointing. But my goal was always to wend my way merrily through life, playing my little banjo and my little guitar and singing my songs."

On the concert stage, Tork had the best time. "One of my points of pride is that as a musical operation the Monkees did amazingly well," he said, "not world cup, but national class, without a doubt." In these sentiments Tork is no longer alone, as critical commentary has finally caught up with the Monkees, marking them down in the record books as a quality good-time band. Tork recalled a typical show.

"First we had an opening band, which did a set, including a Beatles medley. Then a girl singer came out. After an intermission, we'd come out for our portion of the concert. We started off dressed in our suits—we had suits of matching fabric, but different cuts. Mike had a western cut, I had East Coast; Mickey, West Coast; Davy, English. We'd do five tunes on our own and then we'd each do solo spots—I did mine on banjo—with the opening band backing us up. Then that band would retire and we would come out and finish off the show by ourselves. There was one costume change. In the early days we came back in those paneled pullovers; later on we came out dressed however we felt." They introduced some of the earliest light shows, psychedelic slide projections that came to be a staple of the sixties' concert experience. "Most places we went it was the first time the light operator had ever gotten instructions to wave the spotlight at random. They'd never heard of such a thing before." Nevertheless, what lingers most are the incessant screams. "That was annoying," said Tork, "but, what the hell, they didn't come to listen to music. They came to vent their oppressions."

Painfully mixed feelings seem to have been a common

sixties malady. "I don't mean to paint such a bleak picture of it," Tork said. "I still felt I was in the vanguard, along with a bunch of other people. I was pretty happy. I had a circle of friends, and it was a lot of fun. God knows, I went through a lot of scenes and found out what I needed to find out, which is, for instance, that orgies are nice, but they're only temporary and they're not fulfilling."

Tork's infamous orgies were held at the Hollywood house he bought in 1968, previously the property of comedian Wally Cox. At the height of his fame, Tork could have paid for it in cash, but was advised against it. So he took out a huge loan and spent his money redecorating. In the master bedroom Tork's bed was eight feet by eight feet with a foam mattress six inches thick. He had a four-place bathtub put into the bathroom, along with a sauna. He had Mexican tiles laid. He carved his initials into the shower stall. There was red plush carpeting throughout the house, a wet bar in the foyer, six-by-nine-foot picture window in the living room overlooking the San Fernando Valley. The film room was a splendiferous workshop of sandblasted natural wood that housed Tork's resident filmmaker manqué. The screen covered the entire wall, offering a ten-by-twelve-foot platform for the flower of psychedelia's exploding visuals—viewed by exploding heads of all chemical persuasions, days on end. Just down the hall and across a bridge was another wing of the house. Downstairs was a cabana, leading to a fifty-foot pool. There were no houses behind his, so many people preferred to dive into the pool nude—straight out of his bathroom window. "I'd rather have nude swimming," reflected Tork; "it's much easier. There's a certain charge to bodies if they're covered up, and if you remove that, it takes a lot of that extra energy out of things."

Originally, Tork brought a girl friend to live with him at the house. Then his filmmaker friend moved in. He was followed by a young woman and her son. Later a friend of his girl friend stayed there. When Tork quit the Monkees toward the end of 1968, his new group, Peter Tork and/or Release, moved in. Often, wandering downstairs of an early afternoon, Tork would come upon two or three strange bodies asleep in the walk-in fireplace. But that was all right. At the same time, it wasn't all right.

"If you're fixed on the notion that an orgy is going to fulfill you, and one doesn't do it, you're going to try a hundred. If orgies don't do it, maybe drugs will. Like the fixated person I was then, I went from one thing to another. I had to try everything: flower power, dope, orgies, fast cars." His sternest nemesis was alcohol. "In the beginning drinking was a lot of fun," said Tork. "I have some memories of things that I did drunk that I never would have done sober, that I guess I always sort of wanted to do. But drinking isn't selective. It doesn't let you do exactly what you want to do and keep you from doing the things you don't want to do. Furthermore, at a certain point, and I think with certain personality types, it's addictive. You find you cannot drink moderately any longer. It finally reached a point with me where it was obvious that I was going to die if I kept up with it. I was never hospitalized, but I could see the path. I realized I was out of control."

If the rock 'n' roll fantasy was falling apart for Tork in 1968 and 1969, on the street the spool of possibility the sixties had presented in its idealized version was unwinding into an awful mess. The war wasn't ending, it was heating up. The peace candidates weren't winning, they were getting chopped down. Civil rights had turned to civil war. Nothing was working out as planned. The communal ideal depended on an equal sharing of the load, and who in the sixties wanted that kind of hassle? The perpetually stoned ideal presupposed no commitments in the real world; it also needed an independent income. The revolutionary-male-loafer ideal wound up victimizing women even more than traditional macho. Finally, the rock 'n' roll ideal was a sham, too, when you realized that while our rock stars were singing about overthrowing bourgeois society, they were the ones getting rich.

Not that being the rich kid on the block didn't come with outsized problems. "I think I was a sort of Gatsby," Tork said. "I was isolated and did not have a continuing sense of community. I'd have a moment of friendship here or there, a moment of sharing, but I didn't believe that was the main body of my life. I didn't know who my friends were, and anytime somebody asked me for a favor I wrote them off as a hang-around. And I wasn't able to ask people for favors, because I was supposed to have all that it took to keep myself together, because I had the money. At the same time, by giving the money away, I thought I was returning something to the community. I didn't see myself as apologizing, which is how I see myself now. But I had all this money, and I tried to make amends to the world by throwing it at people. And, essentially, what that did was to isolate me all the more."

Meanwhile, the hits had stopped coming for the Monkees. The TV show was canceled. Their movie, *Head*, was a critical and commercial disaster. Tork's money soon evaporated. "I think I was imbued with the notion, as my money ran out, that my fate was not in my own hands," said Tork. "I didn't have the sense that I had to hold on to it because nobody was going to save it for me."

Although he can live with the results of most of his career as a Monkee, *Head*'s failure is still to Tork a source of deep frustration. Had it been as successful as he felt it deserved to be, we might not be speaking today in a furnished room in Manhattan, but instead sipping champagne in an opulent mansion in the Hollywood Hills. "When it was revived for a week in Hollywood," said Tork, "Charles Champlin, the senior critic-at-large for the *Los Angeles Times*, said it was a movie that had been grotesquely underrated, a serious movie. But it was too late. It died a death you wouldn't wish on your worst enemy."

In part, Tork blamed the Monkees' fall on the very marketing machine that had been responsible for their efficient rise to pop stardom, only a day or so before, or so it seemed. "The series left the air early in 1968. We toured the Far East, made the movie and a TV special. We didn't go into the public eye in America at all. That's one of the reasons the movie didn't go, the special didn't go—and nothing ever happened to the Monkees again."

If you missed the movie Judith Crist called "some pot-smoker's dream," Peter Tork has seen it upward of a dozen times, and has total recall. "It begins with this guy who looks just like the mayor of Los Angeles, Sam Yorty, trying to dedicate a bridge. The microphone whistles on him, an officer taps the mike and it's all right. He steps back to the mike and it starts to feed back on him again. The officer checks the mike—it's okay. He steps back to the mike. And just then the four of us come running in. Mickey breaks the tape with his chest, like he's leaping across a finish line. And there are thousands and thousands of people chasing him—Indians, cowboys, the cavalry, Arabs, Italian World War Two army soldiers. All four of us jump off a bridge. There's a long sequence of us falling into the water. We hit the water and get carried away by mermaids, and this thing called 'The Porpoise Song' comes on. After a while it suddenly seems like we have been looking through a fish tank, and on the other side is this very, very pretty woman who kisses each one of us. When the woman kisses Mike, he whispers to her, 'How about you and me ditching these guys and going out together?' She looks at him and says, 'Are you kidding?' and walks off.

"Then we break into this new Monkee chant, and we cut to footage of the Saigon chief of police executing a suspected Vietcong prisoner. He puts a gun to his head, and the guy falls over with blood spurting out. Then there's a war sequence, the four of us in army uniforms, including a scene where I get caught in a pit with Ray Nitschke, former defensive end for the Green Bay Packers. He hits me. We all dive into a tunnel, blow things up, come out of the tunnel, and we're all dressed up in white and it's a concert. We do a tune, and at the end of the song we put down our instruments and run. The kids come screaming onto the stage and start ripping the clothes off what turns out to be dummies. The overall view of the movie is Bob Rafelson's vision of the whole scene. He saw rock concerts as war sequences."

Love and war, black and white, the clash of mortal opposites—the theme recurs again and again; on the one side death, a party on the other. In Rafelson's movie each scene is a mini-movie in itself, commenting on or parodying dozens of other movies and movie genres, complete with dazzling color, abundant Monkee music, numerous insane cameos, a panoply of effects, experiments, state of the artifice, tricks of the trade. It may have stopped the Monkees' career in its tracks, but director Rafelson went on to fame with *Five Easy Pieces*, produced by Burt Schneider, and made *Easy Rider*, with Monkee TV profits.

"There's a big black box that figures prominently," Tork continued. "We keep getting trapped in a big black box, and there's a little personality examination in how each of us tries to get out of the box. Mike cons his way out. Davy says, 'I'll show you how to get out,' and kicks the door down. I have had an experience with a guru, so I say, 'Well, it's really a question of choices, and it doesn't matter whether we're in the black box or not.' And Mickey runs this utter gobbledygook, 'Well, the universal plane is on a different order of vibrational sequences . . . ,' and on and on, sounding just like himself.

Viewing Monkee reruns is slightly less of an all-consuming ordeal for Tork. "The episodes look a little pale to me," he said. "What I remember most are some of the guys in the background—who they were and what kind of times we had during those days on the set. I remember staying at Mike's house in Hollywood when we first started filming the series. It was the upper story of a two-story building on a little hillside. Mike's wife, Phyllis, was wonderful. Mike and I laughed a lot and played music together. I remember that time very fondly."

It was a multimedia bash while it lasted, but comeuppance struck with rude swiftness. Tork found out he'd paid half again what his house was worth, so he wouldn't have been able to get back his initial investment, even had he sold it. For a while he leased it to Stephen Stills, who'd gotten over the rejection of not being selected as a Monkee by becoming a superstar on his own, first with Buffalo Springfield, then in a trio with David Crosby and Graham Nash. Tork and his girl friend, who was then pregnant, went back East with the idea of becoming organic farmers. Late in 1969 Stills moved out, with a few months of rent paid up, so Tork and his girl friend returned to finish out the decade. "We were there for a few months, but it was much less comfortable. Then a fellow came in and took it over, a would-be-guru type, who ran a colony there. When he quit paying the rent, it was foreclosed."

Next they moved into a house in Beverly Glen owned by

David Crosby. Tork's daughter was born there in January 1970. "We stayed there for a while, and I became involved with another woman, and my girl friend and I broke up," he said. A few months later, traveling back to California from the East, Tork was busted for possession of hashish and committed to a Federal reformatory in Oklahoma for three months. "Finally I was granted probation and my record was wiped."

If the bust served to isolate him from the straight world, his past as a Monkee was an onus just as severe in the entertainment business. "As far as I can see, in Hollywood, if you haven't got a lot of political support or another hit lined up, everybody thinks you're dead. I knocked around for a year with my picture, looking for roles, and out of eight people that I went to see, all of whom said they liked me, 'We'll definitely use you,' I got one reading, which I blew, and that was that."

The downward spiral began to turn wicked. "I was never inherently afraid of my situation," Tork assured me. "When I found myself in a boardinghouse with my daughter in a room for twenty-five dollars a month, sleeping on a mat on the floor, I was not discouraged. I had already made my connection with my source."

The source in this case had nothing to do with drugs. It was a spiritual awareness. "Cosmic intelligence, higher power, connectedness, the pattern, the source—these are ways of alluding to the process that expresses itself, in my experience, as intelligence and order," Tork said. "So we discuss a source, an unknowable source, which we call one, the unified one, from which all things spring."

Like many "heads" of the sixties, Tork's introduction to the spiritual plane was provided by LSD. "I brought some of those sugar cubes with me when I left New York in 1965," he recalled. "I'd heard that they deteriorate at room temperature, so I took two. Acid does not deteriorate at room temperature." His trip was virtually a classic of the genre. "I looked in the mirror and saw my mother. I dove out the front door yelling and hollering in Long Beach at two in the morning. I fell into a pumpkin patch and I had my first experience. I finally had a sense of there being a cosmic pattern. I didn't see God in the sense that Jesus came to me, or I saw a man with a beard in a chair high in the sky, but I did have a sense of a driving patterned force being the sum total of all the benevolent intelligences now or ever on the face of the earth."

Ultimately, Tork came to feel that the acid experience was a limited one. "I mean, it opens you up to the possibilities of living beyond your ego, but after a while you come back down and the chemistry you had before the acid trip is largely restored; your ego comes back. I particularly relate to what Ram Dass said, which is that in the throes of acid he was egoless, but as he started to come down his ego walked back in the door and re-fused with his body. That's why he decided to go to India, so he could have the acid experience without having to go through the return trip. In India they had techniques that they'd been developing for years, that made it possible for one to go into a post-ego state."

Tork's trip, in a larger sense, reflects that of many sixties seekers who opened up to the possibility of possibility, the magic of rock 'n' roll and the magic beyond. Some of them are still out there, having missed the flight back, either accidentally or by design. "It is said in a certain school of esoterica that when you first get the hint of it the mountains are no longer the mountains and the moon is no longer the moon," said Tork, as the afternoon sun went down and shadows slanted across his room. "But when you get past it and come out the other side, with some journeyman mastery, shall we say, the mountains are all mountains again and the moon is a moon.

"I think I'm at that stage with my life. When I first got the awareness of the extramundane, things just became all holy and completely beyond rational understanding. It was the first flush of acid, the first social explosion of the hippie era. 'Everything is everything' and 'Wonderfulness is wonderfulness' absolutely swamped the factual reality of a chair. Chairs were no longer chairs; they were imbued with mystery and magic. Having lived with that and taken a few hard knocks on the basis of overdoing it, I've entered what I call the tertiary stage of things. The first stage is where things are what they are. You've got goals and dreams and hopes, but there's no magic. Then you find the magic and it's all magic and nothing is real. Now there is reality and there is magic; they're both real."

What's missing, however, is that sense of community that rock 'n' roll, the peace movement, flower power, a dope-sweet righteousness, and all the media hoopla conspired to create. In the eighties, Tork's talk of magic seems a little beside the point. Once there was time enough for such speculations, when the days stretched yawning across the void and "Six o'Clock" was just another song by the Lovin' Spoonful, not a notch on a train schedule meaning dinner. But Tork, a philosopher-king in the clothes of a jester, has considered all the possibilities.

"It's what I call the Church of Three," he said. "You have a starting point that's essentially unitary, then comes the binary, the secondary phase, where everything is broken up and shattered and shot into millions of pieces. From there, you must have a dialectic. The third stage must appreciate and understand and value the first without undercutting and devaluing the second. It's no good just to talk about the positive. If the negative is there, you can't shut it out. For a while there wasn't any negative. Then it came into our lives in real ways, in ways we had to come to grips with. So, there we were, in the middle of stage two, shattered and broken, not believing in stage one anymore. Then comes stage three. This is where we recognize that there are times to slip into that primary mode and times when it won't do. If you insist on sticking to that mode, you're going to get your nose broken. And that's what happened. So there comes a time when, in full awareness of stage one, you behave through stage two, to get your stage three—a transcendent involvement of both stages."

Specifically, stage two began at Kent State, when four students were shot by the National Guard during a protest demonstration. "When they shot them down at Kent State, that was the end of the flower-power era," said Tork. "That was it. You throw your flowers and rocks at us, man, and we'll just pull the guns on you. Essentially, the revolution, which was sort of tolerated as long as it wasn't a significant material threat, was not tolerated anymore. And everybody went 'Ooops' and scurried for cover and licked their wounds. They became isolated—which was the point of it all. 'Togetherness isn't going to get it' was the moral they tried to lay on us, because the less togetherness there is, the more room there is for exploitation. Kent State was an attempt. Let's try this and see what happens. And what happened was the shooting and vast inflation and a swing to the right—the moral majority. The whole thing was inherent in the situation. A certain amount of loosening up, a certain amount of extra leisure, and people are going to try to improve their lot instead of just barely hanging on. If you had a little extra you're going to try to make everything better. And if you see that your own happiness, or the lack of it, is tied in with the sadness of your neighbor, you're going to start feeling communal. And that's going to expand until the crunch comes. As long as people are educated to believe that isolated self-interest is the only way to go, when the crunch comes they'll withdraw from each other. And only now, in the faintest glimmerings, do I see any sense that people are realizing that togetherness and flower power alone won't get it. It's got to be togetherness, flower power, plus a willingness to do something pretty stern from time to time. If you're not willing to behave sternly, people who won't stop short of stern behavior are going to keep on going. It's taken a while for that message to sink in.''

It's obvious that Tork was a true believer and ironic that he, of all people, should have been a cog in the plastic Monkee machine. He took the sixties to heart, and if the failure of the sixties took the heart out of him for a while, he hasn't let that failure break him. "You've got to struggle over the material,'' he said. "The struggle involved in keeping those people who want what you've got from getting it deprives you of the time to really be yourself. Instead of struggling to keep things out of everybody's hands, if you give what you've got—as Jesus said—if you give away what you've got, life unfolds for you. And the Catholic church would have us believe that heaven doesn't happen until after the death of the body. But I report differently. I report that heaven is an experience available in this life. And it comes from giving your shit away. If you give away your heart, your life, your soul, your goods, and live as close to the bone as you can prudently do, and don't worry about next week, if you live as close to that level as possible, you will find yourself as happy as possible. If you put your faith in the future, you're going to be chasing something all your life. Put your faith in the present; it's all right."

Tork must know whereof he speaks, having gone from uncounted riches down to zero. "I went dead broke for a while," he said. "I still have my guitar. I sold my car, a 1967 MG, a couple of years ago. It was starting to rot away in storage." Though he's back on the scene with a group called Peter Tork & the New Monks, it's not likely he'll either reap the huge rewards the old Monkees did or have to pay the same whopping dues. "Having had a solid taste of fame, I'm aware of the pitfalls of it," he told me. "Being young enough to have assessed the experience and reevaluated my whole life on the basis of it, I've been able to see that what I once heard called 'three hots and a cot' are my only requirements. Give me my meals and a place to put my head at night and I'm okay. That's all I really need, that and my community, my life with other people. To me isolation is the only sin. Human beings are not meant to live alone. And while I feel that I may have a fairly large place in the public life of the world today, it could be just a dream and a fantasy, and it certainly is not a fitting basis for my decisions. The basis for my decisions is to do what I have to do today, do what's put in front of me as well as I can, and to learn the lessons of the results."

One lesson, well learned only recently, has put Tork off alcohol since 1980. "I was able to change my course as early as I did, relative to some of the stories I've heard, because of my dabblings in Eastern philosophy," he said. "Because of that spiritual experience I had beforehand on acid (which has since been validated and expanded) and because of a few experiences in community, I've been allowed to recognize that what I really did want to find on a day-by-day basis was spiritual surrender. Now I am not in charge, not in the sense that somebody else is in charge, but in the sense that what is in charge is larger than I can know by myself, but I have to trust it.

"I can't ascribe my alcoholism to fame," he went on. "I can more easily do it the other way around. One of the things about alcoholics, to the extent that I've been able to make any observations, is that we are either above the crowd or below it—or both at the same time. The reason you shoot to be above is because you feel below, and the reason you feel below is because you're not part of, never one of the guys. You envy the people who seem to have a certain contentment. The character makeup that sent me into pop stardom is the same character makeup that sought to anesthetize myself with chemistry. I found that it was not until I put all of that chemistry behind me that I began to get back in touch with my place in the human scheme of things."

In the mid-seventies, Tork's place in the human scheme of things was anything but clear. "I was kind of half wanting to get my career back together again, but not doing a great deal about it," he said. "I was playing odds and ends here and there and not making out terribly well. The woman I was living with, who would later become my wife, was teaching at a school on the beach in southern California. Through the grapevine we heard that there was a job open at a small private school in Santa Monica." Another ego might have found the shift in rank disastrous, a falling from grace to mere mortalhood, with the screams of the crowds—instead of the alarm clock—still ringing in your ears.

"I believe I'm meant to do whatever it is I do," Tork stated. "I don't want to say it was easy, but sometimes getting up at eleven o'clock is not easy for me now." The two professions were not entirely dissimilar. "You try to be of use," he said. "You try not to just while away the empty hours, either as an entertainer or a teacher. The long-term relationship that you build up in teaching with what could be compared to an audience has a dynamic of its own—that I found to be very interesting. But the thrill of a good job of entertaining, when you know you're hot and everybody else thinks you're hot, is really unmatched for me."

Tork taught English at this school for a year until its director died and the school collapsed. He found another teaching job at a different school, one that had a much more restrictive atmosphere. "What had gotten me out of organized show business in the first place," said Tork, "were the tensions involved with having to deal with power-hungry people. I thought, if this is what show business is like, I don't want to

have any part of it. Then, when I worked at this highly auto-
cratic school, I found exactly the same things going on. It was
at that point that I finally decided to make my push for show
business again. I thought I might as well do what I like to do,
where there's a chance for the big bucks. Even if I don't have
them, at least I'll be doing what I enjoy."

But the transition from pleasant youthful memory to an
ongoing modern-day concern is hardly simple. Tork no longer has a machine behind him. "When you stop working the
formula, people who were depending on you to produce according to the formula desert you, and you're left only with
yourself and those who believe in you in the long run regardless of the formula. It takes a lot of imagination, a lot of heart.
But that's my hope for myself—that I have that imagination."

Unfortunately, his decision to return to the boards has
meant leaving the home he established for himself in Venice,
California, with his wife and two kids. "We're still married,"
said Tork. "I'm still the kids' father. We all love each other.
There's no dispute on any of those issues. I happen to be in
New York, where I have a career, and they are in Venice,
where they have a life. My wife's career is beginning to come
along, and I think she's going to be very successful. I see them
regularly, not nearly as often as I'd like, and I'm not part of
their lives on a daily basis, which is a drag. But it's just the way
things have fallen down. There's no career for me in Los Angeles. But in New York, within a two- or three-hour drive, it's
possible for a person to find enough clubs that pay enough
money so you can make a living.

"So, while it's potentially possible that we might get back
together, it's not likely, certainly not in the foreseeable future.
We both have far too different fates to work out. I think it's
terrible for the kids that Daddy's gone. Daddy didn't leave in
anger, which I think is an improvement, but Daddy did go.
Then again, my parents were together all my life and I had to
put myself through an incredible school of hard knocks before
I came to any sense of self-worth. I'm still coming to grips
with the feeling that there is support for me in the outside
world. I'm still relating on a day-by-day basis with my own
loneliness and isolation. I've had some bleak moments, of

course, and I'll continue to have them, but I trust that if I stay in contact with my source, that my bleakest moments will be a prelude and a vehicle to other times."

While he does not keep as close tabs on his other family, his machine-made Monkee family, Tork isn't out of touch either. Touring with Peter Tork & the New Monks in Japan, he encountered Davy Jones, with his own variation of the Monkee theme. Mickey Dolenz, when last Tork heard, was producing and directing a children's show in England. Mike Nesmith has achieved prominence as an actor and director of musical video productions, a leader in the quirky new field of video-rock. "Mike also hit a low point financially," said Tork, "but he inherited from Liquid Paper. Mickey did the best, I think, because he came from a show-biz family, and they knew what they were doing, so he made out like a champ."

The championship-season metaphor is one that Tork would not reject out of hand. "Yeah, you won the championship that year and you applaud all the other guys because you won. Then you remember the fist fights you had out behind the stadium. In any quartet there are six pairs of relationships and each one had its positives and negatives. I loved them differently and respected them differently and not in proportion to my loving of them—in fact, it was in inverse proportion, if the truth be known.

"What's happened to me in my life since then hasn't been so disastrous," he said. "I could have wished to have better financial resources at the present time, but so what? I've got my three hots and a cot and I have friends. I know I'm going to eat and I know I'm going to sleep and I know I'm going to have company. And I have a career, for Christ's sake. It's not tearing down the walls and breaking up the halls at the present moment, but I'm playing, I've got musicians—good guys, with lots of talent. I have no particular wants. I have odds and ends of desires running loose that may or may not ever be satisfied, but who cares? The really important stuff is right now, this very minute."

CLOCKWISE FROM CENTER LEFT: The
Fillmore, 1972. Laura Nyro, 1967
(courtesy Columbia Records). Tuli
Kupferberg in a King Karol record
store in New York City, celebrating
the Fugs' first album, 1965. Jerry
Brandt, former owner of the Electric
Circus, 1983. Essra Mohawk, 1967.

★ 6 ★

Dope, Sex, and Rock 'n' Roll

To be plugged into FM radio in the late sixties was to be at the burning center of events. For musician and listener alike, FM meant up-to-the-minute status reports on the coming revolution. In fact, for FM diehards the revolution was already here. The pendulum of righteous social behavior had swung wide enough to include group sex, speed, and heroin, Young Socialists with guns, White Panthers. On college campuses the frosh trashed induction centers rather than try out for fraternities. The war in Vietnam offered daily evidence that the system was out for blood. But whenever a leader went down— Martin Luther King, Jr., Bobby Kennedy—it only magnified the nobility of the struggle. Musically, the album cuts programmed on FM seemed to be talking to each other as well as to those within the sound of their voices. On FM you could hear the blues, jug-band music, a sixteen-minute drum solo by Ginger Baker, a two-hour raga by Ravi Shankar, followed by Jimi Hendrix playing "The Star-Spangled Banner," Arlo Guthrie's prodigious "Alice's Restaurant"—soon to be a major motion picture—and a tape of Jerry Jeff Walker's "Mr. Bojangles," *all in succession.* Occasionally there'd be a trifle by Danny & the Juniors, but always to make a point. On FM the music was the message; it was also the only hope.

This was music from behind the front lines. Heightened by the drama of hard drugs, war resisting, and the sense of mission, relationships were especially transitory and fragile. The everyday epiphanies of life in a war zone informed the work of Laura Nyro, Joni Mitchell, Leonard Cohen, Essra Mohawk, the Mothers of Invention, Janis Joplin, the preaccident Dylan. The Fugs (aka beat poets Ed Sanders, Tuli Kupferberg, Ken Weaver) played extreme games of language in charting our sexual and political course from innocent lust to decadence, while the MC 5 responded with a cacophony of outrage and the Velvet Underground celebrated the politics of nothingness, the poetry of pain. This was the true music of the sixties, not the processed nostalgia offered by Paul Revere & the Raiders, the Lemon Pipers, and the Grass Roots. And especially after Richard Nixon attained the White House in 1969, setting in motion his program to eliminate whatever was vital and threatening in American cultural life, these renegade voices would be all we'd have to hold on to, a sound that receded with the memory, gradually supplanted by the official version of events, the AM version, of course.

Playlist

David Ackles

"Down River"
"The Road to Cairo"

Joan Baez

"Be Not Too Hard"
"Saigon Bride"
"Turquoise"
"The Walls of Redwing"

The Band

"Chest Fever"
"I Shall Be Released"
"Tears of Rage"
"This Wheel's on Fire"
"The Weight"

The Beatles

"A Day in the Life"
"Fixing a Hole"
"Getting Better"
"Happiness Is a Warm Gun"
"Helter Skelter"
"I Am the Walrus"
"A Little Help from My Friends"
"Lovely Rita"
"Ob-La-Di, Ob-La-Da"
"Revolution 9"
"Rocky Raccoon"
"She's Leaving Home"
"When I'm Sixty-Four"
"While My Guitar Gently Weeps"
"Why Don't We Do It in the Road"

Tim Buckley

"Aren't You the Girl"
"Buzzin' Fly"
"Goodbye and Hello"
"I Never Asked to Be Your Mountain"
"No Man Can Find the War"
"Song for Jainie"
"Valentine Melody"

Buffalo Springfield

"Broken Arrow"
"Burned"
"Expecting to Fly"

"Four Days Gone"
"Kind Woman"
"Out of My Mind"
"Mr. Soul"

The Byrds

"Bad Night at the Whiskey"
"Christian Life"
"Drugstore Truckdrivin' Man"
"Everybody's Been Burned"
"Goin' Back"
"Hickory Wind"
"King Apathy III"
"Nothing Was Delivered"
"So You Want to Be a Rock 'n' Roll
  Star"
"Wasn't Born to Follow"

Leonard Cohen

"Bird on a Wire"
"Hey, That's No Way to Say Goodbye"
"Seems So Long Ago, Nancy"
"Sisters of Mercy"

Judy Collins

"Hard Lovin' Loser"
"In My Life"
"Michael from Mountains"
"My Father"
"Sunny Goodge Street"
"Who Knows Where the Time Goes"

The Doors

"The End"
"Five to One"

"Moonlight Drive"
"20th Century Fox"
"When the Music's Over"

Bob Dylan

"All Along the Watchtower"
"Dear Landlord"
"I Shall Be Released"
"This Wheel's on Fire"

Earth Opera

"The Red Sox Are Winning"
"When You Were Full of Wonder"

The Fugs

"Boobs a Lot"
"Coca-Cola Douche"
"Doin' All Right"
"Exorcising the Evil Spirits from
  the Pentagon, October 21, 1967"
"I Couldn't Get High"
"I Saw the Best Minds of My
  Generation Rot"
"Kill for Peace"
"Saran Wrap"
"Slum Goddess"
"When the Mode of the Music Changes"

The Grateful Dead

"Truckin' "

Arlo Guthrie

"Alice's Restaurant Massacree"
"Comin' in to Los Angeles"
"Meditation (Wave upon Wave)"
"Motorcycle Song"

Janis Joplin

"Ball and Chain"
"Kozmic Blues"
"Piece of My Heart"
"Summertime"
"To Love Somebody"

The Jefferson Airplane

"Lather"
"The Other Side of This Life"
"Saturday Afternoon"
"Triad"
"Volunteers"
"We Can Be Together"
"Wooden Ships"

Love

"7 and 7 Is"
"She Comes in Colors"

The Lovin' Spoonful

"Darling Be Home Soon"
"She Is Still a Mystery to Me"
"Six o'Clock"
"You're a Big Boy Now"
"Younger Generation"

MC 5

"Kick Out the Jams"

Steve Miller Blues Band

"Gangster of Love"
"Living in the U.S.A."

Joni Mitchell

"Both Sides Now"
"Chelsea Morning"
"Songs to Aging Children Come"
"Tin Angel"
"That Song About the Midway"

Essra Mohawk

"Arch Gooliness and Purpleful Magic"
"Full-Fledged Woman Now"
"Opening My Love Doors"

Van Morrison

"Astral Weeks"
"Cyprus Avenue"
"Madame George"
"T. B. Sheets"

The Mothers of Invention

"Bow Tie Daddy"
"Concentration Moon"
"What's the Ugliest Part of Your Body"
"Who Needs the Peace Corps"

Randy Newman

"Beehive State"
"Cowboy"
"Davy the Fat Boy"
"I Think It's Going to Rain Today"
"Living Without You"

Nico

"Chelsea Girls"
"Eulogy to Lenny Bruce"

"I'll Keep It with Mine"
"These Days"

Laura Nyro

"And When I Die"
"Buy and Sell"
"The Confession"
"He's a Runner"
"Lonely Woman"
"Poverty Train"
"Stoned Soul Picnic"
"Sweet Blindness"
"Wedding Bell Blues"

Phil Ochs

"Flower Lady"
"Outside of a Small Circle of Friends"
"The War Is Over"

Pearls Before Swine

"Ballad to an Amber Lady"
"I Shall Not Care"
"Morning Song"

Peter, Paul & Mary

"The Great Mandella"

The Quicksilver Messenger Service

"Fresh Air"
"Let's Get Together"
"Pride of Man"

The Rolling Stones

"No Expectations"
"Salt of the Earth"
"Stray Cat Blues"

"Street Fighting Man"
"Sympathy for the Devil"

Tom Rush

"The Circle Game"
"No Regrets"
"Shadow Dream Song"

Paul Simon

"America"
"Cloudy"
"For Emily, Whenever I May
Find Her"

The Stone Poneys

"Autumn Afternoon"
"Driftin' "
"New Hard Times"
"One for One"

Traffic

"Feeling Alright"
"Paper Sun"

The Velvet Underground

"Heroin"
"I'll Be Your Mirror"
"I'm Waiting for the Man"
"Sunday Morning"

Jerry Jeff Walker

"Little Bird"
"Maybe Mexico"
"Mr. Bojangles"

Tᴜʟɪ Kᴜᴘꜰᴇʀʙᴇʀɢ *(the Fugs)*

Eꜱꜱʀᴀ Mᴏʜᴀᴡᴋ *(aka Uncle Meat)*

When the Fugs played their first gig, at Ed Sanders's Peace
Eye bookstore in 1965, the East Village (Lower East Side to
purists) was hardly a bustling neighborhood. Deep in the
murky entrails of Manhattan, nestled among the entrenched
Ukrainian, Polish, Jewish, Italian, black, and Puerto Rican low-
er-class immigrants, was Tompkins Square Park, their central
meeting ground. It was a haven for life's seamier element:
pimps and prostitutes, addicts, ex-cons, mental patients, Bow-
ery bums, drifters, perverts—the wretched refuse of our teem-
ing shores. Unsafe during the day or night, the East Village,
naturally enough, soon became a grazing ground for excess
"boom" babies, dropouts, druggies, runaways, longhairs, and
would-be poets—the hippie fringe. With rents on Avenue D in
the six-rooms-for-twelve-dollars range, these fringers were
liberated from their battles for the real estate of the actual—
money, security, status. Drawing sustenance from their prox-

imity to the outlaw existence of drugs, cheap sex, the possibility of mayhem or death, they created a bohemian retreat from the suburban affluence that was their heritage. As the sixties reached their midpoint, this new bohemian lower class was gathering strength and numbers, imbued with the beatnik mystique of Jack Kerouac and Allen Ginsberg, mobilized by the progressive idealism of folk music and the civil rights movement, and by the contagious, youthful recklessness of rock 'n' roll. The whole country seemed ripe for change, turned on by President Johnson's extravagant visions of a great society. The unthinkable now seemed possible.

"We used to read at the Metro, on Second Avenue," Tuli Kupferberg, an original Fug, recalled. "After the readings, we'd go to the Dom, on St. Marks Place. *Dom* means 'home' in Polish. It was the Polish National Home. Then it became a bar, where lots of young people would go. The jukebox had Beatles and Stones albums on it, and some of the kids would dance. Once they started, the other paper-assed intellectuals tried to get up and dance, too. And Ed Sanders got the idea it might be good to try to combine some of our poetry with rock music."

Born of immigrant parents and raised in New York City, Tuli Kupferberg had been married and divorced when he became a belated rock star with the Fugs in 1965. "I was older than most of the people this happened to," he acknowledged, "but I had been living a bohemian life; I knew the bohemian tradition. I'd never been integrated into the great morass of bourgeois society." When he attended Brooklyn College in the forties, Tuli's poetic model was T. S. Eliot. "My writing was more literary, more abstract, but the concerns were probably the same." During the beat period of the late fifties and early sixties, poets clamored for coffeehouse stages, Tuli among them. "Suddenly poetry jumped off the page and became a performing art, which is what it should be," he said. "But when you read at the Metro, you read to fifty people. When you were the Beatles on 'The Ed Sullivan Show,' you reached a hundred million people. I had an elitist idea that it didn't matter, but it does matter. You have to accommodate yourself to that fact. So the next step is to perform on a musician's platform."

The platform provided by the Fugs proved to be ideal for Tuli and for the college-age, neo-nihilist rock constituency of the mid-sixties. "I was fortunate, I think, to have moved to the East Side at that time. It was an accident of geography and fate. I was fortunate to find the Metro. Switching to an apartment next door to Ed's bookstore was interesting. We were all fortunate to come together at the same time. I think it was sort of unusual. I was a Jewish boy from New York City. Ed was from Kansas City. His father had an Ozark background. Ken Weaver was a good ol' boy from East Texas. He'd been thrown out of air force intelligence for smoking dope. He had his dishonorable discharge framed and hanging on the wall of his apartment. So it was an unusual amalgam, I guess, a peculiar kind of free American energy."

Seated at the kitchen table of his comfortable Spring Street loft, bearded and wrapped in a bathrobe, Tuli Kupferberg's is a laconic and understated version of a riotous age. Pointed toward the eighties, he is a cartoonist now for the most part. In the seventies he published a series of humorous pamphlets, containing a mélange of news clippings and commentary, drawings, doodles, assorted bits of trivia and arcane scholarship, semisatiric musings and digressions. Tuli certainly did not retire on his Fugs winnings; in his best year he netted less than ten thousand dollars. On the other hand, he's made it into his sixth decade without ever having had to get another job. He owns his Soho loft, so he's safe from the vagaries of the rent commission—payment enough for all his good off-color works of the sixties. And if his artistic forays since the sixties have been fairly limited and without a backbeat to seduce the masses, to his neighbors, especially the younger ones, neophyte bohemians just arrived in New York and in their twenties, he's still as venerated as he was when he prowled the wild streets of the Lower East Side, invariably with a long-haired nubile female on each arm. This Tuli, a figure out of Dickens, was a personification of how Bob Dylan's glorious ascent had given the image of the word-bedazzled poet a cachet on the street normally reserved for second-story men and movie stars. Simply put, poets had become sex objects.

"You didn't even have to be a poet to get girls," said Tuli. "And the fellows . . ."

Free love may be a traditional bohemian ideal, but as preached by the Fugs and taken up by their spiritual heirs, it turned the sixties into a massive, oily group grope. With their ragged rhymes and baggy pants, their joyously lusty references, in songs like "Slum Goddess," "Saran Wrap," "I Couldn't Get High," "Supergirl," and "Coca-Cola Douche," the Fugs defined the issues for the grungy crowd who hung around Tompkins Square Park, jangling finger bells and sniffing incense, who loved to proclaim that sex was "as natural as going to the bathroom." But the Fugs were also manna for the frustrated souls of those who never had any fun at love-ins, who spent the sixties resolutely *looking* for the orgy, winding up stationed behind a pole at one of the dozen or so misty-hued pleasure domes that proliferated in the city like fast-food stands (my favorite was Rock Flow, four dollars at the door), ogling the translucent blouses shivering and shimmying under the walloping decibels.

"My poetry became simpler," said Tuli. "It became cruder, more sexual, more emotional. Politically it became less polite; it became more openly bitter and disrespectful. Part of the sixties was not worrying whether you were writing for the ages or not. It was a very immediate thing. But we felt that our songs were as great as any being written. We were saying what had to be said."

Mirroring the extremes of the music, the kids of the sixties gravitated to the East Side, lured by visions of dope, sex, and rock 'n' roll. In the West Village, the freaking out of the East was viewed with alarm, if not contempt. More traditional and restrained, the singers and songwriters who resided in the West were still committed to the dream of a humane and equal society, and, like Phil Ochs, played their music in service of that dream. On the East Side, a blissful hedonism prevailed. Apparently they'd solved with no hesitation the intellectual's timeless mind-body dilemma in favor of the body. By 1967, when the Fugs helped to celebrate the symbolic death of the hippie at Tompkins Square Park in conjunction with a similar rock 'n' roll wake being held in San Francisco, the

Summer of Love had arrived; the slums had turned to Wonderland. East Village cheek had invaded MacDougal Street, the West's main entertainment drag, where the Fugs held down a nightly gig for many months. On St. Marks Place on the Lower East Side, the Dom now sported a rock club upstairs called the Balloon Farm, where the Velvet Underground, with Lou Reed, John Cale, and the exotic chanteuse Nico droned their seductive hymns to the underside of life.

"Andy Warhol had a week at the new Cinematheque when he could put on whatever he wanted," Lou Reed told me in an interview at his Fifth Avenue apartment, "and what he wanted to put on was us, with films and stuff. It was a show by and for freaks, of which there turned out to be many more than anyone suspected. Everybody just looked at everybody else and said, 'Wow, there are a lot of us.' "

The Velvet Underground's material, songs like "I'm Waiting for the Man" and "Heroin," was as seamy as the streets of the Lower East Side. Combined with the ghoulish glitter of the Andy Warhol crowd they were favored by, their music celebrated with morbid prescience the despair that lurked at the core of sixties hedonism, a desperation that would overtake those streets by the decade's end.

"I was ten to fifteen years older than some of those people," said Tuli, referring to the Velvets and the Warhol crowd and the strung-out, zombie troops they influenced. "I came from a much more rigid tradition. Some of the things they did shocked me at first. I couldn't see the physical destructiveness of the drug thing. I was terrified by the loss of control. There were a lot of areas we agreed on. We agreed on the attack of bourgeois society. But on how to live your life after that, I disagreed. Self-destruction is not particularly charming, although sometimes it was accidental. The young people just didn't know the dangers. Some of them woke up dead."

"Canters!" the three teenage girls called to the man with the long black hair, Fu Manchu moustache, and goatee. "Ben Franks!" Frank Zappa, in the Village for a summer job at the Garrick Theater on Bleecker Street, with his freaky ensemble, the Mothers of Invention, stopped in his tracks when he heard the names of his favorite L.A. hangouts. This trio of teeny-boppers were obviously aliens from back home. So Zappa pro-ceeded to escort them into the Garrick to see the show that night for nothing. It was 1967 and the Village was in the midst of a love-in, influenced in part by Zappa's compelling transla-tion of the L.A. Experience, opening on the Lower East Side at the Balloon Farm, later exported to the Garrick, on the West.

Two of the girls were from Los Angeles, while the third was from Philadelphia. She was nineteen; her name was then Sandy. Within two weeks she'd be a Mother.

"When I went to hear the Mothers, Jeremy Steig was opening that night," she told me. "It was the only concert I ever saw on acid, and I ended up being in both bands."

Essra Mohawk, aka Sandra Hurvitz, aka Jamie Carter, was rechristened Uncle Meat once she became a part of Frank Zappa's bizarre musical operation. "One of Frank's jokes was that he liked to use opposites to call people. Like Suzie Creamcheese, another of his characters, was a real bitch. Her last name was Zarubika, and, let me tell you, she was a real Zarubika. You try to be nice to her, she'd go 'Who are you talking to?' So she had this attitude and he called her some-thing soft—Suzie Creamcheese. I was real nice and sweet, so he called me Uncle Meat. After a couple of months of it I said, 'Hey, I really don't want to be Uncle Meat,' and Frank said, 'I'm sorry, but I must insist you are.' And I said, 'Well, excuse me. Here I thought you were Frank Zappa, the wonderful mu-sician, and now I find out you're God and you're going to tell me who I am.' So a few days went by and he said, 'Okay, you don't have to be Uncle Meat. If you don't want to make money out of the name, I will.' I said, 'Thank you and more power to ya.' And so he came out with an album and called it *Uncle Meat* just to prove a dumb point to me. He could have called it *Shit on a Shingle* and it would have sold."

Abundantly long-haired and freaked-out, Essra's three-song cameo in the Mothers of Invention concert was, to me, the high point of the show. Though her songs were frankly in-coherent (her main theme was entitled "Arch Gooliness and Purpleful Magic"), I saw her as the ultimate merger of all that was wonderful in the reigning female types of the age, possessing the street-wise angst and funky sex appeal of Maria Muldaur, the verbal dexterity and intellectual honesty of Joni Mitchell, the troubled urban soul and ethereal innocence of Laura Nyro. Though the voice was closer to Etta James than pseudo–Joan Baez, in all other ways Essra represented the essential candy-store evangelist of the mid- to late sixties, who lugged guitar cases twice their size down to Washington Square Park to sing their wrenching rhymes in voices about six decades too old for their bodies. She was a cross between Leonard Cohen's "Suzanne"—"wearing beads and feathers from Salvation Army counters"—and the classic Janet Margolin character Lisa, from *David & Lisa*, the ultimate schizophrenic, who talked in rhymes and had soul-deep, scared little faraway eyes and a sad smile that could break your heart.

Born and raised on Long Island, Essra, at the age of sixteen, in 1963, invented folk-rock, under the name of Jamie Carter, with a single on Liberty records, called "The Boy with the Way." But it came out sounding like Lesley Gore and nothing happened with it. She yanked off her braces, played a dance in Youngstown, Ohio, gave away a box of records, and that was that. A few years later, publishers Koppelman & Rubin, who already had John Sebastian in their stable, offered her fifty dollars a week to write songs—no more and no less than Carole King had gotten when she broke in. But Essra was after something better. In 1967, after half a cup of coffee at Philadelphia Community College as an art major, she lit out for California with a friend in order to view up close the sunrise of a new era at the Monterey Pop Festival. But they made a wrong turn, after three thousand miles, and wound up at the Free Hippie Festival, just down the road.

Such detours were to define the remainder of the sixties for her. "I think I'm real fortunate that it didn't happen for me then," said Essra, speaking to me on the telephone from Beverly Hills, where she was preparing, as it happened, for her third marriage. "At that point in my life I had no caution and I would ride with the flow. Now I'm older and there are lines I don't go beyond. I was a fearless teenager then. We were all adolescents forever. Our parents had been through the Depression, therefore they overprotected us, so we were allowed to remain children longer than any other generation in history. So we didn't know responsibility. We didn't know caution. We only knew freedom. What's wrong with all these people older than us? Don't they know how to be free? Then we found out, if we lived long enough, that there were things they were hip to that we had better get hip to. So I personally feel I was saved. I grew up really wanting to give something to this world, and I wouldn't have been able to do it. So I'm grateful I didn't make it then. I'm not bitter at all. I know what I would have done with my success. I would probably be dead."

Essra left the Mothers of Invention after six months as an auxiliary Mother. By that time her Village dues were paid in full. "I opened for everybody at the Café Au Go Go, next door to the Garrick. I did three sets a night there, three sets a night with the Mothers, and three sets with Jeremy Steig & the Satyrs—nine sets a night, for fifty dollars a week." Her first album, on Verve records, done under the auspices of Frank Zappa, was actually an unfinished demo tape. It came out in 1968, attracting relatively little attention, except for a phone call it prompted from an admirer.

"I was living with my girl friend on West Fourth Street in the Village," Essra related, "and one day a voice on the other end of the phone says, 'My name is Laura Nyro, and we heard that you need help. David Geffen is my agent and he helped me and I'm sure he could help you.' And I was a flower child, and my thought was, 'Isn't that nice, these strangers want to help me'—not knowing that these things don't happen." By putting her career into David Geffen's hands, Essra feels, she played right into Laura's. "They got me a contract with Reprise and then sat on me for a year and a half." Her second album, *Primordial Lovers*, didn't come out until mid-1970, by which time Laura Nyro was ensconced as the Queen of White Psychedelic Soul, and the mystical urgency of Essra's sentiments was already sounding dated. Even so, the album gained a rare five-star review in *Down Beat* magazine.

Briefly, Essra became part of Laura's entourage, an artist-in-waiting. "I went with Laura to Los Angeles for her Stoned

Soul Picnic. She had an interview scheduled the day before it and she was late, so I talked to the guy in her room at the Beverly Hills Hotel. The same reporter came to the picnic, and because I was the only one within her circle who was straight with him, he talked to me through the whole picnic. He got his guitar out of the trunk of his car and played a song. Then I played a song, and we had fun. Sunday the paper came out with a whole lovely full-page article on Laura, and the last paragraph was about me. 'Also traveling with them is a very exciting singer. . . .' That's all it said. And David took me aside and said, 'You know, Laura's really pissed about that article.' That's when I first got an inkling that these people were not really my friends."

While recording what would be her second album in California, Essra met and six weeks later married her record producer, Barry Feinstein, aka Frazier Mohawk. They took a house nestled among the elite of sixties rock in Laurel Canyon. Paul Rothschild, who was producing Janis Joplin's first solo album, *Pearl*, lived across the street. "He was looking for material, and my stuff was perfect for her," Essra said. "But we were a little tardy in getting the tape to them, and, I'll tell you, she died before I finished making that tape."

Joni Mitchell was a regular visitor at Essra's house. "I had just come back from Woodstock and I read her a poem I'd written and told her my impressions of the festival," Essra said. "The next day she came back with her song 'Woodstock' and said to me, and I quote, 'I want you to hear my new song. It was influenced by your music.' So that's a quote from her. I guess I was the first free-form vocalist in rock 'n' roll, and I showed Joni not how to do it, but just told her to go ahead and do it. And, basically, ever since then she went off into the more dissonant chords and the more jazzy vocal style. That was my influence. I've never heard her say it to anyone, and I've never heard anyone else say it to me, and I haven't seen her in many years, but I don't know why she would deny it."

Scheduled to perform at Woodstock, Essra missed the exit ramp for the heliport and got stuck in traffic, finally pulling in fifteen minutes after Joan Baez's closing performance on Friday night. Saturday was 'band day,' so she wasn't permitted to do her set, even though she was friends with the promoter and "that was my people out there, man; I was one with them," she said. "You had others who flew in, did their act, and left. They wouldn't even dirty their boots. But I really felt it was right for me to sing to those people." Saturday afternoon she came down with sunstroke, and she left that night in a helicopter with Crosby, Stills, Nash & Young. "So I didn't even get to see Jimi Hendrix."

She flirted around the edges of the action, this disarmingly rococo go-go girl, and if she never did get to experience the high of rock stardom, by 1970 another high was making its wicked inroads into her life. "I think it was four years that I was on and off a junkie," Essra told me when I went to meet her at her parents' house in Philadelphia. A modest middle-class dwelling in a neighborhood of almost identical attached houses, this was where Essra retreated for shelter several times when the pains of making music in California became too hot to handle alone. "I don't remember those years," she said. "I'm very vague. There are a lot of things I don't remember. Little by little I'm starting to remember. With some of the stuff I'm starting to remember why I forgot."

The "Arch Gooliness and Purpleful Magic" girl of the Garrick Theater is long gone, although a picture of her from those days is on her piano in her parents' living room. Lately Essra hacked off most of her luxurious long hair. She's got a more suburban look now, more grown-up. She's been off heroin for almost ten years.

"I was real innocent," she said. "I was very dumb and very smart at the same time. I was street-wise, but I was gullible. And my first husband got me strung out. Ned Doheny warned me; David Crosby warned me. Don't go with Barry, he'll make a junkie out of you. I said, 'Come on, how could someone make someone else a junkie?' Sure enough, that's where all our money went.

"I'm not self-destructive," Essra said. "Maybe I was, but I didn't even know it. I was just fearless. Certain things even I wouldn't do. I would have never touched STP. I was not into angel dust. I hate speed. I had tried heroin once, before I met Barry, in 1967. I had a friend who was a junkie. He told me he didn't want to do it, and I said, 'If you don't want to do it, don't do it.' And he said, 'You don't understand.' That's the worst thing you can say to me. I wanted to understand everything. I was scared to death of needles. I was the kid the doctor had to chase around the bed. But for understanding I would go through anything. My friend said he wouldn't give me any. I said, 'If you don't help me to understand, I'll go out in the street and find someone who will, and God knows what'll happen to me. At least you'd be there to make sure I'm okay.' I could always talk my way into anything.''

At a party, Essra was enlightened. "I had to fight this feeling of lethargy just to continue to be social," she said. "It was like fighting sleep, and it bothered me. I decided it was not my cup of tea. Two years later, I fall in love with a junkie. He goes, 'Did you ever do heroin?' And the cocky kid goes, 'Sure.' He could have looked at me and seen I'd never really done it. But someone had told him that the only way to hold on to me was if he could get me strung out."

Essra left the marriage in early 1971, returning home to clean up. "I walked away from it," she said. "I felt sick for a couple of days and that was all. Later I developed a real habit on my own, because it reminded me of Barry. That's why I got into it, because it was nostalgic. It was the only thing of him I knew, and I was still in love with him. People do crazy things when they're young and stupid."

Of all the confessional poetry that came out under the label of rock 'n' roll in the sixties, by far the most trenchant, searing, and revelatory was written by women. Where Dylan and Leonard Cohen, Tim Buckley, Neil Young, Eric Andersen, and the others only occasionally ventured to speak of real feelings beneath the skin of their masterful wordplay, women like Joni Mitchell and Laura Nyro placed emotion and even outrage front and center, confronting their own and the era's moral unease. The drift through drugs and sex, political activism and self-determination, inspired by and trumpeted in the rock lyrics of the time, had led them to previously unknown doors of possibility. And as Tuli Kupferberg told me, "Once you grew your hair long, or once you smoked grass and realized it might be something nice, it made it that much harder to go back to what was really the emotional straitjacket of middle-American life."

More ensnared than men in that confining fabric, women were the emotional leaders, the cutting edge, who took the first fire in their agonized marches to awareness and equality. The sexual revolution depended on a radical redefinition of women's sexuality. While the introduction of birth-control pills may have made things simpler on a purely technical level, the decision to have sex or not was as eternal and confusing as ever, with reverberations that were bound to strike deep and linger. Society's rules and preconceptions may have been shed by this trailblazing generation, but in their place was only a murky abyss clouded further by mind-altering, inhibition-shattering, ghost-evoking drugs. The doors of possibility led to other doors—marked Do Not Enter. As they opened the doors, one by one, many women were left with permanent scars. Their anguish is echoed in Laura Nyro's haunting "Been on a Train" and Joni Mitchell's searching "Blue," both written in the early seventies.

"It was real easy to find an orgy in the sixties, if you were a girl," Essra Mohawk commented. "I always remember being recruited for them. People would say, 'Hey, let's get in a pile.' My first awakening was to that kind of thing—open, multisexual situations. To me that was perfectly normal." Her famous "Arch Gooliness and Purpleful Magic" spoke to some of the new concerns of the age. "It was a psychedelic love song," said Essra. "It was about wanting a guy to take an acid trip with me, and he wouldn't. And wanting him to commit himself in love, and he wouldn't. And saying that, after consuming all these things, why, it was back to Go anyway."

For men, the sexual revolution was a simpler matter. They had broken from tradition, too, by stepping off the school-marriage-career treadmill. Many were faced with contemplating the imminence of their own demise, as the draft threatened them every day. But sexually, the idea of a revolution, was, to a man, somewhat akin to a folkie's discovery of the Big Rock Candy Mountain.

"Much of the sexual revolution had validity and had to be gone through," Tuli Kupferberg said, "but it didn't come anywhere near solving the problem. As I look at it now, a common basis for a lot of the mistakes was that, since it was so much of a youth movement, people didn't realize that what's sexually wonderful at nineteen, may not be what you would want when you're thirty or thirty-five."

Tuli saw implications here that were larger than the quest for the Big O, whether or not to take acid before or during sex, the penchant for couples to live together after the first date. "That kind of youth dominance of the movement was inevitable and necessary," he said, "but it was one of its major weaknesses, too. Politically, the movement was never able to affiliate with the vast majority of people who were not nineteen, who had problems with work and family, education. It said this was life, when maybe it was just youth."

The promise was that these were new mores being carved from virgin land, a considered, progressive alternative that would gradually overcome the bourgeois status quo by the century's end. Listening to Nico's smoky readings of "Chelsea Girls," Jackson Browne's "These Days," and Dylan's "I'll Keep It with Mine" was enough to convince skeptical romantics that an authenticity was at work, shaped by the struggles of street life into a viable code of behavior that would be further developed and refined as the years went by. Instead the generation achieved new highs in venereal disease and divorce.

Lou Reed had never cared much for the love generation in the first place. "When we went to Frisco," he told me, "Bill Graham was doing his Fillmore, and he had a light show, right? So we walked in and we saw a slide of the Buddha and we said, 'That's gotta go!' He hated us, said we were the lowest trash ever to hit Frisco. Ralph Gleason, the dean of American reviewers, wrote in a review—I'll never forget it—he said the whole love thing going on in San Francisco has been partially sabotaged by the influx of this trash from New York, representing everything they had cured. Let's say we were a little bit sarcastic about the love thing, which we were right about, because look what happened. We knew that in the first place. They thought acid was going to solve everything. You take acid and you'll solve the problems of the universe. And we just said, 'Bullshit, you people are fucked. That's not the way it is and you're kidding yourselves.' And they hated us."

Even the artistic energy of rock 'n' roll after 1968 or so began to fade dramatically. The homespun reactionary solace of country music beckoned to many soul survivors. Few of these musicians managed in the seventies to interpret in rock 'n' roll terms their survival experience. "That's another way to say the sixties failed," said Tuli. "The people never grew up into the seventies. They just never matured."

While it's possible that the Weathermen sang Dylan while blowing themselves up in bomb factories in New York and the Manson gang whistled "Helter Skelter" by the Beatles as they chopped up Sharon Tate in the California hills, the political relevance of rock 'n' roll had always rested in its promise of personal salvation through joy—the joy of the struggle, the joy of release. Joni Mitchell's mood swings in *Blue*, 1971, from high spirited ("Carey" and "California") to chilly ("Blue") to downright scathing ("The Last Time I Saw Richard"), reflected the divisions and, finally, the choices that our moral ambivalence had brought us to. The violence in the streets and overseas, inflicted within relationships and on the self, had corrupted the purity of the sixties dream; in the gray shades of daylight, it would never be so simple again. Laura Nyro, who had always flirted with an absolute loss of control, submitted to it in *New York Tendaberry*, 1969. There was one enchanting song, "Captain for Dark Mornings," and a lot of confusion. In 1970 she came out with *Christmas and the Beads of Sweat*, containing at least a few sweet-sad laments—"Brown Earth," "Upstairs by a Chinese Lamp," and the stunning "Been on a Train." Laura left on that train of tragic visions soon after, and in the absence of new material, issued a wistful set of oldies.

In 1972, Joni Mitchell coiled up and went inward with an intense collection of introspective lyrics on *For the Roses*. It was clear that the seventies would be every man and woman for him- or herself.

"As open as I was when I began," Essra Mohawk told me, "by the mid-seventies I'd become a totally conventional young lady." She'd returned to California in 1973, but an album deal with New York-based Paramount sent her shifting coasts again. When Paramount merged with ABC, Essra's management took the record to Elektra/Asylum, a label helmed, ironically, by David Geffen. The ensuing *Essra Mohawk*, a sensuous war-whoop of anguish and bliss, was regarded warily by an audience who wanted to put such extremes well behind them. Songs like "If I'm Gonna Go Crazy with Someone It Might as Well Be You," "Back in the Spirit," and "Magic Pen," which contained the statement "There will always be more of us . . . ," were a mild shock to the easy-listening sensibilities of 1974, a period dominated by the comfortable blandness of Carole King's lyrics and Olivia Newton-John's physique. Even though Joni Mitchell's *Court and Spark* would appear, filled with fragrant and touching moments, they seemed in the stale and complacent atmosphere like the dying embers of a forest fire kindled in the woods of Monterey.

Essra's fourth album, *Essra*, begun on Elektra/Asylum, went over budget and was peddled to Private Stock, which released it in 1976—one more shriek of weird life into the void that was becoming disco, and then silence. Essra moved back to California in 1977, got married again in 1978 and divorced again in 1979.

"I met him in December of 'seventy-seven and we got married in February nineteen seventy-eight," she said. "It was just a mismatch. My mom had always told me to live with a guy first. Hip mom. He was a would-be record producer, but he just couldn't cut it in the big leagues. I mean, here we were, broke, worse than I'd ever been in my life, and he was saying, wait until you get a record deal. What I didn't understand was that we were two people with one career."

The women's liberation movement, which was probably

the most tangible result of the sexual revolution—and undoubtedly the opposite of what most men were after—has left Essra somewhat befuddled. "I feel sorry for guys in a way," she said, "because there are certain things that are nice that should be maintained about a man caring for a woman. And, in a way, I feel sorry for the woman, because now here she is alone, looking for a man and she can't find one who's as much of a man as she is. And they're missing out, because it's very nice to be cared for. There's a great advantage, I think, to being a woman. You can have everything, if you play your cards right, and not have to do a thing. Now if a woman thinks she wants everything, she has to do all the work.

"It's different for me. I always did what I wanted to do. I was always independent, a loner. I was more often single than I was with someone. One marriage lasted a year, one lasted a year and a half. Eight years in between I was alone. So when women's lib first got popular attention, I didn't think much of it, because I'd been free forever, because I always followed my heart." But that had built-in dangers, too. "I was always a romantic," said Essra. "And if you get hooked up before you really know somebody, you think you know them because you have this dream and they're the object for your dream. Then, when you get to know them, they don't fit the dream. Some people are content to stick with that; me, I just realize, 'Oh, I was projecting my dream on this individual. Let him find the person who really loves him for what he is and let me find a person I can really love who is my dream.' "

The third time around, Essra has been less hasty. "We've been together for two years and we really just get along," she said. "We have arguments, but they don't last long, because neither one of us wants to hurt the other's feelings. Most people are more concerned with making their point in an argument than how it affects the other person. If you really love somebody you won't be like that."

"Free speech has a long history in America," Tuli Kupferberg said. Behind him, on the kitchen bulletin board, were notices concerning upcoming poetry readings in the neighborhood, a women-only concert at a nearby coffeehouse. Down on Spring

Street, the hub of Soho, smock-smeared painters and punk-rockers made me feel nostalgic for the old days of the underground. "It seemed we'd won our battle, but now we're back in moral-majority time."

In 1965 it was a victory to push an advertisement for a Fugs concert past the censors at the *New York Post*. Tuli claims authorship of the controversial name. "It was from Mailer's *The Naked and the Dead*. I think it was Dorothy Parker who said when she first met Mailer, 'Oh, you're the young man who doesn't know how to spell *fuck*.'" The Fugs did, and would, at every opportunity. In fact, the literary magazine Ed Sanders founded was called *Fuck You: A Magazine of the Arts*. The Fugs, in their inimitable way, would take the lonely protest of that solitary Berkeley student with his placard reading: *Fuck* and make it as American as "At the Hop."

"We thought we could do anything and we just about did," said Tuli, summing up the mood of so many singers, groups, artists, and loiterers of the sixties. In the Fugs case, it was no pipe dream. "It was amazing how little trouble we had on the road. We were warned a few times by promoters not to use certain words, and a few times we defied those warnings and nothing ever happened to us. I'm amazed we never got arrested. Occasionally people misinterpreted what we were doing. I remember once I saw a photo from Vietnam of a soldier with *Kill for Peace* on his helmet. So I had to think twice about that. I know that song was misinterpreted, but I don't think our messages were ambiguous at all."

A classic misinterpretation occurred in Appleton, Wisconsin, center of the paper industry and, ironically, home and burial place of Joseph McCarthy, the infamous red-baiting senator. "I'm surprised we were invited to play in Appleton," said Tuli. "We'd constantly be amazed at where we were going to play and finding hippie radicals when we got there." Traveling with the Fugs' entourage was the hippie's patron saint, the poet Allen Ginsberg.

"Ginsberg wanted to do a thing on McCarthy's grave," Tuli recalled. "So about fifty of us went out in an open truck in the middle of the winter, and we were going to pray—do some kind of Buddhist thing for the elevation of his soul to the next stage. We brought flowers and candles—it was really a nice thing. And the highlight of it was when some young girl lay down on the grave to give him some affection. So this was completely misinterpreted by a reporter as our pissing on his grave, and it went out over Paul Harvey's noon news broadcast out of Chicago.

"Later we got this call at the hotel, 'We think you may be getting arrested. You better leave.' So we left in the middle of the night, taking the student who'd brought us, and we traveled in this secret caravan to Madison. Once we got to Madison it was like we'd just reached the revolutionary Zion.' "

Definitely there's an aura around those days, life on the existential edge, in battle with know-nothing authority, with the history of the century at stake—feelings that are conspicuously absent from life in the eighties. "Anything that starts underground is immediately overground now," Tuli said. "There are ten thousand people ready to exploit it. The main problem has always been to keep control of it. For instance, whenever any radical went on TV—like Abbie Hoffman—it was really a war. Are they going to screw him or is he going to screw them? I remember once a guy interviewed me on some local radio station during a demonstration and I said, 'We're going to end this fuckin' war.' He said, 'You can't say that on the air. Don't you want to get some publicity?' I said, 'No, we want to make the revolution.' "

In the seventies Ed Sanders came into a measure of acclaim for the fine writer he'd always been, with *The Family*, a stark and raving portrait of the Manson clan. Tuli started a radical theater group called the Revolting Theater. Working mostly with college students, he toured the campus circuit for a while, doing skits, acting out advertisements; there was a slide show. "I had no band, so I did parodies of other people's songs," he told me.

Janis and Lenny
died in the can
and were buried along
with their fame
everyone came

Abbie and Jerry
wiping the dirt from their hands
as they run from the grave
who did they save?

—*from "Ah, Look at*
All the Hippy People,"
a parody of "Eleanor Rigby,"
by Lennon & McCartney

"Where have all the hippies gone?" Tuli intoned. "Some of them are still on the East Side. You see a lot of kids with long hair, some of them are not kids. And you don't just see them on the East Side. If you travel a little you'll find there are outbacks where they don't realize the sixties have ended. But the vast majority are more or less out there in middle America, and when push comes to shove, either in their private life or in some sort of political crisis, it's not going to be too easy to predict how they'll react. They may not have adjusted that well. They may not have bought all the crap that's been handed to them. I see that whenever I meet someone who has on a three-piece suit and tells me he used to be a Fugs fan. It doesn't just happen once, and I'm sure it doesn't only happen to me. There's that little twinkle in his eyes. He still remembers the great times. He wonders if he's done the right thing."

A lot of secret Fugs fans were expected to turn out a few weeks hence, when Tuli and Ed Sanders were getting together for one night only, to perform at a local club. Tuli was facing this reunion with mixed emotions. "Anyone can come back," he said. "The point is, what do you come back as? Do you come back as nostalgia?" The original breakup in 1970 he ascribed to "artistic differences." "I felt we should be buffoons. Ed thought we should be high art. I was afraid we'd get lost in trying to become fine musicians. I always thought of us as theater."

Although Tuli saw a need in the eighties for some sort of satire on the order of what the Fugs once did, "the continuity has been broken in terms of what is required now," he said. "I've been listening to Lenny Bruce recently, and he doesn't hold up, because he's won. That's how it is with people who've won."

In any case, next time around, Tuli is sure the Revolution *will* be televised. "But only on cable," he added.

"I can remember thinking in nineteen seventy-three that the sixties were definitely over," Essra Mohawk said. "By 'seventy-four I was sure of it. By nineteen seventy-five I missed the sixties desperately. And by 'seventy-six I was looking forward to the eighties. Personally, I always kept the thread going. I'm one of the people who never changed. In the fifties I was in the sixties. I remember friends of my parents saying, 'Watch her, she's gonna grow up to be a beatnik.' They were right. I know from the ages of five to ten I thought I was from another planet. I mean, I looked around and it was like I was observing this place and not really in it. I had a persecution complex—but I was really persecuted. Every time we moved I would meet the wrong people. But music always got me over. Whenever I sang, everyone liked me. For that moment everything was cool. By the time I was fourteen I had a piano and a guitar and I was filling up books with my songs."

In 1963, after the family moved to Philly, Essra finally met the right crowd. "I found a beatnik school downtown," she said. "People liked to discuss things and talk a lot. Suddenly they were all like me for a minute." Essra was twenty-two when the sixties ended, she'd been to California and back, but she was still a long way from where she wanted to be. "I'll tell you the truth," she said, "I had no idea it would take me this long to be a star. My karma is such that things take longer with me, but I chant now, so it won't take me quite so long."

In recent years Essra has become a follower of Zen Buddhism. "I was never a joiner," she explained, "especially in the sixties, when everyone was joining things. I figured they were all joining these things to get where I was already. Most of those people were straight and I had never been straight. I'm more of the person who was freaked out and was trying to be straight. That's why I found this practice when I needed discipline in my life." To Essra Zen's chief benefit involves the concept of karma. "We're reincarnated with the karma from all our previous existences, and we're stuck with it and can't change it. But now you have a means of changing your karma. Every breath you take creates karma—but Zen is faster; it's like a shortcut. You can do it all in one lifetime. You can eradicate all your negative karma and create all good fortune and therefore achieve enlightenment and become a Buddha and not have to say that in so many lifetimes from now I'll be this or that. You can do it now."

The decade or so since the sixties ended has not been especially kind to those girls of summer who tiptoed through my daydreams in long, straight hair, simple shifts, no makeup—beat madonnas with banjo eyes and a certain folksong gullibility. Joan Baez is without a record label. Laura Nyro dwindled to a whisper of her former shrieking self, no closer to figuring out the secrets of the cosmos or of a lasting male-female relationship since becoming a mother. Joni Mitchell's whirling descent into jazz alienated much of her audience, though her latest release is said to have made some stabs at winning back a mature following. I heard a rumor that Carole King was living under her fourth husband's name at a trailer park in Indianapolis, a quasi-spiritual retreat unfathomed even by close relatives. Maria Muldaur, word has it, has been "born again." And Buffy Sainte-Marie, for all her righteous fire and fury, makes the best part of her living as an occasional guest on "Sesame Street."

Essra Sandy Hurvitz Mohawk wants no part of dirges. On the tapedeck in a friend's car, she placed the cassette of her brand new album, due out, she said, in a month, maybe two, tops. At turns lush and roaring, bluesy but optimistic, the collection is a testament to endurance, faith renewed. "I'm calling it *Burn and Shine Essra*," she announced, "because that's what I am, I'm real alive. It's an important statement to make, because a lot of people think I'm dead, if they think about me at all."

Since her last album appeared in 1976, Essra's written over one hundred songs. For a while she gigged around Los Angeles with a band made up of cronies of her husband, Dahoud Shaw, a session drummer, who also produced her album for an independent San Francisco label. "People who had never heard of me before gave us beautiful reviews. There was nothing in there about my past. I was the new kid on the block and got reviewed just on my merit."

Though as yet the record has not been released, and perhaps never will be, Essra was convinced at the time we spoke that greater things were in store for her in the years ahead. "I believe in the eighties and I believe in this generation," she said. "The sixties was just a taste of something yet to come. It was short-lived because the people suddenly had a direction without any practice or chops and the seventies was spent getting their chops together. Now all of these people who were in their twenties are in their thirties and can better and more stably do what they set out to do then.

"When we were teenagers the world belonged to us; not that it always belongs to teenagers—it belonged to *us*. We're not teenagers now and it still belongs to us, because we're the majority, therefore the consumers, the market. We've finally got our feet on the ground as well as our heads in the clouds, and we can pull the two together instead of going off the deep end. It's like *chudo*, the middle way in Buddhism. This generation is now taking control of the world—and the world will change. I know these people, and I'm one of them and they're all like me, and the world will be ours because we're the ones who've survived and maintained and therefore can do it and mean it."

CENTER: John Sebastian at home in 1983 (Photo by Catherine Sebastian). CLOCKWISE FROM TOP LEFT: Stephen Stills and John Sebastian, circa 1970. Lightnin' Hopkins, date unknown (photo by Chris Strachwitz). Cameraman and companions on scaffolding overlooking the stage at Woodstock, 1969. The Lovin' Spoonful (left to right, John Sebastian, Joe Butler, Zal Yanovsky, Steve Boone). Camping at the Woodstock Festival on the hills of Max Yasgur's farm in White Lake, 1969.

★ 7 ★

By the Time I Got to Woodstock

Many in the throngs that collected at the Woodstock Festival in August 1969 undoubtedly were lured there by the rumors of an appearance by Bob Dylan. Woodstock, after all, was where the legend had lived in hiding since his disastrous motorcycle accident of 1966. At Woodstock, it was promised, Dylan would stage his return to live performing, his poetry restored, his energy and charisma resurrected to take on the challenges of the repressive seventies looming just over the rise. Instead, it was Dylan's absence that rock fans had to deal with, as he, like many another sixties figure, chose to abdicate his role as savior of the country. But in his absence his titles left a message that is obvious: "Tears of Rage," "Nothing Was Delivered," "I Shall Be Released," "You Ain't Goin' Nowhere," "Too Much of Nothing."

It may be unfair to caption Woodstock "Too Much of Nothing," but the image and the reality of the event are not at all difficult to separate. To the general public and posterity it was presented as nothing less than a victory celebration, something akin to the founding of a city in the state of bliss.

But this ritual rain dance was a mudbath, a financial disaster. The bands in attendance, though awed, were ultimately removed from their musical moment. There were just too many people, too much rain, too little planning. A sloppy good time, for sure, but more discomfiting than euphoric, except in retrospect.

A walk-on at Woodstock, singularly at one with the event (he claims he was tripping), John Sebastian uniquely blends both the up side and the down side of the sixties musical experience, of which Woodstock was the culmination. Born at the center of the action, right across the street from Washington Square Park in Greenwich Village, he grew up with folk music in his parlor, bluegrass in his playground. At eighteen he was "adopted" by Lightnin' Hopkins. He was a charter member of the influential Even Dozen Jug Band. By twenty his soulful harp had gotten him access to every important recording session of the early-sixties folk scene. A year before Dylan upset the Newport fathers by "going electric," Sebastian was lugging amps down to MacDougal Street with his band, the Lovin' Spoonful, and incurring the wrath of all the purists there. But when "Do You Believe in Magic" leaped from Greenwich Village to the world, Sebastian epitomized the sixties hip trip, mellow good times, granny glasses, polo shirts, insouciant charm.

As Sebastian can attest, however, good vibes alone were not enough to surmount an intractable enemy. Sebastian's enemies, it is significant to note, came from within the counterculture as well as from without. When the Spoonful were cast in the role of informers in a drug bust, their underground constituency dismissed them without a trial. Eventually, some people saw the shades of gray beneath the black and white, but by then the band was finished. Sebastian moved out of the Village to live in a tent in California, stripping himself of group, worldly goods, and his first wife. A smooth transition to a solo career was also derailed by a series of snafus in which he came across as an unabashedly effusive hippie, his good, tough Village chops notwithstanding.

Though Sebastian's fortunes were restored, chiefly through the miracle of California real estate, he ultimately survived the gaffe that was Woodstock and was rewarded for his efforts with a return to the top of the charts in 1976, just ten years after his last visit there, via an inconsequential ditty written as the theme for the TV show, "Welcome Back, Kotter," enabling him to move back to the East and to Woodstock. Not everyone was as lucky or as resourceful as Sebastian, but the ironies that ground his career thus far seem to indicate that although, as Neil Young suggests, you can't be twenty on Sugar Mountain, the view from thirty and forty may be even more interesting.

Playlist

1969

January:	"Proud Mary" *Creedence Clearwater Revival*
	"Indian Giver" *The 1910 Fruitgum Company*
	"She's a Lady" *John Sebastian*
February:	"Aquarius/Let the Sunshine In" *The Fifth Dimension*
	"Galveston" *Glen Campbell*
	"Lodi" *Creedence Clearwater Revival*
March:	"Get Back" *The Beatles*
	"Hair" *The Cowsills*
	"The Boxer" *Simon & Garfunkel*
	"Atlantis" *Donovan*
April:	"Bad Moon Rising" *Creedence Clearwater Revival*
	"In the Ghetto" *Elvis Presley*
May:	"Good Morning Starshine" *Oliver*
	"The Ballad of John and Yoko" *The Beatles*
June:	"Honky Tonk Women" *The Rolling Stones*
	"Get Together" *The Youngbloods*
	"Marrakesh Express" *Crosby, Stills & Nash*
July:	"Sugar, Sugar" *The Archies*
	"Green River" *Creedence Clearwater Revival*
	"Easy to Be Hard" *Three Dog Night*
	"Lay Lady Lay" *Bob Dylan*
	"Give Peace a Chance" *The Plastic Ono Band*

August: "Suspicious Minds" *Elvis Presley*
"Hot Fun in the Summertime" *Sly & the Family Stone*
"Everybody's Talkin' " *Nilsson*

September: "Come Together" *The Beatles*
"And When I Die" *Blood, Sweat & Tears*
"Wedding Bell Blues" *The Fifth Dimension*
"Something" *The Beatles*
"Eli's Coming" *Three Dog Night*
"Ballad of an Easy Rider" *The Byrds*
"Suite: Judy Blue Eyes" *Crosby, Stills & Nash*
"Fortunate Son" *Creedence Clearwater Revival*

October: "Leaving on a Jet Plane" *Peter, Paul & Mary*
"Down on the Corner" *Creedence Clearwater Revival*
"Cold Turkey" *The Plastic Ono Band*
"She Belongs to Me" *Rick Nelson & the Stone Canyon Band*
"Na Na Hey Hey Kiss Him Goodbye" *Steam*

November: "Jingle Jangle" *The Archies*
"I Want You Back" *The Jackson 5*

December: "Everybody Is a Star" *Sly & the Family Stone*
"Jesus Is Just Alright with Me" *The Byrds*
"New World Coming" *Mama Cass Elliot*

1970

January: "Bridge over Troubled Water" *Simon & Garfunkel*
"Traveling Band" *Creedence Clearwater Revival*
"Instant Karma (We All Shine On)" *John Lennon*
"He Ain't Heavy, He's My Brother" *The Hollies*
"Who'll Stop the Rain" *Creedence Clearwater Revival*

February: "Let It Be" *The Beatles*
"Spirit in the Sky" *Norman Greenbaum*
"House of the Rising Sun" *Frijid Pink*
"ABC" *The Jackson 5*

March: "Everything Is Beautiful" *Ray Stevens*
"Cecelia" *Simon & Garfunkel*
"Up Around the Bend" *Creedence Clearwater Revival*

April: "The Long and Winding Road" *The Beatles*
"Ball of Confusion" *The Temptations*
"Woodstock" *Crosby, Stills, Nash & Young*

May: "Mama Told Me Not to Come" *Three Dog Night*
"Candles in the Rain" *Melanie*
"Ooh Child" *The Five Stairsteps*
"Teach Your Children" *Crosby, Stills, Nash & Young*
"Save the Country" *The Fifth Dimension*
"Cinnamon Girl" *Neil Young*

June: "(They Long to Be) Close to You" *The Carpenters*
"Ohio" *Crosby, Stills, Nash & Young*
"Big Yellow Taxi" *Joni Mitchell*

July: "Looking Out My Back Door" *Creedence Clearwater Revival*
"Snowbird" *Anne Murray*
"Peace Will Come (According to Plan)" *Melanie*
"Uncle John's Band" *The Grateful Dead*

August: "Up on the Roof" *Laura Nyro*
"Fire and Rain" *James Taylor*
"Lola" *The Kinks*
"El Condor Pasa" *Simon & Garfunkel*

September: "We've Only Just Begun" *The Carpenters*
"Heaven Help Us All" *Stevie Wonder*
"You Better Think Twice" *Poco*

October: "My Sweet Lord" *George Harrison*
"Domino" *Van Morrison*
"Only Love Can Break Your Heart" *Neil Young*
"Carolina on My Mind" *James Taylor*

November: "Stoney End" *Barbra Streisand*
"Your Song" *Elton John*
December: "One Bad Apple" *The Osmonds*
"Mr. Bojangles" *The Nitty Gritty Dirt
Band*

JOHN SEBASTIAN *(the Lovin' Spoonful)*

The legend on the poster they sell to tourists at the Woodstock general store reads: "Let Woodstock be a shining example." Although the rock festival that put the town on the culture map nearly thirteen years ago actually took place in nearby Bethel, the example of Woodstock is still hailed whenever shock troops from the abortive rock revolution gather together to mourn the pipe dreams of those halcyon days when the music was churning and burning and rock 'n' roll seemed capable, all by itself, of great and impossible things: love, peace, equality, acid in the drinking water.

But Woodstock is a symbol nonetheless for the enormous expectations, exalted sense of history, and agonized, messy downfall of a generation caught up in the momentum of its own power over events. Those who had dislodged Lyndon Johnson thought for sure that they could change the world through force of will and an electric guitar, endless theoretical conversations, and a little stamping of the feet. But as high as it got on those smoky nights, it never got high enough to with-stand the pull of gravity—the crunch of repression.

By the time the troops got to Woodstock—to offer to the media and the world, out of the mud and music, humanity, heat, rain, bad acid, and faulty plumbing, a smiling, eight-by-ten glossy album-cover photo and documentary film still—the revolution was effectively over. The civil rights movement and the peace movement had gone down with Bobby Kennedy and Martin Luther King, Jr. Ronald Reagan had clamped a lid on Berkeley protest. The great society had turned to mush. The blissful borders of an acidhead Nirvana had been invaded by Charles Manson and the Weathermen. Having believed in the magic of rock 'n' roll, having opened themselves up through sexual exploration and chemical experimentation, street theater and political activism, the Woodstock constitu-ency was faced with the prospect that it all may have been an illusion.

In their disappointment at being deserted by all things countercultural, some would drift to self-destruction, some would look to reincarnation, others would take it out on the music. But at Woodstock, for three days, this vast and tattered and freaky graduating class could sit within the shadow of the Big Rock Candy Mountain one last time before contemplating the long journey outward alone.

If anyone could have represented Woodstock to its con-stituency, it was a performer whose image was in tune with the multicolored, evanescent joviality of that famous lawn party for half a million of the faithful: John Sebastian, founder of the Lovin' Spoonful and coiner of the phrase "the magic of rock 'n' roll," a man of a thousand T-shirts. In the documen-tary film of the festival, Sebastian is seen onstage unshaven, in a flowered jacket, outrageously delirious at appearing to such a historic throng.

"I was basically on about a triple acid trip right when they asked me to play," Sebastian explained. "Which answers the question: Can a man play his own songs when he couldn't find his car?" He was at Woodstock as a guest, manning a back-stage tent and relaxing in typical fashion. "I was not sched-uled to perform," he said. "I was enjoying being off that particular series of days, so I accepted an awful lot of acid from Wavy Gravy, who kept saying 'You know, these kids are really having bad trips, but it's not that bad.' As weird as this may sound, except for the first year or so with the Spoonful, doing eight shows a night and running down to the basement to get stoned between sets, I had begun to discover as I did shows that I couldn't get stoned, because when you become introspective in front of more than one hundred people you look like an idiot. If anybody had told me (a) that I had a chance of performing and (b) that it might be filmed, I think I would have somewhat saved myself."

Usually Mr. Control, the essence of bespectacled post-Beatles hip, Sebastian, as recorded for posterity by the cameras of Woodstock, oozed ecstasy, congratulating the audience for its inescapable righteousness. In voicing such heady palaver, Sebastian was no doubt echoing the sentiments of everyone wedged in there on Max Yasgur's grazing grounds. "Still, in retrospect I was very unhappy about the impression I gave people at Woodstock," Sebastian told me. We were seated in the rather drafty living room of the magnificent house he now owns in Woodstock, where he lives with his second wife, Catherine, their son, Ben, and, currently, a brood of ducks, which had taken up residence in the kitchen.

"I think I play and sing a lot better than I played and sang that day," he continued. "I was sort of one with the experience of Woodstock, I guess, so that stood me in some sort of short-term good stead, but in the long run I'm sorry that the highest visibility performance I've ever given was one where I was smashed beyond belief."

Sharing the mixed emotions of most who were there, Sebastian saw Woodstock as the culmination of the decade's frantic momentum. "We were coming out of an unpopular war, where people had a rallying point," he said. "They'd had a lot of practice in various civil rights and antiwar demonstrations at being part of large numbers of stoned people, somewhat in disarray, but able to keep it together." As high as Woodstock was, as a moment and a symbol, its aftermath was depressing and depressingly American.

"No sooner was there a Woodstock than there were a mil-

lion natural-yogurt companies cropping up," Sebastian remarked. "I think we are devourers of our own culture and
cannibalized a lot of things that could have happened out of
Woodstock. A media culture can absorb and regurgitate stuff
so fast that it loses meaning almost before it's out of the pot.
Somehow every mood that was created was suddenly turned
into a marketable item. I regret that more of the spirit that ex-
isted at that point in time could not carry over to the sort of
cocaine-and-glitter thing that filled the void once it was gone.
But I guess those are the jokes."

The cosmic jokes played on John Sebastian surrounding
his ill-advised cameo at the Woodstock Festival were even
blacker still. After a career noted for its ease of ascent, Sebastian's transition to solo stardom was anything but smooth. At
Woodstock he took the stage having left behind the Lovin'
Spoonful less than a year before. Once the band was the epit-
ome of good-time splendor in the grass, but a drug-informant
controversy permanently enshrined them as rock 'n' roll finks.

"That was a very, very detrimental thing for the band,"
he admitted. "And yet nobody ever really understood exactly
what had happened. Basically, Zally and Stephen, en route to
a party, were stopped by the police, answering a screaming-
woman call. The police find an ounce of grass on them, take
them down to headquarters, and say 'We're going to bust you,
and you, Zally, will get deported'—which would be the end of
the Spoonful—'unless you tell us where you got the dope.'
Zally and Stephen then extract a promise from the cops that
they won't bust who they tell on, because the cops said,
'We're looking for Mr. Big.' Knowing that there is no Mr. Big,
Zally and Stephen go, 'Okay, fine, I got this from so and so.'

"You have to remember the framework of the period,"
Sebastian said. "People's perception of the police was changing radically. In the Village before 1967 policemen were still
people who looked after you. Frank Serpico took friends of
mine home and put ice on their balls so they would make it
through a bad shot of heroin. But after 1967 this whole pig
thing had started and you were dealing with a very different
flavor of police department. So, under the threat of being

busted, Zally's being deported, and the group's breaking up, Zally and Stephen felt that the only thing they could do was tell the cops where they got the dope and then buy the guy out of the sentence. What happened was, instead, the guy who got busted chose a lawyer who decided he was going to make pot legal in San Francisco. The result of that was that the guy who sold them the pot went to jail overnight. It wasn't a big deal, but it *was* overnight, and overnight in jail is not cute. Eventually we could help to get him off, but the damage was already done. It was picked up like a banner by the press. And I think it did a lot to close up the whole good feeling behind the Spoonful, because we felt not only had we been lied to by the authorities, but also quickly deserted without any kind of a listen by the majority of the rock press.

"In later years Ralph Gleason [the late dean of American rock critics] wrote a very good piece on the bust and the whole thing, which, to my mind, set things right, but it was way too late. That piece doesn't click in anybody's mind, either—for instance, Oh yes, 'The Vindication of the Lovin' Spoonful,' by Ralph Gleason, of course. . . ."

The group officially broke up in mid-1968, after Zally left the band. "Zally was threatening to leave for quite a while, and eventually it became a real bore and I fired him," said Sebastian. "I can laugh about it now, because I invested another five years remaking Zally's friendship after this all went down. But he was really feeling like he'd taken the thing as far as he could go and didn't want to be this cartoon of a rock 'n' roll star that he'd been able to make fun of for so long." Yanovsky was replaced by Jerry Yester, who had played piano on "Do You Believe in Magic," but the magic was gone. "I'm glad the group broke up when it did," Sebastian said, "because the alternative is sort of playing in cheesier and cheesier entertainment parks as a lot of famous groups going down the tubes do. So, instead of cashing in on the downfall and taking the slow road, we just pulled the plunger."

Within two weeks, Sebastian was in the studio, recording a solo album for MGM and, at his home in Sag Harbor, Long Island, supplying the punch line for another of life's jokes.

"Outside of Paul Rothschild's living room, I think Crosby, Stills, and Nash first really sang together at my house," he recalled. "I heard Graham and David singing together first, then I heard Graham, David, and Stephen planning Crosby, Stills, and Nash in Cass Elliot's swimming pool, on tetrahydrocanabinol, if I recall correctly. At that point Stephen was trying to convince me to join them, as their drummer, and to be in the group. But I was having what looked to me like the beginning of a good solo career. Unfortunately, I didn't know that I was going to have to wait a year for my album to come out."

When Sebastian finished making his album, the folks at MGM said, "Great, another Spoonful album." Sebastian said, "Hey guys, this is a solo album—I'm the only one of the Spoonful on the record." MGM said, "No, we're putting it out as the Spoonful." Sebastian said, "Then you're not putting it out." A year of suspended animation followed, protracted litigation, until Warner Brothers agreed to release Sebastian's album. At which point MGM released their own version of the same album. "So, not only did I lose a lot of momentum," Sebastian said, "but then people were going, 'Which is the real album?' "

Shortly after Woodstock, MGM managed to get another album out of Sebastian, in a similarly devious fashion. "To capitalize on my appearance at Woodstock, I did another show, in the town of Woodstock," he said. "I'd just been up all night doing the Atlanta Pop Festival, but there were four hundred people in a field here waiting for me to perform, so I flew in, saying, 'Hey, I'm not going to let these people down.' But, unbeknownst to me, somebody recorded it—on a real cheap recorder, too—and it went out on MGM. I mean, it was Wallensack time. In fact, I was playing through a Fender champ amplifier, in the rain, on no sleep."

As if they were Nixon's plumbers trying to sabotage the Weathermen, the fickle fates that cackle in the music business were unraveling all of Sebastian's mid-sixties daydreams. Not only was his career falling apart in 1969, his short-lived first marriage was also breaking up. No wonder he took off to live in a tent in Burbank, California.

"It was terrific," Sebastian said. "I had accumulated all these belongings, and it was wonderful to get away from this atmosphere of possessions that I'd begun to feel very stifled by. My first wife was very concerned with buying things and shopping, so I was reacting against that, I think, and really enjoying having nothing but my little fishing-tackle box full of guitar tools, an instrument or two, and enough clothes. Not to make it sound too much like roughing it, I was not very far from a place where I could go and make phone calls and do what I had to do."

Sebastian had found the tent only after spending a few nights crashing on a friend's couch. Cyrus Faryar, former member of the Modern Folk Quartet, had gotten a gig as a renting agent for a complex of buildings that included half a dozen small houses and one empty eight-by-eight-foot Volkswagen-bus tent. Sebastian promptly added a bed, a catalytic heater, and a 160-pound dog named Bear.

The place was dubbed Chicken Flats, because it was adjacent to a chicken pen. "One of the things that really kept you honest was when this rooster would go off at five each morning," Sebastian said. "If you hadn't slept enough by then, you were in trouble." He lived in that tent for two years, punctuated, of course, by more sumptuous stays in the Holiday Inns of the constantly touring rocker. But by no means did the tent go unused. "In fact, it became a little hermitage spot for people who were having one problem or another, saying, 'Hi, can I use your tent while you're out of town?' "

Meanwhile, as it had with Woodstock, a good thing proved too much of a temptation for exploiters. "Within a year of when I put that tent up, there was another fellow who decided he wanted to put up a tent," Sebastian remembered. "So, of course, he came up there with a bulldozer, cutting out a straight place and a place to run water down, and all of a sudden it was a development."

Living in the tent did not eradicate all of his post-sixties comedown problems. "I did a crazy year of cocaine," Sebastian indicated, "and then I said, 'Oh my God, I'm not funny anymore. Nobody's funny anymore." He was spared from further descent by the love of a good woman, Catherine, who actually lived in that tent with him for nine solid months. "I thought, anybody who can put up with this is ready for me." From there they moved to a little place on the side of a mountain in Laurel Canyon, where Ben was born. "As soon as Ben could walk we started to get anxious to move to more level ground," Sebastian said. "So we ended up in Tarzana, down in the valley."

By the mid-seventies Sebastian's career was down in that valley with them. "During this period I was having a creeping realization that the whole atmosphere was getting stagnant for me creatively," he said. For one thing, the folkie spirit, the hippie ethos, and the tie-dyed sincerity of Woodstock vibes were the object of endless, mirthless scorn by a younger generation of cynical, heavy-metal products of the New Disillusionment. The economy was crumbling. The war may have been over, but Watergate was in the wings.

"I began to feel like, is this artistic paranoia, or am I sensing genuine resentment from my record company about the type of music that I do? We were entering the Alice Cooper era, which was intimidating enough for the record company that people there were actually putting on mascara and trying to feel like, 'Hey, I'm in with this new thing.' Most of them were guys who two years before were wearing beads."

If the music business had shut him out, there was a better way to make a buck in California in the early seventies. "Selling the house in Laurel Canyon got us almost enough to buy the next house," Sebastian revealed, "which was twice as valuable. When we sold that house we got about twice what we paid for it. Our joke has always been that during those years I made as much money from real estate as I could have writing songs."

As they sometimes do, the jokes began to even up for Sebastian. "It was about nineteen seventy-four when I really said to myself, okay, you're going to have some slim years as far as recording goes, while this business goes through whatever it's got to go through, so you better go where you can work, which for me, since the end of the Spoonful, was always the

East Coast college circuit. I came back here and began working—and what do you know, the thing I'd done just before I
left L.A. suddenly came to fruition, which was this little TV
theme song." The tune, "Welcome Back," from the series
"Welcome Back, Kotter," not only earned Sebastian plentiful
TV residuals, but, released as a single in 1976, it went to number one, his first hit as a solo act, coming only a decade after
"Summer in the City" reached the top of the pops for the
Lovin' Spoonful in August 1966.

"I was back in business," said Sebastian. "I could buy this
house."

With its gold records on the bathroom wall, squatting
livestock in the kitchen, assorted authentic instruments loung-
ing in the living room, overhead fan out of *Casablanca,* mini-
recording studio with drum kit next to massive record
collection, surrounded by foliage, and up a mile or so of winding road, Sebastian's house is a castle befitting the one-time
king of Bleecker Street. Not for Sebastian, even then, the vagaries and vagrants of the Lower East Side. A year in that part
of town expunged forever his romantic notions of slum living.
"The East Village was smack and speed and scary guys, what
we used to call 'evil spades,' and people who in general were a
little bit more than us young, middle-class kids were ready to
cope with," he said. "I always felt more like a West Villager."
Nestled on one of those serene, shady blocks in the West Village, Sebastian's brownstone was a bohemian's dream of glory, right across the street from Zal's brownstone, patrolled by
a couple of teenybopper sentries. In Woodstock he continues
to define the dream of making it with class, one rocker who's
sustained a standard of living, who's succeeded in transforming a life-style into a life.

Sebastian is the first to attribute his superior coping
mechanism to his upbringing. His father, John Sebastian, was
a classical virtuoso on the harmonica. "I felt much better prepared for what happened as a result of growing up as the son
of a man who was committed to music for a lifetime," Sebastian told me. "I knew how very good you could be and still not
have popular acceptance. So I think the various waves of pub-

lic approval or disapproval might have rolled off my back a little bit better than off a lot of my contemporaries whose parents had nine-to-five jobs, who sort of said, 'How can this be a life-style?' "

The elder Sebastian's life-style was hardly one of limos and luxury. "If you think rock 'n' roll was funky in the forties and fifties," said Sebastian, "believe me, classical was funkier, because you had to get more places for less money. Generally, he traveled with a pianist in a station wagon. He toured places that nobody had been at that time. He was in the Orient before that was anything like fashionable for Americans. This was not somebody who was afraid to get his tux muddy. He was usually on tour three to four months a year, and then there was the occasional plush gig with an orchestra at the Whatchamacallit Room of the Waldorf-Astoria."

Sebastian senior didn't achieve the fame of Sebastian junior. "I'd say he was never really able to attain anywhere near the recognition that I, for one, always wished for him, but that was never his goal. He was a classical musician. He wanted to be a soloist, and I think he did have it the way he wanted it. Eventually he was written for by some of the great composers of the time. He transposed a lot of flute and violin sonatas by Bach. He adapted a lot of classical works to the harmonica. He doesn't have much of a reputation as a writer, but I found his occasional original pieces to be completely magical."

"Completely magical" is an apt description of the younger Sebastian's more prolific output, especially in the heyday of the Lovin' Spoonful, when his songs, in great juicy bunches, seemed to define in breathing Technicolor the succulent, open-ended street life of the extended adolescent in the mid-sixties. Sheer shimmering optimism was never so shamelessly extolled in melody or lyric. "Do You Believe in Magic," "You Didn't Have to Be So Nice," "Did You Ever Have to Make Up Your Mind," "Daydream," and "Summer in the City" were rhapsodic odes to possibility, belief in the essential goodness of people, nice choices, and just plain goofing off—youthful passions recaptured in the face of "Younger Girl," like that pair of dungarees you hadn't worn in six years *that somehow still fit.* Nowhere is uttered a disparaging word, countercultural slogan, obscure poetic reference, or sigh of alienation.

"If anything, I was pooh-poohing people who were trying to put art into rock," said Sebastian. "I wasn't aspiring toward anything but what I was doing. I really wanted to be in *rock 'n' roll* and write *rock 'n' roll* songs." That he did. Three-minute gems of classy precision. Even those that failed to crack the Top 10, like "She Is Still a Mystery to Me," "Six O'Clock," and "Darling Be Home Soon," were laced with sophisticated imagery, glistening snapshots of the always fascinating male-female ballet. Dylan's androgynous amphetamine queens who thought of love as a four-letter word were of no use to Sebastian, who could have persuaded the pants off of any local girl with a chorus of "Coconut Grove" in a café over coffee.

Beyond words was his sinuous, sensuous harp, an inherited gift from his father, in more ways than one. "Having a famous father in a given area, you do feel competition," Sebastian said. "I decided at the age of five that I never wanted to play the harmonica again. But I found, at about thirteen or fourteen, that I could play it in a very different way and not be anywhere in the same ball park. In fact, my father got me my first Sonny Terry record. It wasn't even a record; it was a silver acetate of Sonny Terry musically recreating a fox chase that got me pursuing this other way of playing."

Born on Bank Street, Sebastian virtually grew up with the folk scene that was centered in Greenwich Village. Burl Ives and Woody Guthrie were among the houseguests his parents entertained during his early youth. While most of his friends attended the notoriously liberal Little Red School House, Sebastian went a much more proper route, from the Notre Dame School to the Friends Seminary to the prestigious Blair Academy in New Jersey, with the occasional summer in Florence or winter in Rome, while his father toured Europe. Other summers were spent in camp in New Hampshire. Home from school in the spring and fall on weekends, his playground and training ground was Washington Square Park. "I was just one of the little kids there for a long time," he said. "By the time I had anything to say, I'd already seen a lot of mistakes. Then it was a question of hanging around the park on a Sunday and going, 'Hi guys, can I play?' "

Through his father he was introduced to Lightnin' Hopkins, his first mentor in the blues. "My father had done a Sunday-morning television show called 'Robert Herridge Presents,' which also included a Welsh poet, an at-that-time-unknown folksinger by the name of Joan Baez, and Lightnin' Hopkins. I was snowed by Lightnin' and started following him around." To many ears, the blues of people like Lightnin' Hopkins, John Lee Hooker, Son House, Skip James, and Mississippi John Hurt was purer of art and intention than the rhythm 'n' blues that had been appropriated by white America and made into rock 'n' roll. Soon Lightnin' and John Sebastian were roommates.

"My roommate from Blair Academy had an apartment, where I lived part-time. Lightnin' ended up there because it was a place he could stay for free. I never played on stage with him; I carried his guitar and bought him gin, and that was about it. But the fact was that what Lightnin' delivered was something very exciting and very beautiful and had very little to do with me. As time went by I could accompany him in living rooms now and then. He'd sort of nod and smile when I'd play a lick back at him, but ours was not a tight, tight relationship. He was very suspicious of most white club owners, but because I'd spent a little time with him, I think he'd gotten to know not to lump me in with them. So I became somewhat his friend."

After high school Sebastian struck out on his own to seek his fortune, as a sailmaker in Marblehead, Massachusetts. But destiny, in the form of an allergy to rust paint, deposited him back in the Village. "The day I arrived home, I received a call from Stefan Grossman, who said, 'Hi, you're in our group and rehearsals start today.' I said, 'Yeah? That's very convenient.' " Included in the group was an old-time banjo player named Peter Siegal, an accordion player named David Grisman, a blues singer named Maria D'Amato. It was the soon-to-be-legendary Even Dozen Jug Band, with perhaps half of its members going on to substantial careers in the music business as soloists, sidemen, or record-company moguls. Their eventual album was produced for Elektra by Paul Rothschild.

"Meeting Paul resulted in an enormous amount of work for me as a harmonica player," Sebastian said, "because Paul was producing all these folk acts for Elektra and needed accompanists to flesh out albums by people who were used to working just with one guitar and vocal. So Felix Pappalardi and I became the Village rhythm section for a long time—Felix on guitaronne (he rarely played electric bass) and me on harmonica and second guitar. Soon I was making fifty-three dollars for a three-hour session. I remember writing to my father about it. 'Gee, this is great, this is what I want to do. I'm a studio musician.' And he wrote me back a great letter that I remember to this day. He said, 'You be careful. You'll be selling it note by note, and you'll lose your soul.' "

Some of those notes, however, blooming out of the left ear of Tim Hardin or Judy Collins or Mississippi John Hurt or Fred Neil were as gorgeous as anything blown by Sonny Terry or Sonny Boy Williamson, billowing and bittersweet. Before anyone knew he could also write songs of a similar quality, Sebastian was famed for his harmonica belt and his surprise appearance behind Mississippi John Hurt at the Philadelphia Folk Festival of 1965. About a month earlier, at Newport, Bob Dylan had put a puncture wound through the bleeding heart of traditional folk music. Sebastian himself had gone electric the year before. At the time Dylan had wanted Sebastian to play bass on *Bringing It All Back Home,* his first rock album.

"It was very funny," Sebastian recalled. "I'd just finished my first week of rehearsals with this rock 'n' roll band I'm committed to, so I said, 'No, I can't do it.' I was in a phone booth on Long Island. I remember hanging up the phone and saying, 'Jesus, who would have ever thought I'd be turning down Bob Dylan in a recording situation?' Meanwhile, the fact is that the Spoonful had already been in existence and playing electric rock for audiences at the point at which people were booing Dylan."

In 1964 and 1965 they were the house band at the Night Owl, gateway to MacDougal Street, then still the hub of the urban folk scare. "It was right around the time of the World's Fair, and New York was having a bit of an upsurge in tourism in general, and I think the Village suddenly held a lot of allure. And, to avoid any false modesty, the Spoonful was what was happening on that street. Everything else was very exciting, of course, and if you were into traditional music, Mississippi John Hurt was what was happening. But for the younger people, who didn't know anything about that, it was rock 'n' roll. The Spoonful were heartily frowned upon by all the traditional blues and folk music people, inasmuch as any place we'd play we'd be louder than anything else they'd ever heard, and people would be terrified. But we were sure we were the cutting edge."

Sebastian's route to the Spoonful was typically random and circuitous. Lightnin' Hopkins had a role in it, as did Cass Elliot, later of the Mamas & the Papas. But the man perhaps most responsible was an obscure black singer named Valentine Pringle. "After hearing him at the Village Gate one night having a lot of trouble with his accompanist, I walked up to him after the show and applied for the job," Sebastian recounted. "Lightnin' Hopkins was there and put in a good word for me. And Val, who had about as much of an idea of the blues as an Anglo-Saxon Protestant, gave me the job. That got me to Washington, D.C., where we were opening act for a group called the Big Three (Cass Elliot, Tim Rose, Denny Doherty)—hence I met Cass, who introduced me to Zally."

When Zal's group, the Mugwumps (the Big Three minus Tim Rose, plus James Hendricks, Cass's husband), broke up, he and Sebastian formed the Spoonful, with Joe Butler on drums and Steve Boone on bass. And, as so economically detailed in the song "Creeque Alley," Cass and Doherty formed the Mamas & the Papas with John and Michelle Phillips. After Dylan and the Byrds had put its more serious face on the pop map, the Spoonful and the Mamas & the Papas turned folk rock's somber visage into a huge smile. The soaring harmonies over milk-and-honey California reveries were the Mamas & the Papas' trademark. The Spoonful, at first, took after the Jim Kweskin Jug Band, with amps.

"They were the big guys," Sebastian said. "When I was in the Even Dozen, it was always 'Yes sir, Mr. Kweskin.' They were the Yankees, for sure." From the Even Dozen Jug Band, the Kweskin contingent, based in Boston, drafted Maria D'Amato for fiddle and funky vocal. There she met and married the quirky blues singer Geoff Muldaur. From the Kweskin Jug Band the Spoonful inherited a few tunes. "Certainly the Spoonful owes them a debt," Sebastian acknowledged. "But by the time we were an entity, we knew we wanted to make hit records and get girls, and we knew that wasn't what they were about—so we had a clear field." Eventually, the Kweskin Jug Band would be about harmonica player Mel Lyman's eerie Family, one of the many exotic cult communities born out of sixties ashes, as lost diehards flocked around leaders possessed by a demonic charisma.

After woodshedding for a stretch in the basement of the Albert Hotel, the Spoonful returned to the Night Owl, adding to their mix of electric jug-band music and rock 'n' roll a previously missing ingredient. "We knew we needed original material, and I was sort of elected, because nobody else wanted the job," Sebastian said. "I wrote 'Didn't Want to Have to Do It,' hoping Dusty Springfield could sing it. Then I wrote 'Do You Believe in Magic' because I knew that one of the things we did real well was play shuffles."

But in early 1965 "Magic" was decidedly mundane to the ears of the record business. "Every major label turned it down," Sebastian told me. "That's where the Village stood me in good stead, because, as with electricity, the sheer fact that we could be met with such consistent disapproval said something to me. It said that we must have something going for us if everyone hates us." Then one night Phil Spector, in the waning heyday of his era, stopped by the Night Owl to catch a set. "After that, there was an average of eight record execs in the audience, per show," said Sebastian, "until Artie Ripp and Kama Sutra came in and committed."

In addition to the Spoonful, the Night Owl had a cast of characters as various and dedicated as the Gaslight, up the block. Richie Havens, without a label, had a fan club that mobbed West Third every night, just to glimpse him tramping through the dusty streets, carrying his guitar, no case, and smiling—no upper plates. Fred Neil was a crusty blues singer who inspired awe in musicians from coast to coast (both Sebastian's Spoonful and Marty Balin's Airplane recorded Neil's "The Other Side of This Life"). "Freddy had a classic case of ambivalence," Sebastian related. "You see, he hung out with a lot of jazz musicians, to whom making it was synonymous with selling out. I came from the next generation, which didn't know from selling out. We just knew from Is it a hit or is it not a hit? So I think life was a little simpler for me.

"Freddy knew a lot more about rock 'n' roll than he was letting on," Sebastian revealed. "He had done a lot of time in Nashville and in the early rock 'n' roll amphetamine and road scene. He played guitar on 'Diana.' He was only sort of passing as a folksinger. I used to tease him about it. I only wish that he'd been able to see a lot more of the humor in that situation, because I think he could have capitalized more on what he did."

With nutty humor a spoonful shy of burlesque, Sebastian and crew translated that peculiar zesty Village magic, even in their clothes, which he absolutely denied were costumes. "If the Spoonful were first in anything," he said, "it was with wearing street clothes on stage. We insisted on doing that. The fact was that we had some pretty unusual-looking street clothes that were all sort of fashioned out of the new psychedelicum—Village folkie, jug-band vests, and funny hats and raccoon coats."

As far as pop stardom went, at the outset at least, they had no debilitating ambivalence. "Somehow I think the success part of it was more interesting than the stardom part," Sebastian reflected, "and the stardom part was the most surprising and the hardest to adjust to. When we went to California to play, we had fairly high expectations, which we quickly discarded when we realized that this was just another cheesy topless club, and we were the band. There was also the responsibility of coming up with a new single, but that was okay, because now I'd gotten one accepted, and a little acceptance goes a long way. So I started writing a mile a minute, and it was just a matter of which one would emerge as the next good one through the process of recording and arranging and performing. Taking no chances, I wrote another shuffle.

"I think the Spoonful was coping with a change within ourselves, which I think was also happening within others. It was a turning away from this preoccupation with the association of traditional music and protest. We said, 'No, we just want to take that other part of traditional music, the funky part, where they were just talking about Let's go have a party.' "

The era of great parties dwindled into a sloppy series of financial and musical baths, poorly planned and atavistic festivals, celebrations, love-ins, and human carnivals through the early years of the seventies, which all attempted to exploit Woodstock vibes. Merely a year after Woodstock, in fact, two of its producers, Michael Lang and Artie Kornfeld, were suing the other two, John Roberts and Joel Rosenman, for ten million dollars. Rapidly, that pure and innocent body language, rock 'n' roll, began to take itself as seriously as its sidewalk critics did, becoming in the process something more and something less. When *Hair*, the first major rock musical-opera, moved uptown to Broadway in 1968, the die was cast. Following its success musicians and groups with theatrical and classical and poetic pretensions abounded, performing to a chorus of impassioned critical rhetoric. Trying to be all things to all people, rock 'n' roll got lost in its flamboyant gestures.

In 1969 Sebastian lived through such a musical fiasco—*Jimmy Shine*, starring Dustin Hoffman. "They weren't sure whether to consider me important or not," he said, "because they weren't sure whether they wanted a musical or not. They said, '*Hair* made it; maybe we should listen to him.' So they were telling me, 'This isn't a musical. This is only a show with songs in it.'

"So I was writing songs for the show, but I had written half the songs already, and just by coincidence they fit. I wrote one or two that were custom-made for the show, and they were so awful they were great. What was funny about them was that they were making a slight parody of the desperation the lyricist always has in plays. You can see him up at three in the morning saying, 'Christ, it's going into rehearsals tomorrow and I've got to get this done.' I had one song in there that they cut in half. The guy they assigned me to teach the song to could not sing, hence they had him sing half the song on his entrance and half on his exit. So I said, 'Okay guys, I'm just going to go ahead and make the record my way.' The song is 'She's a Lady.' It's a nice song. It has impact on a stage. It stops a show or two now and then in my shows. So I knew the song was valuable, and I also knew that none of the people there saw the value—forget *musical*—the *dramatic* value of the song."

Despite his experiences back then, Sebastian has become involved, of late, in another musical venture. "Maybe in a year from now, if it gets to Broadway, I'll be described as an overnight success," he joked, careful not to pin too many hopes on any one project in this cold climate.

His heart remains in rock 'n' roll, however. "I'm still a mad fan of the three-minute single," he said, "and the most exciting thing for me is to have a hit record on the radio. But rock 'n' roll addresses an essentially adolescent experience, and we've extended adolescence about as far as anyone would want to. It's impossible for me to create in a false environment and have any success with it. Which means I have to continue to speak to my contemporaries, and that audience is getting older. The funny thing was, I thought I was doing that with 'Welcome Back.' Here the flavor of the song is retrospective and second thoughts about things, and suddenly I picked up a whole bunch of thirteen- and fourteen-year-olds who watched the TV program."

Many of Sebastian's contemporaries, like him, are sixties survivors, an audience that developed, through FM radio, the discernment to appreciate album cuts rather than only hit singles. And not only album cuts, but specific guitar solos on those cuts—down to a specific superb progression of notes two-thirds of the way into that solo (you could drop your record needle onto that solo right now). But most of the music made in the sixties was virtually wiped off the radio dial when disco trucked into fashion in the mid-seventies—much in the same way that good old rock 'n' roll was eradicated by the twist, in order to pave the way to a temporary advancement of the form called rock. No such advancement has taken place in the wake of disco's much-celebrated death. Which leads us to the essential sixties dilemma: was the decade part of the evolutionary process, in music, in life-style, in politics, or merely an aberration of that process? Was it a brief, shining mirage, meant to indefinitely tantalize and depress those who clung to its odes (many of which may now seem incomprehensible, like the era that evoked them), or merely a prelude to another renaissance?

In any case, rock 'n' roll, as we have witnessed, made a comeback, with an oldies circuit and radio stations all its own. Certainly the sixties audience is enormous enough to support at least a dozen circuits, as well as a station or two featuring those album cuts. And with significant reunions lately by the Mamas & the Papas, Simon & Garfunkel, Peter, Paul & Mary, Crosby, Stills & Nash, the Hollies, and various Monkees outfits, it seems apparent such a comeback is already underway. Not for John Sebastian, however.

"There is no Spoonful reunion in the works," he told me. At present Zally owns and operates a restaurant in Kingston, Ontario, called Chez Piggy's. Joe Butler has been acting off and on off-Broadway and supplementing his living with "high-rent cabinetry," according to Sebastian. Steve Boone has been involved with recording studios. Sebastian sees them all occasionally. "It's sort of low-key, but it does continue," he allowed.

It continues, especially in Woodstock, a town filled with legends and ghosts from the sixties. Albert Grossman's Bearsville Records is just up the road. Eric Andersen lives in town. Paul Butterfield, just out of the hospital, makes the scene almost daily at one of Grossman's restaurants, the Little Bear. Grossman's even got that veteran pop-scene columnist Al

Aronowitz on retainer. In his fifties now, Aronowitz has a little cabin, where he's self-publishing a collection of his recent works—on a Xerox machine, for one hundred dollars a book. What's left of his hair has freaked out. The town itself is a rustic throwback to almost ancient days, from the hippies too stoned to break a five at the local food shop to the bearded artists who collect in the luncheonette in the center of town. Carpenters by day, they look at ten in the morning as if they just stepped off MacDougal Street, between sets. The occasional pioneer woman in lumberjack shirt, breastfeeding her infant, is another dash of unmistakable local color. Over maps and coffee here, I feel a curious ambivalence, nostalgia and intimidation—not unlike what I experienced in my first visit to Haight Street in 1966. That the sixties didn't take over may be just as well: in a nation of beatniks, who's going to sell the soap?

After living here for ten years, Sebastian is quite content. "It was a bit precious at first when Dylan and the Band and those boys were in the area," he said. "Not that it was their fault or that they were precious. But the town became very cliquey, and there was so much secrecy involved with where everybody was getting together—because there was such rabid interest from people who had no business being there—that people like me, who might have had a real good reason to be there, really couldn't find out where the jam was that night. Over the years, though, I think that the mood in town has cooled out."

So Sebastian putters around these days, working on a new-fangled guitar, flying out to L.A. to lay down tracks in search of the elusive hit single, waiting for Broadway to beckon. And I wouldn't bet against a Spoonful reunion of some sort either. But as far as an actual sixties comeback, I'm not so sure. In a safe surface form, it may happen, of course, but in truth the memories may forever be too sore to play with. Too many of us will never be able to laugh at the excesses, the dreams, the confident predictions of the sixties. The scars are too visible. We would rather forget it, block it out, nestle in with Sinatra or Johnny Carson—the eternals.

"The rock stars became the cowboys," Sebastian reflected. "The generation before, it had been either you were a singer or you were tough. Then Elvis Presley made it okay to be tough and sensitive. Then the Beatles made it okay to be cute and tough and sensitive. So it was just mounting permission to be more and more for musicians, until it was possible to be Hopalong Cassidy."

But Hopalong Cassidy rode off into the sunset, and so many other cowboys traded in their cap pistols for three-piece suits. Hank Williams, Jr., said it in a recent country song, "All My Rowdy Friends Have Settled Down."

"For my generation," John Sebastian said, "it would be more like 'All My Rowdy Friends Have Died.' None of the guys I considered rowdy ever stopped—and they all died." Among sixties freaks and faithful, their names are almost clichés now, our honored dead: Hendrix, Joplin, Morrison. The assassination of John Lennon. In Sebastian's circle alone there was Cass Elliot, Michael Bloomfield, Lowell George, Tim Hardin. "I'd say Timmy knew exactly what he was doing and lived, to my mind, about twenty years longer than I ever expected," Sebastian said. He felt much the same way about Lightnin' Hopkins, who died in 1982, nearing the age of seventy. "Knowing his habits from 1965, I was frankly just awed that he lasted so long. The man would wake up and have breakfast of two eggs and a jelly glass full of gin. But he never seemed to get sloppy drunk." And the deaths continue: in 1983 Felix Pappalardi was shot and killed.

You couldn't bring back the sixties without releasing once again that chill of imminent death, not only to rowdy friends and superstars but to assorted street fighters and draftees, acid casualties and living zombies, and otherwise normal neighbors caught in the crossfire of events, who strayed too close to the edge. It's why the rest of us are sometimes thought of as survivors.

"I was sort of a figure for [the late] Keith Moon and a couple of others of that ilk, who really took great delight in coming and wrecking my evening, which was all nicely mapped out and ended somewhere around twelve-thirty," Sebastian reminisced. "Keith used to show up with stuff like a demijohn of champagne and Sha Na Na at my door when Catherine and I would be just at the moment of beginning to disrobe in front of the fireplace.

"All my rowdy friends used to come around and try to bother nice, well-centered, wholesome John."

Epilogue: No Easy Way Down

Because we were promised so much, there is a tendency to look at the sixties as an utter failure. Just as we failed to win the war in Vietnam, we also lost the war at home, with the quality and inequality of life. For all the optimism of working within the system (freedom rides, Peace Corps) and the exhilaration of trying to take the system apart (dropping out, trashing the shopping center), what is remembered most is the exhaustion of defeat, the frustration of seeing the system spinning on unperturbed, the chagrin of middle-class outlaws hustling for the few remaining seats on the gravy train. We inflated all our heroes until they burst—the superstar as ultimate victim. The Beatles failed, Dylan failed, just as acid failed and Gene McCarthy and the antiwar crusade and all the music scenes so hopefully erected in Cambridge, San Francisco, and Greenwich Village were toppled by the American way of exploitation, repression, and money.

The intensity of life in the sixties gave the music an added intensity, which the music, in turn, gave back to the various causes in the air. But when events turned vicious, life lost that special intensity. Youth vanished, and without it the music didn't seem to matter as much, leading some to the belief that it never mattered much. The seventies dawned, not on the next hundred years of bliss, but to tunes of resignation: "Let It Be." Four dead in "Ohio." "Bridge over Troubled Water." Bye-bye Miss "American Pie." As folk and blues and poetry and idealism left the music, it no longer held the interest of the white middle-class, which had tried so hard during the sixties to remake the pop charts—as well as the world—in its own image. But the members of the middle class underestimated the entrenched powers and the power of gold. They failed to consider the working class, whose lives went on basically unchanged and whose neighborhoods remained as snug as they'd been in 1958. In their insistence upon relating to blacks only as symbols, they failed to learn the lessons of soul—patience, endurance, self-containment.

Deserted by its elite constituency, rock 'n' roll reverted to its overwhelmingly teenage, essentially escapist concerns, typified by disco, the thudding drumbeat of apathy that drowned out all thoughts and feelings. But what better reaction and antidote for the many who had repudiated every aspect of the middle-class experience than to be forced to submit to it a decade later? Yet, no songs chronicled Watergate, an event that should have brought a charge of vindication to sixties idealists and a lot of guitars out of the closet. This suggested a conspiracy of silence, a vast forgetting by its participants, of what the decade meant. If we believe that everyone merely made the transition to seventies' scarcity in ease and silence, it will come to appear that no one gained or lost a thing back then. The sixties were just a rollicking good time, almost as much fun as the fifties—a pit stop, really, for a generation on the unobstructed road to the good life.

Does it mean that people have banished from memory the feeling they had when they heard Dylan for the first time and wondered if anyone else knew about him? And then when they discovered a friend who shared that enthusiasm, realized that there were more of us—more of us, in fact, than *them,* or so it seemed. And this feeling repeated, with widening reverberations, as each new wave of music and discovery crashed across the continent. Dylan went electric. The Beatles got turned on. Then the world turned on to sex and dope and rock 'n' roll, and the young occupied center stage with an impossible mandate for its programless programs. Undoubtedly, we'll never be so unified or so positive again. But thousands in the sixties tampered with the fine tuning of their lives, stepped outside the rituals of making it to look inside for a spell. Few were left untouched by the fleeting visions. And if there were pipe dreams, ego trips, dissension, self-destruction, it was done in the cause of noble exploration, experimentation, idealism—in the name of art. If people have now locked themselves back behind their doors of perception once again, for the duration, there's no way they can deny what a long, strange trip it was.

Since the ending of the sixties—in 1972 or so with the debacle of McGovern—music has been relatively uneventful. The failure of nerve and tenacity on the part of the middle class extended to FM radio and the record business at large. With no audience for protest music of any type (except for music that protested protest music) artists were discouraged from producing it. FM got by for a while on the credibility it had accrued from the sixties, but then lapsed into giving the "people" what they wanted.

Yet there are artists around who witnessed the sixties, some as participants, some as observers, who have remained true to a vision, popular back then, of rock music as more than cosmic tranquilizer—as a means of actually getting at the truth. The careers of Joni Mitchell, Laura Nyro, Paul Simon, Lou Reed, Leonard Cohen, Dylan, McGuinn, Neil Young, Judy Collins, and Dave Van Ronk have had their peaks and valleys in the last decade, the quality of their work diverging widely. All of them are still producing. People like John Prine, Billy Joel, and Bruce Springsteen have emerged from the working class dismissed by the elitists of the sixties to create informed and relevant (and rocking good) material. In "Song for Adam" and "Before the Deluge," Jackson Browne has written two of the best (and most heartbreaking) summations of the hippie era, from a post-hippie vantage point. Randy Newman has put togther an impressive body of work. Tom Waits and Rickie Lee Jones evoke the pre-sixties Beatnik era in their songs and stage personas. The Roche sisters, Maggie, Terre, and Suzze, offer hypnotic harmonies, while Talking Heads offer just the opposite—jarring pieces of contemporary anomie. Bonnie Raitt and James Taylor continue to have large, loyal (and mellow) followings. Peter Tork's got a band, John Sebastian's written a musical, Essra Mohawk has a new album, and even Jiggs Meister has been to the studio recently. And Tracy Nelson is sounding better than ever. Certainly there are causes out there that can and will engage the talents of these artists—No Nukes comes immediately to mind—internal and external issues that will somehow find voice.

Whether there will be an audience for this music—the same audience that grew up with it in the sixties, supporting and nourishing these artists through the eighties and beyond—may depend less on the whims of the music business than it does on the unpredictable needs of the human spirit. I, for one, haven't given up on us.

Playlist

David Ackles

"Montana Song"
"Out on the Road"
"Subway to the Country"
"Waiting for the Moving Van"

Eric Andersen

"Blue River"
"Is It Really Love at All"
"Moonchild River Song"
"Time Run Like a Freight Train"

Joan Baez

"Diamonds and Rust"
"Lovesong to a Stranger"

Karla Bonoff

"I Can't Hold On"
"If He's Ever Near"
"Lose Again"
"Someone to Lay Down Beside Me"

Jackson Browne

"Before the Deluge"
"Farther On"
"For a Dancer"
"For Everyman"
"Fountain of Sorrow"
"Looking into You"
"My Opening Farewell"
"Song for Adam"
"Take It Easy"
"These Days"

Leonard Cohen

"Famous Blue Raincoat"
"Humbled in Love"
"Take This Longing"
"You Know Who I Am"

Judy Collins

"Angel, Spread Your Wings"
"The City of New Orleans"
"The Moon Is a Harsh Mistress"
"Pirate Ships"

Bob Dylan

"Day of the Locusts"
"Hurricane"
"Idiot Wind"
"Joey"
"Sign on the Window"

"Time Passes Slowly"
"Went to See the Gypsy"
"You Gotta Serve Somebody"

Billy Joel

"Captain Jack"
"Only the Good Die Young"
"New York State of Mind"
"Piano Man"
"Scenes from an Italian Restaurant"

Joni Mitchell

"Amelia"
"Blue"
"Car on a Hill"
"Carey"
"Court and Spark"
"Goodbye Porkpie Hat"
"The Last Time I Saw Richard"
"Raised on Robbery"
"River"
"The Same Situation"

Essra Mohawk

"Back in the Spirit"
"I Cannot Forget"
"If I'm Gonna Go Crazy with Someone
  It Might as Well Be You"
"New Skins for Old"

Maria Muldaur

"Mad Mad Me"
"Vaudeville Man"

Tracy Nelson

"God's Song"
"Going Back to Tennessee"

"I Need Your Love So Bad"
"Love Has No Pride"
"Satisfied"
"Soul of the Man"

Randy Newman

"Burn On"
"God's Song"
"Political Science"
"Sail Away"
"You Can Leave Your Hat On"

Laura Nyro

"American Dreamer"
"Been on a Train"
"Brown Earth"
"Captain for Dark Mornings"
"Child of the Universe"
"Christmas in My Soul"
"Stormy Love"
"The Wind"

Phil Ochs

"Jim Dean of Indiana"
"When I'm Gone"
"When in Rome"

John Prine

"Angel from Montgomery"
"Christmas in Prison"
"Dear Abby"
"Far from Me"
"Fish and Whistle"
"If You Don't Want My Love"
"Illegal Smile"
"Sam Stone"
"That's the Way the World
  Goes 'Round"

"Your Flag Decal Won't Get You
into Heaven Anymore"

Bonnie Raitt

"Angel from Montgomery"
"Good Enough"
"Home"
"I'm Blowing Away"
"My First Night Alone Without
You"
"Run Like a Thief"

Lou Reed

"Caroline Says"
"Coney Island Baby"
"Growing Up in Public"
"Her Life Was Saved by
Rock and Roll"

The Roches

"Hammond Song"

John Sebastian

"The Four of Us"
"How Have You Been"
"Rainbows All over Your Blues"
"Welcome Back"

Paul Simon

"American Tune"
"Armistice Day"
"One Man's Ceiling Is Another
Man's Floor"
"Peace Like a River"
"Run That Body Down"
"Something So Right"
"Slip Slidin' Away"

Bruce Springsteen

"Born to Run"
"For You"
"4th of July, Asbury Park (Sandy)"
"Independence Day"
"Jungleland"
"The River"
"Rosalita"
"Spirit in the Night"
"Thunder Road"
"Wild Billy's Circus Story"

Steely Dan

"Aja"
"Bodhisattva"
"Kid Charlemagne"
"Rikki Don't Lose That Number"
"Show Biz Kids"

Talking Heads

"Don't Worry About the Government"
"Once in a Lifetime"
"Take Me to the River"

James Taylor

"Anywhere Like Heaven"
"Handy Man"
"Her Town Too"
"Something in the Way She Moves"
"Sweet Baby James"

Dave Van Ronk

"Urge for Going"
"Song to Woody"
"Sunday Street"
"That Song About the Midway"
"That'll Never Happen No More"

Loudon Wainwright III

"B-Side"
"Down Drinking at the Bar"
"Lullabye"
"Needless to Say"
"Red Guitar"

Tom Waits

"Christmas Card to a Hooker
  in Minneapolis"
"The Piano Has Been Drinking"
"Red Shoes"
"Romeo Is Bleeding"
"Step Right Up"

Neil Young

"Cowgirl in the Sand"
"Down by the River"
"Human Highway"
"The Loner"
"The Old Laughing Lady"
"Southern Man"
"Sugar Mountain"

Index